Hair of the Dog

The Revenge of Deanie O'Banion

Jean Luntz

Note: This novel is a work of fiction, and historical characters have been fictionalized within the context of this story based on the author's imagination. Any resemblance to people, living or dead, is coincidental.

To my husband and all my friends who read the original drafts and helped to hone this final version, a huge thank you and hug of gratitude.

Also, to my parents who taught me to love music. ♪♪

1

T*his is the way the world ends -- with a bang – not a whimper, isn't that what T.S. Eliot said?* thought Gregory Davenport almost as quickly as he wondered, *how had Capone's men found them?* Terror threatened to choke him, throwing his heart into overdrive. Clouds of smoke and debris swirled throughout the speakeasy he and his brother Harrison had worked so hard to build from their parent's failed farm. He crawled along the brass lower foot rail edging the once shiny mahogany bar, remembering how long his brother's friends had polished the wood to create its luster.

His elbows dug into the thick green and floral carpet while wood and glass flew overhead. He dodged the tall bar chairs, several upended on their elegant backs carved to look like peacocks, ducking behind the bar and hiding at its far edge. He and Harrison had been thrilled to find those stools for their club, and now they were being ripped apart by bullets.

Ladies screamed in horror while the male patrons shouted obscenities as couples ran for the eight exit doors hidden behind green velvet curtains. Mrs. Davis raced by his hiding place – Mr.

Davis, her banker husband, running interference for the couple, shoved one of the delicate black lacquered tables out of his way. Mahjong tiles skittered across the floor, the Bakelite clacking loudly. He and Harrison had known these patrons since the club opened eight years ago and now each and every one of them were being targeted, forced to flee. *Bastards shot out the chandeliers with the first blast of the tommy guns. Did they have any idea what those damned things cost?*

Around him, shouts from fleeing patrons continued with the constant rat-a-tat-a from the guns. Tears in the rich gold fabric flounces and burgundy velvet wall coverings made it look as if the club itself were bleeding. Several of the Irish waitstaff hastened destruction of the chinoiserie tables, black lacquered chairs with oriental designs, breaking the furniture to serve as shields or as weapons before they tossed the broken pieces aside to flee. Playing cards swirled in the air and dice clattered to the floor. Drinks dripped among shards of broken glass. *The stains,* Gregory groaned. Satisfaction and joy the club generally brought him, had soured in his gut. *Thank God he had been the only soloist tonight with their small band.* When they couldn't get known entertainers like Besse Smith or Ethel Waters, Gregory wailed away on his saxophone, imitating the famous sounds of Jelly Roll Morton or Jack Gee Jr. His heart panged, longing for those magical minutes playing music. *Would they be able to attract anyone good ever again now that the club--.* Gregory shook his head. He started panting, trying to catch his breath. *It had taken them months to build the club and only moments for their enemies to destroy it. Now all of it was coming down around his ears.*

Gregory glanced over his shoulder to peer into the darkening room, past the carnage of furniture. *Where the hell was his brother?* Bile climbed up Gregory's throat, tasting sour, and panic grew, tightening his lungs. He could see waiters in their black suits dashing here and there like mother birds attempting to chase predators from attacking their nests, ushering patrons to safety, clearing the basement club of people. Among the last to leave were young political aide Jeffery O' Mallory and his fiancé, who dashed off in the opposite direction from the waiters. Gregory guessed the red-haired man believed they could better escape that way. With the patrons gone and most of the waiters with them, his burly, wide shouldered brother should have been easy to spot. But he wasn't there. Gregory swallowed twice. He hoped that Harrison would stay out of harm's way; not playing hero by jumping one of the men in black suits, who held the smoking muzzles of their guns toward the ceiling. So far, several people had been hurt, but Gregory didn't think anyone had been killed. Beneath the ringing in his ears, he thought he heard moaning coming from his left-- from the far side of the rectangular room, off near the doors leading up to the kitchen. With all the haze and debris, Gregory could not tell how many intruders stood by the main staircase, off to his right—were there five, six? He squinted to see. In a moment of respite from the barrage, one of the intruders shouted, "No one crosses Al Capone or Frank McErlane."

Another man shouted, "We'll liven up this wingding" and bullets sprayed across the room.

Remaining low, behind the cover of the upended bar stools, survival instinct screaming in his brain, Gregory attempted to make sense of what was happening. *Frank McErlane was off the rails, even crazier than cousin Deanie's pal Two-Gun Alterie, who once punched a horse in the face for giving him `the eye.'* He looked desperately around him at the intruders for a rotund balding man, but McErlane was nowhere in sight. Gregory knew Capone would never show his face here in an Irish club, hating them as he did. These were simply hatchet men – guns for hire, but they were enough. Splinters of wood littered Gregory's path towards the back office where he and Harrison hid their books and other records for the speakeasy and the liquor they bought. He was afraid to stand. If, he thought, no -- when the police arrived, he needed to have burned the records or at the very least have made certain they could not be found. He began to move toward the office on his hands and knees, when another loud crash reverberated throughout the speakeasy.

Frozen with fear, Gregory noted a new presence at the very back of the room. The large, burly shape stood close to the door, blocking the way up the stairs concealed within the walls between the entryway and the main parlor of the house above them. *McErlane?* Lights flashed around the room, something hard pelted into the wood of the bar like a woodpecker beating a tattoo, then the noise hit his ears like a jackhammer. He felt a slow burning along the side of his head. Gregory swiped at the spot with his hand, his fingers coming away sticky. *Blood?*

More splinters of wood splattered down on him, forcing him to drop completely onto the carpet, where he flattened himself as much as he could. He brought his hands up to protect the back of his head and pain lanced his left shoulder. He couldn't think clearly, could not understand the entirety of what was happening. Capone, of course, might resent what they had done with their parent's farm. *I can understand that, but why was McErlane doing this?* Gregory shook his head. *How could he even wonder?* Hadn't Harrison been placing himself deeper and deeper in harm's way, first when he joined O'Banion's Irish gang as a boy, and now partnering their cousin and his friends in this speakeasy.

Harrison often bragged about his exploits.

"I share a street corner near 42nd with another boy-- Bugsy Moran's cousin, Teddy O'Hannilon," Harrison had told him, looping a thumb into his suspenders. "We hawk the papers—well, one does the yelling, while the other goes sneaky like amid the crowd on the sidewalks, picking the pockets of the most likely gents. It's great fun, Gregory, I can tell you." His brother's eyes twinkled with joy. Harrison slowly revealed that the North Side Gang members led by his cousin were notorious for doctoring drinks in order to rob saloon patrons, slipping necklaces or jewelry off those listening when Deanie sang on stage in bars, and often hijacking cars from the street. Gregory had wondered how the racketeers had become heroes in the public eye, despite being labeled *Public Enemy #1* by the Treasury Department and then his question was answered by Al Capone, himself. "I have been spending my life as a public benefactor," Capone told a newspaper reporter, recently and the Italian's words echoed in Gregory's head. "I provide pleasures and good times."

But Gregory knew the truth.

Each year Harrison worked his way deeper and deeper into their cousin's confidence, and Deanie gave him more responsibility like running the numbers and fixing gambling games. He even began to dress like their cousin down to the fedora tilted over his light brown hair. People in the city knew Harrison Davenport, just as they recognized Bugs Moran, or Hymie Weiss, leaders under Deanie O'Banion. In the end, Deanie wasn't able to protect any of them. O'Banion had been cruelly gunned down before he even turned 33. *He and Harrison missed him. McErlane had been behind that, too,* Gregory thought. Gregory knew George Bugsy Moran declared war against Capone after that, acting like a bull charging a matador's cape. Murder statistics spiked all over Chicago. Gregory could not forget the blazing headlines merely a month ago screaming *St. Valentine's Day Massacre.* Harrison, that fool, might have been shot that day just because his best friend was Moran's cousin. Gregory went cold with the thought.

His older brother, Harrison, for all he adored him, easily loved the darker side of the business. Even his latest squeeze, Lysette O'Hannilon --a green eyed, vixen-faced beauty, whose diminutive stature brought the top of her raven hair just beneath Harrison's chin, connected Harrison to Moran and the vendetta with Capone and McErlane. *And, that's why Frank McErlane had it out for them.* Gregory thought bitterly. He tried to ignore the nagging pain in his shoulder and the continuous burn along the side of his temple. He closed his eyes, to rest, just for a moment.

Groaning, Gregory wondered how long he had lain in the dark. His head and shoulder throbbed. When he attempted to sit up, glass tinkled to the floor. Opening his eyes slowly, he noticed the dust had settled, covering the upturned and broken furniture in the room. It looked like the twisted destruction he had seen a tornado wreak. A broken piece of mirror from behind the bar had fallen nearby, distorting his appearance. His mane of brown curls which he slicked back with pomade, strong chin, and aquiline nose twisted from handsome to gruesome, the chin tilting right and his nose looking split in half due to the fractures in the glass. His hair was covered in debris and dust from the attack. His once deep brown silk, three-piece suit was coated grey. *Thank God Mother and Father never knew cousin Deanie bought our farm—they were spared seeing this.*

Gregory rubbed his eyes, not only to clear the dust but also to wipe away the memories. The room around him had grown quiet, almost tomblike. Gone were the sparkling lights, the excited chatter of the crowds, and the wailing saxophone accompanying the rest of the small eight-piece orchestra. None of the waiters roamed about with trays of drinks in crystal goblets. The club had been so very packed when the first burly gunmen appeared at the doorways. Card and mahjong tables whirred with the sounds of shuffling cards or maj tiles clattering against the felt covering the wooden table tops, with calls of "Pon" ringing out, but tonight Harrison wasn't there overseeing the gambling.

Suddenly, Gregory remembered Harrison wasn't in the club, nor was he upstairs, a potential victim in the house. He had left early that morning for Canada for a shipment of pure whiskey. *Had the lot belonged to McErlane?* Gregory wondered what Harrison would do when he discovered the wreckage McErlane's men had made of their beloved club. At least no one found the secret stash of booze, he thought with a bitter smile. The liquor storage lay beneath a hidden door covered by the Persian rug in the Club's office. Gregory hated going down those steep dirt stairs which lead downward to yet another basement level deeper under the farmhouse.

That had been Deanie's idea. Gregory wiped at his face. He blinked twice. *Was that a figure coming toward him?*

"Deanie?" Gregory croaked. His cousin's dapper appearance was marred by blood stains and bullet holes – a ghost. *Not possible. Or was **he** dead, too!*

"Yes, me boyo!" Deanie's voice seemed distant, but clear enough. "I've come to give you a gift." Deanie knelt down beside him and took Gregory's face between his hands. His cousin kissed his forehead with cold spectral lips that burned like dry ice.

"Gift?" Gregory asked, confused. "What sort of gift?"

Deanie broke into his broad boyish grin. "You'll learn soon enough, ya savvy? But I will tell you one thing—your innocence will help me get my revenge."

"Revenge?" *What was Deanie saying?*

"And another thing," Deanie stood, and tipped his fedora more over his left ear. "Death has taught me – time is not what it seems."

"Wait—am I dead?" Gregory tried to raise a hand, but it felt too heavy.

"No, me lad. That would not have played into our cards." Deanie smiled even broader.

"What?" *Good. Alive!* Gregory thought.

"Remember, laddie, revenge and time." But, before Gregory could ask anything else, Deanie's smiling ghost dispersed into the floating debris.

Smoke was beginning to clear, revealing the wreckage, but the acrid odor threatened to choke him. This vision of the club depressed him, especially since he and his brother had put so much sweat and blood into it. Gregory suddenly felt so very exhausted he couldn't take it all in. Ringing in his ears made him dizzy. He lay his throbbing head against the dust covered sleeve of his silk suit jacket, pressing hard into his arms before everything went black around him.

2

Harrison and his friends spent a month sweeping up debris and repairing the damage done to their club. The carpenter patched up the holes in the wood work. While he and his assistants repaired the bar and decorative rails, the waiters cleaned up shards of mirrored glass and broken furniture. Outside the parlor window, a large bonfire of wrecked furniture sent plumes of smoke and the scent of wood burning into the air. Gregory heard the workers, remembering how the first time he and Harrison had done most of the carpentry themselves and were so very proud of the result. They enlarged the house hidden among the apple and pear orchards and acres of wheat and corn, north and west of Chicago. As he reclined on the sofa in the front parlor, sometimes reading and sometimes listening to recordings of his favorite musicians, Gregory slowly healed his wounds from the raid and tried to forget about his cousin's words. Tinkling of piano keys and the strident notes of the trombone blended with the hammering and sawing. Gregory dozed and recalled how; before they had been dreaming of riches back in 1920, when they had taken the seed money from their cousin, the brothers faced economic ruin. Gregory could see his brother clearly on that day – when they feared the bank would come to reclaim their farm.

Dressing in his best suit, Harrison had combed back his light brown hair in an attempt to look much more dapper than he felt. He hitched the plow horse up to the buggy, and drove to their cousin's flower shop deep in the heart of Chicago. After tying the rig up in the street, he sauntered into O'Banion's office. Resting one foot on the arm of a side chair facing his cousin's desk, Harrison began, "Deanie, I have a proposition for you that I think you will like."

O'Banion, straightened the lapels of his silk three-piece suit and sat up in his leather chair. "I'm, as they say, all ears."

"You know our farm is cold meat. There isn't a pathway even to Hell that will bring it back from going to the bank." Harrison raked his hands through his pomaded hair. "But I've got an idea."

O'Banion slid his grey fedora further to the side on his head. "Yes, yes," he said impatiently, reaching for a cigarette and a lighter on his large wooden desk.

"I want to transform our farm house into a gambling club – not an ordinary club, but one that is for the fancy crowd. Have drinks, music, dancing, cards, everything." Harrison spread out his hands, waving them toward the clutter of paperwork on the desk in front of him. "You know there is going to be a need for clubs in the next year or so." Harrison lowered his voice, "Prohibition is coming. They've passed that damned Volstead Act."

O'Banion gave Harrison a toothy grin, cigarette smoke sliding through his teeth.

"We're family. Our mothers were sisters. I'm asking you as family for help." Harrison knew this was his last hope. "We will go into the club as partners, fifty-fifty."

"Seventy-five mine and twenty-five to you and your brother and it's a deal," O'Banion slapped the top of his desk with his free hand. "I like the idea of a high-end club. One that won't take riff-raff. We can offer genteel amusements that patrons won't find elsewhere. Your brother can play the saxophone – some of that new Jazz." That was how Harrison got Deanie O'Banion to loving the idea of a social club offering gambling games, cards, mahjong, dancing and good Jazz music along with liquor.

Over the course of a year, with help from the others in O'Banion's gang, they personally transformed their parent's tiny home into a three story, yellow brick edifice that would not raise an eyebrow of suspicion. Gregory recalled the shirtless days in the heat of spring and summer, sweat trickling down their backs, when seven of the gang, if he could include himself, tore down some walls with sledge hammers, taking up hammer and nails to construct others. *Working toward a positive goal made all of them feel better about a world turned upside down.*

Teddy, tall and lanky, wore his shirt tied around his waist, his sleeveless undershirt sweat soaked and grimy. His pencil thin moustache gleamed in the sunlight overhead while he stood knees bowed out to grip the wooden ladder. His biceps rippled as he swung his hammer at nails, the large window frame rapidly forming around him. "I don't know how you conned me into this honest work" he had said, laughing.

His cousin Bugs Moran shouted, "Less chatter and more hammering!"

Gregory worked at using the large wood saw, cutting up planks for the under flooring. "They are doing the best they can," he replied. He wiped sweat from his forehead with his hand.

Harrison stood bent over the plans with Cousin Deanie. "Large mirrors behind the bar and on the back wall will create an illusion of a bigger space."

Deanie tapped the ash off his cigar. "Agreed. We don't want our patrons to remember they are deep underground."

Gregory, who hated cramped spaces, had shivered at the idea of all that earth pressing down on the speakeasy. Harrison had assured him the club would feel as airy as a second-floor parlor. The project resembled the community barn raisings their father had described from his youth. The old tornado shelter doors had been replaced by a façade—a wall of pillars made of granite, seemed to be merely decorative, but gave access to a hidden stairway. Similarly, beneath the modern kitchen was another stairway leading seemingly into a root cellar. The two staircases ultimately led two floors underground to the *Hair of the Dog Club*, a large open room with a mahogany bar with mirrors behind it at one end, and a small office space at the opposite end. To the right of the bar, with two short steps leading up to it, a bean-shaped stage made of thin oak planking was provided for the eight-piece orchestra which included the upright piano pushed against the wall next to the stage. Window dressings provided privacy while also preventing the heat or cold from penetrating into the interior.

Guests who wished to and who were included in Deanie's inner circle could remain at the house overnight. And on the top floor, Gregory and Harrison took the old servants' quarters for their own space. All in all, the farm house radiated innocence. Few would suspect that this magnificent home concealed a fancy, modern blind pig. Theirs' was a place offering to show people miracles for the cost of admission. Publicly, it was known soft drinks were sold inside. Privately, well—that was another matter entirely. Known only to a select clientele who whispered a code to a guard in order to gain entry, patrons walked down several flights of hidden stairs into a delightful speakeasy complete with the best available alcohol, jazz music, and company within fifty miles.

After opening their doors in 1921, Harrison and Gregory had painstakingly built up their business. Harrison had been well aware of the competition who might – at any moment – retaliate with machine guns and other forms of violence since the beer war between O'Banion and Torrio was escalating. Bribes were all part of the bookkeeping, but Harrison insisted that the distance of their establishment from the Loop and downtown Chicago would protect them.

"Mother and Dad fortunately passed on before they could know what we have done with the old homestead," Harrison had told him early on after they opened. He had pressed his broad shoulders against the dark wood lining the wall adjacent to the stairs into the club, and a wide, toothy smile flashed across his face.

"They would be turning in their coffins otherwise," Gregory had muttered.

"What's that?" Harrison inquired with a raised eyebrow and shooting a jacket cuff. "Look, the farm could never bring in the money we have now. That last downturn in the economy – you know the one in 1910 almost wiped them out completely. They could barely afford seeds for wheat or corn. That's why mother encouraged me to seek out cousin Deanie in the first place."

"I remember." Gregory shuddered, running a hand through his dark, curly hair, pomaded back sleekly from his forehead. While the farm produced wheat and corn today, it was an uncertainty for the future – the past proved it. "Mother told you to learn all you could from him. He was kin, after all." He had only been nine years old, himself, but he would never forget the stink of the hogs on the sweltering wind nor the despair on his parents' faces, turning their complexions ashen when they realized their farm was failing. "The bank wanted to repossess everything."

Harrison hooked a thumb into his gray striped suspenders and tugged pridefully. "I saved them, then, and I've saved us now." He tilted his grey fedora even further to the left side of his head.

Harrison had always been saving them – and he would, thought Gregory, *until he couldn't.*

But it was the day he convinced Deanie they should change the farm into a club that was the day Harrison put a real target on his back and drew the attention of Capone and McErlane.

Deanie volunteered to bring in good Canadian whiskey brewed in real distilleries, giving *The Hair of the Dog Club* even more elan.

"Nothing like that bathtub swill other joints serve," their cousin had remarked, tilting his fedora. "We want the best reputation."

Harrison often hinted that Deanie already had a fleet of vehicles disguised as taxi cabs, flower deliver trucks, milk wagons, and camouflaged trucks or cars with concealed compartments to carry booze without detection. "He can easily supply the club without expanding the business he already does in Chicago itself," Harrison confided. "Two-Gun persuades suppliers to switch from McErlane or Capone to places run by the North Side."

Deanie had overheard Harrison and added, "I pay ten percent of whatever we can sell the alky for, and nobody who tips me off ever gets caught." He laughed loudly, then tipped his fedora forward on his head before walking away. Over his shoulder, he remarked, "We are a class operation."

Their cousin had been correct, the club served only the highest rollers and because of the wealth, the club also attracted famous entertainers like Louis Armstrong and Bessie Smith. Gregory remembered when Armstrong first visited, calling for a glass of the good stuff. He then returned from the coat area, trumpet in hand, joined the small group of musicians on stage, and played to round and round of applause. "Don't call me Louie," he reminded them all, his large round face shiny from his exertions before closing with *When All the Saints Come Marching In.* Bessie Smith would lean against the mahogany bar, singing into her beer. She would peek around at the guests in the smoke-filled room as if including them in on her secret torment of love gone wrong. Gregory always waited with anticipation for the slow eye roll or furtive glance from under the flowered hat she always wore.

The entertainment at the club just got better and better, packing the dance floor not only with those doing the Charleston, Black Bottom, Fox Trot, and other popular dances, but also with those sitting at the club's tables drinks in hand, listening to Jazz and Chicago Blues. Fats Waller came out often, sitting at the piano beside the raised stage area as if he were at home, cigarette hanging loosely beneath his trim mustached top lip. Sitting at the keys with his fedora jauntily placed on his dark, bowl cut hair, Waller's expressive eyes and bushy brows conveyed extra meaning to his music than mere words could. His left hand seemed to stretch easily to cover the walking tenths in the base, while holding the octaves and melodies in his right. The place started "jumpin" every time Waller sang in his hoarse, whispery voice, or played instrumentals like *Handful of Keys*. Gregory loved joining in on the saxophone in the background, swaying with the syncopated rhythm along with the other seven orchestra members. He could not recall a time he had felt so fulfilled and happy. None of the guests could sit still either, the beat was so powerful and alluring; everyone crowded the dance floor.

That had been the first version of the club. *How he missed it.*

The operation ran trouble free for eighteen months, lulling Gregory, Harrison and even Deanie O'Banion into thinking their supply line was golden. Other trucks got hit by gangs from both the North and the South side to shake up the competition, but not the ones bringing the *good* alky for the Davenports. Harrison, if not Gregory, should have been able to read the signs portending the danger they might face even as early as their first liquor run.

The meet up and transfer had gone smoothly near the Illinois border. Gregory had sounded the duck call and the Canadians with the shipment gave the correct response. Two burly men transferred the large cases of Canadian liquid gold into every available space of the Ford truck Deanie gave them for the business. His brother didn't even stop the engine while the Canadians loaded the wooden crates because using the crank to restart the truck would take too much time. The narrow rear bed, surrounded by open slats of wood painted a deep blue, could only hold eight large cases, and the men grumbled about only having three thin blankets on the truck's bed to soften the ride.

Laughing, his brother ran a hand under his hat, through his hair. "What are they? Babies? It'll be fine."

After the larger of the two men replaced the rear panels in their slots and banged on the back, Harrison eased the truck back onto the main road. The engine spluttered, rocking the truck with subtle vibrations, as he throttled into a higher gear. They headed back toward Chicago on the narrow, pitted and poorly paved roads.

Through the clear, inwardly slanted windshield, stars blinked far above in the blackened sky. The truck hadn't gone more than five or six miles when Gregory noticed lights following them.

"There is someone behind us, Harrison," He hissed as if the others could hear him out in the deserted road.

"I think they have been following for the last mile or so, since the last turn off," Harrison confirmed.

"What do we do?" Gregory gripped his brother's smooth camelhair overcoat.

"Nothing for it," Harrison said. "Hang on!" He turned the dial and pressed his foot even harder on the floor lever, making the Ford jump and buck. The narrow, rubber wheels screamed against the brick pavement, but the truck tripled its speed, shaking as if that effort was going to rip the whole vehicle apart.

Gregory gripped the door and seat so tight his knuckles whitened, staring out the "C" shaped opening beside him. "Do you think we'll get away?"

"Don't know. We have a better chance if McErlane isn't with 'em. Honestly, that man terrifies me." Harrison concentrated on the road ahead with its potholes and curves lit up in the bobbing headlights. As they approached the city, the road way improved slightly while becoming even less straight.

Behind them, the other car also sped up, the headlights growing larger and larger, like the huge eyes of some nocturnal predator.

A loud crack sounded from behind. Gregory didn't know if it was a backfire from the Ford or a gun shot from the people following. Suddenly the truck jolted and began to bump violently toward the back wheel.

"The bastards shot out a tire." Harrison wrestled with the steering trying to maintain control of the truck.

Another shot rang out. "Abandon the truck!" Gregory suggested. "They may steal our whiskey, but I would like to hang onto our lives."

"Agreed," replied Harrison. Abruptly, he slowed the truck

enough for them to jump out, then roll onto the small brush beside the road.

The truck raced forward without them for a while with a dark sedan in pursuit.

"Come on," Gregory said, pulling his brother away from the side of the road, gravel on the shoulder crunching underfoot. "We can't let them see us."

Harrison nodded, clapping his fedora onto his head at that jaunty angle their cousin always used. "Let's go. Deanie will know what to do."

That was when Deanie decided to use the farm as a base for producing corn and grain mash. "Because we run a class joint," their cousin had said.

In order to prevent more bootleg from getting hijacked from *Hair of the Dog*, O'Banion built stills and a brewery in the old red barn out behind the apple orchard. The farm was not profitable enough, at least not as it had stood, but O'Banion was willing to pay men to work it and force the land to yield harvest. They brought anything else they needed from other local farms. Harrison studied how to turn the corn or wheat into a distilled mash and then how to process it into the best bootleg liquor, supplementing the rest of the beer and whiskey that now flowed freely in the *Hair of the Dog Club.*

"We've got control over the process from beginning to end," Gregory had said. The farm could produce grain or fruit for their purposes while covering up the illegal trade.

"This way, we are guaranteed the best hooch we can get," Deanie had cocked his head to one side and smiled broadly, showing a mouthful of teeth as he chortled. His expensive silk suits and easy way with his friends and women had always caused Harrison to admire O'Banion. "I don't take kindly to getting robbed, either."

Gregory had suspected their cousin retaliated violently. The newspapers had reported some trucks exploding, but they could never know for certain Deanie had done that. Other stories told of competitive hijacking first from Italian enterprises, then from Irish ones, especially after Frank McErlane switched loyalties from the O'Donnells to Capone. These crimes finally led to Stephen Wisniewski, a small-time racketeer who regularly targeted O'Banion's camouflaged tin lizzies, being found along the road by Lake Michigan. He had been shot in the back of the head, and Deanie's buddy Hymie Weiss had been bragging.

"We took Stevie for a ride," Weiss had crowed. "One way!"

Weiss and Deanie had laughed over that for days, and Harrison continued to brag about them and their audacity. Harrison also spun stories about Two Gun Alterie and Nails Morton.

"Those two are off the rails," Harrison would claim. "I saw Two Gun stomping around inside a bar with his spurs jangling and shooting his revolver until the barman agreed he'd only buy from Deanie." His brother viewed the other, older gang members as "right, good eggs."

Violence escalated between Deanie and the Italians. After McErlane and Capone took Deanie out, they continued to harass Moran and anyone who still supported the Irish operation, finally hitting *The Hair of the Dog*. The idea of revenge made Gregory recall what Deanie's ghost had said. Something about vengeance, and Gregory's own innocence being key. *Well Deanie's anger towards Capone and McErlane was justified,* thought Gregory. *But just what gift* had *Deanie given him? He felt the same as he always had aside from twinges in the shoulder and in his forehead. Wasn't there also something about ... time?*

From the sidelines, seated in a padded chair, Gregory watched as their friends altered the club's appearance from Asian influence to a more modern look based on some designs of Frank Lloyd Wright that Harrison had found. The once heavily Chinese style furniture gave way to simple pieces with angular lines and geometric shapes of Art Deco. Gregory admired how the opulent chairs with mother of pearl inlay were beautiful but still functional, thinking that Lysette – Harrison's latest squeeze --must have helped choosing them. New mirrored panels combining chrome and etched glass replaced the huge single panes against the wall behind the bar and decorating the hall concealing the office entrance. Gone were the heavy velvet drapes, replaced with curtains of lighter, gauzy material. Only the oriental carpets on the floor remained the same as before. Even the brass fittings used as stair rails for the three steps up from the dance floor to the small stage disappeared. The candle like chandeliers vanished, replaced with four layers of octagons made of opaque glass. Wall sconces echoed this geometric pattern, bringing even more light into the club. Overall, Gregory thought the club gained a simple elegance it lacked in the first design. He approved.

Harrison came to him one morning after the club had been open a few months, gripping Gregory's good shoulder with his left hand. "I'm going to change our entry procedure by adding cappos to the doors and maybe a few to walk around the club, enforcing peace."

"Now you're talking," Gregory said, excited by the prospect. He stared up into his brother's hazel eyes, the single lock of sandy brown hair curled between heavy brows. Harrison beamed, removing his hand from Gregory's shoulder.

"Applicants are already here. Klein has them in the front parlor, if you want to help me."

Gregory nodded, levering himself up out of his chair. *This would give him something active to do beside just watching the others rebuild the club. Something not physically taxing.*

The front parlor seemed crowded by burly men milling about in small clusters. Harrison strode smartly across the room, shaking hands with the most likely, leaving the better dressed for Gregory.

Engaging a pair of taller applicants still wearing their bowler hats, Gregory soon realized they would not suit at all. Their Irish brogues were thick enough even Gregory had difficulty understanding them. "Thank you for coming," he was saying when movement from the corner of his eye drew his attention to the door.

Klein stood back, ushering a very tall, willowy woman with auburn hair into the parlor. Sporting a dark burgundy suit of fine silk, she appeared businesslike and no-nonsense as she strode in, the tails of her coat fluttering behind her, and a fedora tilted jauntily on her close-cropped head. She was followed by a petite woman in a drop-waisted dress of pale gold, who toyed with a long rope of pearls hanging almost to her natural waist. This woman, who wore her jet-black hair in a tight bob, attracted every eye in the room, and her bee-stung lips formed a coy smile. They took seats on a sofa near the far corner.

Gregory sucked in a breath. Before he could move across the room fast enough, Harrison had reached the pair first.

Putting out his hand, Harrison said, "Harrison Davenport."

The tall one with pomaded, short hair stood and shook his brother's hand firmly while the black haired one remained seated, proffering her own hand for Harrison's quick brush of lips across the knuckles.

"Clarice Daniel is my name," the red head said and inclined her head, "this is my Letty."

Letty lowered her kohled eyelashes demurely and said, "Letty Carlyle."

Clarice took a sheaf of papers from a satchel and handed them over to Harrison, who began to read over the recommendations.

Whistling softly, Harrison's smile broadened. He tapped the papers against his arm. "If half of this is true, you both are better than any other candidates in the room."

"We had a vaudeville act back in '21, lasted four years," Letty practically purred.

"Both Letty and I can shoot the pips out of a five of hearts at 50 feet," Clarice confided. Men chatting nearby paused to listen. "We met out West while we were with Barnum and Bailey; where we mastered marksmanship."

"Are you willing to demonstrate?" Harrison asked.

"Here?" Clarice laughed, a deep contralto that stirred Gregory's musician's soul.

"We have a field out back where we can do the test. If you are as skilled as you say, you're hired." Harrison turned to Klein, who remained by the door. "Everyone can go. I believe I've found our gals."

After briefly proving their expertise, Clarice and Letty were hired. His brother claimed they were to act as hosts and cappos, further screening guests. In reality, Gregory knew why Harrison had added Clarice and Letty to the staff. While their appearance might fool strangers into thinking they were merely modern women, both of them carried pearl handled revolvers to protect the club from intruders. It really didn't matter to Gregory. He admired their frighteningly accurate shooting skills as much as he valued their cutting wit. He could easily believe that they had been with the circus or had a vaudeville act.

Furthermore, after hearing her several weeks later, Harrison asked Clarice to sing on the stage, adding another draw for patrons. The brothers easily justified the expense. Her sultry, deep voice lulled patrons into a trance much like the sirens of the Greeks as she crooned songs like *Downhearted Blues, I'll Build a Stairway to Paradise,* or *Lady Be Good.* Dressed in a black silk, man's three-piece suit, Clarice stood by the upright piano near the steps of the small bean-shaped stage, belting out Chicago Jazz or Blues songs as powerfully as Bessie Smith herself. Unlike the other women in the audience who wore their hair in short bobs, Clarice always pomaded hers into a style very similar to the one Gregory himself wore. She rouged her cheeks red, outlining her eyes in black kohl as Letty did, softening the severe, angularity her slicked coiffure gave her features. Sometimes her girlfriend, Letty, clung to her arm and looked up adoringly at her. Letty often dressed in ice blue or apricot-colored sequined dresses, fringed from the hips down to her knees that made her figure look completely boyish, creating a contrast with Clarice's more mannish style. No matter what their appearance, the audience loved them.

Harrison called Clarice and Letty his first line of defense. "They lure people in with their innocence and then – wham!!!" His brother smacked a fist into his open palm.

"I rather like Clarice and Letty. They add," Gregory had waved his hands in small, tight circles, "even more elan to our club." *And, they will definitely protect us.*

Harrison thought Gregory didn't know, but Clarice and Letty also watched out for him. Gregory had overheard the conversation his brother had with the two women in the closed office.

"Protect my brother, Gregory, at all costs," Harrison had said. "We seem to be on Capone and McErlane's lists."

"Consider it done," came Clarice's drawled reply. She had a smoky laugh. Gregory could just imagine her leaning a shoulder up against the wooden mantle over the office fireplace.

Teddy O'Hannilon, too, came around more often after the attack. "I want to make sure you are safe," he told Harrison and Gregory, crushing out his cigarette with his fingers. "Do you want me to move into one of the upstairs rooms? I don't have to commute back and forth. The gang can almost run itself."

"Horse feathers!" Harrison laughed. "Don't think your cousin George would agree."

"He is fine with how I see things." Teddy said quickly, crossing one long leg over the other and wrapping his interlaced fingers around his knees as he shifted his weight back into his chair. "He trusts me."

"More than we do," Gregory laughed, knowing that teasing Teddy was the fastest way to turn the topic to something else. Not only did Teddy have a target on his back as Bugs Moran's cousin, Gregory knew Teddy was too private to want to live under the same roof as Harrison and himself. Besides, the man had another new girl – Irene something, he thought it was, and he would be wanting room to court her properly if nothing else.

"Teddy," Harrison grabbed his friend's elbow. "Come into the office. I want to discuss buying more General Electric stock."

"So, you are investing?" Teddy asked, shocked. His thin brown eyebrows arched and his moustache twitched with his silent laughter.

"I've made millions so far. General Motors has been a gold mine."

Harrison beamed. His smile and cockiness reminded Gregory so much of Deanie.

"All on paper, mind you," Gregory mumbled to himself. The office door should have closed him off from his brother's conversation, but it hadn't. He seemed to hear the two men perfectly as if he were right next to them in the small green walled office with its huge RCA radio, large oak desk and leather chairs.

"I want to catch this latest upswing in General Electric. Raskob claims returns will be more than 12 percent," Harrison continued. "I can't believe that you aren't dabbling in the market, Teddy. I've been investing half of our profits back into the club and using the remainder to buy up stocks."

Gregory heard the distinct squeak silk made as Teddy slid into one of the large, leather arm chairs facing his brother's desk. "I have not been playing with bulls and bears," Teddy finally responded. There was a scratching sound of a lighter – ah, the requisite cigarette. A puff of air that usually accompanied a stream of smoke. "You know my fingers are in other types of pie."

"Yes, yes, you slay me," Harrison muttered, then slammed an open palm against the oak desktop. "Damn it, man. You can make a fortune! Everyone else is. You can't lose."

His brother never sounded so positive before. Gregory knew he thought stocks were a surefire way to increase their money quickly because one never bought the shares at full price. He knew Harrison bought on what he called "margin," where he paid something like only ten percent of the stock price, but when he sold the shares he held, he received full money as return on his investment. While Gregory thought the whole thing risky, Harrison had bought shares in the Coca-Cola Company, Woolworth Company, as well as the Radio Corporation of America to list a few. Trading shares had brought in cash enough to manage the speakeasy, bringing the best provisions and entertainment so Gregory really couldn't complain. There was even enough money to pay the farm hands a decent wage.

Teddy remained skeptical. Gregory heard his brother's friend pull a flask from his hip pocket and take a swig. "The market has been too good for too long. Such great bringers of wealth only last in fairytales. It has to end, and when it does..." Teddy took another drink. "Come on, let's listen to the ball game."

Harrison must have agreed because Gregory heard the crackle of the radio set and the announcer 's "It's the bottom of the third...."

Gregory shook his head. He agreed with Teddy. Fairytales like the fish that brought the fisherman gold, or the goose that laid golden eggs always ended badly with the central characters losing everything and learning that other things in life were more important than money. Still, Gregory knew his brother was merely taking care of them as he always had. He had to trust Harrison because his brother had always protected the family and provided for them.

3

It was August 9th, four months after the raid on the club. Gregory was preparing for a séance; his first since the attack, making certain all the knobs and pulleys worked smoothly. He had completely taken over that portion of the family business; so, didn't think anything about his brother allowing him to make preparations by himself. He felt particularly proud of the small seances he, Teddy O'Hannilon and sometimes Harrison held during the afternoons. The bereaved were shown up the small portico and through the white door framed by etched window glass. They walked on thick carpets to the back of the house where the brothers had lined the back, parlor walls with a deep blue satin. Two large windows allowed light to enter the room unless the damask draperies were pulled closed. Dominating the room at its center stood a large round walnut table surrounded by six or eight chairs depending on number of members participating in the séance. Under the table, concealed from their guests, were buttons and levers connected to bells, wooden pegs, or other devices that created a convincing performance. Gregory never minded conducting these seances as the hosting medium because he believed communication with the departed loved ones brought joy – even if misguided – to the patrons.

The parlor had not been touched by the intruders, but the damask couches against the wood paneled walls needed dusting as did the large table at the center of the room. He had taken rags and lemon oil to do the task, not wanting to delegate to one of the waiters, when a slim girl dressed in a magenta coat knocked on the doorframe. Because she was wearing white kid gloves, the knocking sounded more thud-like, but it got Gregory's attention. Her oval shaped face was framed by her helmet cap of dark navy felt–reddish blonde hair peeking out about the edge–and the fox tail collar of her tailored coat. Her eyes were outlined in kohl, and red lipstick gave her lips a bee stung appearance after the fashion of Clara Bow, Hollywood's "It" girl. She smelled marvelously of Heliotrope and Jasmine.

"I'm sorry," she said softly. "I don't mean to disturb you."

"Are you looking for someone?"

She smiled, brightening her round face with an angelic light, her blue eyes twinkling. "I've found someone, haven't I?"

Gregory laughed. "Yes. I suppose you have. But are you looking for someone specific?"

"Well, yes," she shrugged her shoulders, gathering her fox collar closer to her slightly pointed chin. She edged into the room, openly glancing around, taking in the older style couches, granite sided fireplace with its stone mantle, heavy window dressings, and the large table dominating the center of the space. He noticed her long, shapely legs covered in flesh colored silk stockings rolled at the knees and her pale-yellow strapped pumps.

"Ok," Gregory took a step across the deep, thick green carpet towards her. "Might I know who?" She was really delightful. Gamin rather than jaded like the patrons of the *Hair of the Dog Club*.

"A family friend, but suddenly, I'd rather be here with you." She broke into another smile that warmed Gregory's heart. Her cheeks dimpled, and Gregory noticed that if she wore rouge it was lightly applied.

"Seeing that's the case," Gregory began, looking down at the rag in his hand, "might I know your name?"

"I am called Irene by my friends," she said softly, before turning toward the pecan armoire standing next to the room's single large window. She traced the scrolled carving in the wood with a gloved fingertip. "Formally, I'm called Miss O'Brien."

Gregory followed behind her, getting close enough to take in her scent of lilac, jasmine, and heliotrope. "I hope to be numbered among your friends in future, but for now – Miss O'Brien it is," he said wistfully. The top of her reddish-blonde head barely reached his shoulders; the perfect height for a woman, he thought.

She turned and faced him, studying his features as if she liked what she saw, then noticed the rag still in his hands. "Oh, but I've interrupted your work. Please forgive me."

"No, no," Gregory whipped the rag behind his back. "There is nothing to forgive. I was about finished. The séance will be held," he took his pocket watch out from his waistcoat, "in another 30 or 40 minutes. Would you care to join us?"

"Séance?" There was a catch in her voice. Her eyes seemed to cloud over.

Did she have a lost parent or loved one whom she missed? Gregory could not help wondering.

"Teddy never mentioned those to me," she muttered, glancing downward at her heeled pumps. Then wonderingly, she inquired, "You really wouldn't mind a newcomer? I recently lost my brother. He had fought in the war to end all wars, returning to us so changed." Drawing the dusky green, drapery slightly aside, Irene pressed her forehead against the etched window pane, lost in thought.

"By all means—we will try to contact your brother for you." Gregory was at once fascinated, wanting to help her. So many young men had been irrevocably changed by their experiences in Europe. He was always so thankful that he and Harrison were too young and that horrible experience had by-passed them both. "For the time being, perhaps you would like to wait below in the *Hair of the Dog*

Club, or ... I could make you a pot of tea in the kitchen. It's just downstairs."

"Normally, I would never pass up a drink from a kind gentleman, but, perhaps, I could take tea and a little something to eat?" She whirled around, facing him again, her expression open and hopeful.

"I have just the thing. We have a delightful cinnamon bread Cook made earlier this morning. I had some with coffee at breakfast." Gregory held out his elbow to escort her.

She looped her arm through his, allowing him to lead her out of the back parlor, down the wide hallway lined with paintings of landscapes to a staircase concealed behind the door to the front parlor. Carefully, he made his way down one flight, making certain she did not slip on the wooden steps. The big open kitchen welcomed them with its huge white stove and big table covered with baking and cooking tools, and generator topped ice box dominating the far corner. Gregory urged Irene into one of the plain wooden chairs before going over to the stove. He took the kettle from beside the stove top, filled it with water from a small pump, and placed the kettle on the stove, which he lit afterwards.

While the water boiled, Gregory walked over to the cupboard where Cook kept the dishes. There was a shelf below the glass doored, upper cabinet where Cook kept cookie jars, bread boxes, and covered pans of cinnamon bread or pies. He took one of the plates from the cupboard, slid a fork from the drawer holding the sterling, then cut a slice of the cinnamon bread to place on the plate. Gregory walked the plate over to Irene and set it before her on the table, easing the fork down beside it.

"Tea will be ready soon enough. Go ahead, try it." He indicated the cinnamon bread with a tilt of his head.

Irene studied the confection covered with stripes of candied sugar, turning the brown and cream leaf patterned plate before her. "Looks divine," she purred. She eased her fingers out of kid gloves, setting the soft white material down to the left of the plate. Taking up her fork, she eased a bite away from the larger piece.

Gregory could not look away. He stared in fascination as she slowly raised the fork to her mouth, parted her red lips, and slipped the moist cake inside. She drew the fork out between her pressed lips while rolling her eyes. "This is just marvelous. I must get the recipe." She took another bite, much as she had the first, with such relish that Gregory found his pulse racing.

He did not realize that women could flirt while eating a piece of cake. Nor did he understand the very power such actions might have over him. Gregory shook his head to clear his thoughts. He had to be completely in charge for the séance to be successful. And yet—he was so reluctant to part company with Miss O'Brien.

Wait! Had she said Teddy earlier? The thought that she might be close to Teddy, a new flirt or worse, a new girlfriend hit Gregory as solidly as a glass of cold water. He could ask Harrison, of course, or he could simply ask Miss O'Brien.

Gregory walked around to the end of the table, closest to the edge where Irene was enjoying her cake. He dragged the chair out, scrapping the wooden floor loudly as he did so. Carefully, he folded himself into a sitting position, flicking back the sides of his navy-blue silk suit jacket. "I say. Did you mention Teddy? I mean before when we were upstairs?"

Irene's eyes were closed, showing the light green color decorating the lids between the kohl lines. "Hummm?" She was still deeply involved in enjoying her cinnamon bread. "Oh, Teddy," she said brightly. "Yes, yes. Our fathers are great friends. But," she leaned in closer to him as if to impart a secret.

"There you are, darling," Teddy exclaimed coming down the stairs into the kitchen, the silk trouser legs of his black suit pants brushing softly against one another. "I meant to find you earlier, but here you are with Gregory." A slow smile curved the thin moustache on his upper lip upward.

"Teddy," she acknowledged before turning her attention back to her plate.

Gregory couldn't be certain, but she did not particularly look overjoyed to see him. Teddy, for his own part seemed glad to have found her, but more relieved than ecstatic for all he called her "darling."

"Miss O'Brien will be joining the séance," Gregory put in to break the lingering silence.

"Will she, now?" Teddy brightened. "Inquiring after Geoff?"

Miss O'Brien, Irene, nodded. "I'm thinking I would very much like to say good bye to him."

"His death was quite sudden," Teddy admitted. "I don't think he belonged to any of the crowds we knew either," he said knowingly to Gregory. He reached over to the brass ashtray on the table and put out the cigarette he had been smoking.

So, no one-way ride for him, Gregory mused. "What happened? May I be so bold?" He did not want to reopen an old wound.

"It was the war," Irene sighed. "Geoff was an idealist." She said it as if idealism were the very worst sort of disease anyone might have. "He enlisted early in order to end all the evils in Europe and the world. Geoff believed that the war would end injustice."

Teddy smothered a guffaw with his long tapered, well-manicured fingers. "As if *that* were possible."

"Now, Teddy," Irene cut off his remarks. "You *know* how Father is. He fostered that kind of thinking and was rather proud of Geoff." She looked up at both Gregory and Teddy. Her look was candid. "Just because we perceive my brother as an idealistic idiot doesn't mean I don't love him."

Teddy curled the fingers of his right hand and examined his nails. "But darling," he said, still finding his cuticles fascinating, "surely?"

Irene almost stood. Heat gathered in her cheeks. "Well. I certainly do *not* blame him for running into that freight train!" She looked straight into Gregory's eyes then making his heart jerk. "He had been a survivor of that horrible mustard gas. His entire group of eight men had been hit. Geoff blames himself that he had gone to check around the corner of the trench, missing all but the vestiges of the attack and surviving when his brothers-at-arms fell instantly in the most horrible way." Irene bit her lower lip and tears filled her eyes.

"Don't think of it anymore," Gregory said hastily. A sudden sadness engulfing him. "I am certain he was very brave. Otherwise, he wouldn't have gone to Europe in the first place," was all he could think to say.

Irene nodded and eased herself back into her wooden chair, once again taking up the fork she had unwittingly dropped while wrapped up in her memories. She glared at Teddy, daring him to make another comment.

Teddy never saw the gesture. He was busy checking the nails of his left hand. He buffed them against his silk jacket before regarding both Irene and Gregory again. "No matter. I shall accompany you to the séance." Pointedly to Gregory, Teddy asked, "What time shall I have her there?"

Gregory pulled out his pocket watch. *There was something not quite right with the relationship between Irene and Teddy, but now wasn't the time to explore it.* "I'd say twenty minutes. Which means, regretfully, I must leave you both and make preparations."

As he walked back up the stairs and headed for the back parlor, Gregory was suddenly struck with the memories of Teddy with his other flirts. He could not remember Teddy ever being serious about any girl as a matter of fact. Even though several of them seemed much more taken with him than Irene – Miss O'Brien – seemed to be. That Miss Hardgrove, for instance, had always been throwing herself at him, kissing his cheeks, and dancing the fox trot so close a butter knife would not have fit between them. Did Harrison even know who Teddy favored? Harrison was, after all, Teddy's closest and best friend.

4

Finally, the back parlor met all of Gregory's specifications for the séance. He readied himself, changing into the loose smoking jacket of dark green and purple jacquard with the purple velvet cuffs that made him feel more like a real medium. The waiter, Klein, who doubled as a butler for the seances, rushed to the front door, and Gregory could hear the burble of voices, the excited couples and singles coming to see if Gregory could act as a go-between and contact their deceased. Women in cloche hats and frocks with waists below their hips turned their outer wraps over to the butler who would carry them to the armoire for storage. They retained small beaded clutch bags, perhaps holding their lipstick, a hand mirror, and small change. The gentlemen wore grey or black trousers and suit jackets with hidden pockets for their silver hip flasks of whisky or unidentified alcohol.

Teddy and Irene brought up the rear of the group, making the total of participants in today's séance nine. The ratio of women to men was about two to one. Gregory wondered if Teddy would bother to remain, or if he would, as was his custom, leave before the lights were dimmed and head for the *Hair of the Dog* to oversee the new dice tables and roulette wheel, they had added to the gambling games.

"Welcome, welcome, one and all." Gregory raised his arms, gesturing for everyone to enter the parlor and to take a seat. The table held places for 11 participants and a larger chair closest to the window and the armoire for himself. Gregory moved to stand behind his chair, waiting for the others to choose seats for themselves.

Teddy managed to escort Irene to the chair on Gregory's left. A prized spot for those wanting to address the dead. Irene gave up her fox-collared coat, and slid into the chair. Her dress was an ice green chiffon, overlaying a slightly darker green silk beneath. The dress had a deep scoop neck, revealing a twisted rope of pearls bobbing with each breath Irene took. A lightweight sea foam colored scarf rested lightly around her shoulders as if it would keep her bare arms and shoulders not covered by the dress warm.

Once settled, Irene glanced shyly up at Gregory and nodded.

He winked at her before addressing the audience with his usual speech about being a long time mystic and hoping that he would be able to reach their loved ones today.

"Please lower the lights, Mr. Klein," Gregory said to the butler, who dimmed the lights using the toggle switch nearest the door. Klein would guard the door during the proceedings, preventing those who became frightened from leaving or disrupting the enjoyment of the others.

If Klein had darkened the room, Gregory did not really notice. He was completely focused on Irene, who shuffled slightly in her seat. Her dainty hands rested on the table top and while she did not fidget, her fingers radiated energy.

"If you would all clasp hands, we will begin." Gregory reached out and took Irene's hand with his left and the hand of the lady seated at his right side. Closing his eyes, Gregory muttered a prayer and asked for help communicating with the dead. Before he could use the foot-pedal concealed under the rug at his feet, a solemn knock sounded throughout the room. "We have a presence," Gregory said, following his script, a little startled that he hadn't needed to use the pedal. "Please come forward and make yourself known to us."

A moan ripped through the room. Gregory's hair on his arms, legs, and neck bristled. He felt an unusual coldness begin to seep through him as he became aware of a consciousness sharing – because he could not think of another word – his body. "Who are you," Gregory asked in his own voice, then felt the presence take over his vocal cords—Deanie's gift, or part of it.

"I am Geoff O'Brien, beloved brother of Irene and little Neil. I must –" the voice broke off into sobs.

Irene straightened in her chair and her grip on Gregory's hand tightened. Around her the other participants also sat upright and leaned in closer to Gregory over the top of the table. They had heard the seances included knocking and lights flashing in the crystal ball at the center of the table. No one had said anything about spirits talking. Two of the women's faces went ashen and one of the men looked as if his stomach churned, his cheeks taking on a greenish pallor.

"Geoff?" Irene asked into the darkness. She looked incredulous. Teddy moved in closer behind her chair. Protectively?

"It is I, dearest sister."

"That is indeed your voice, my darling brother." Tears streamed down Irene's face, smearing the kohl into dark dripping stains. "Oh, please tell us, why, oh, why did you take your life?"

"Please tell us, spirit," Gregory said in his own voice, urging the spirit within him to share his story. Around him, the participants added a collective "Yes," as they leaned toward the center of the table.

"I had no intent of stepping onto those tracks!" Geoff screamed. "No – I merely went to meet up with Johnny The Fox. Father said he needed me to help smooth over the turbulence between Torrio and O'Banion. Like O'Banion, Father believed that the Italians needed watching," Geoff moaned. "They must have known Father was loyal to O'Banion and the North Siders."

Irene gasped. *Had she not known her family's involvement with the North Side Gang?* "Father is an honest politician!" she insisted. Her entire posture screamed outrage.

Mrs. Steven Deneen, cousin by marriage to Senator Charles Deneen, drew up her ample bosom and snorted. Under her breath she muttered, "He was part of the Pineapple Primary. The man's as deeply involved in scandal as our cousin."

"You don't believe me?" Gregory, or rather Irene's brother, stared coldly at her. He stood up and towered over his sister. "Just ask Father what happened to my West Point ring."

"Ring?" Irene seemed confused. "Didn't you die with it on?

"Oh, no. Not at all. The South Siders are so fond of torture. Father has my ring – sent to him with my fourth finger. A gift from the South Side gang." The grimace on Gregory's face was an expression he never had worn before.

Irene cupped her face in her left hand, having dropped the hand of the lady beside her, breaking the circle, which should have banished the spirit, but strangely Geoff O'Brien remained. Energy crackled in the room.

"No matter, honest or not, Father's political career was financed by O'Banion and his influence. The South Siders did not appreciate that loyalty. They wanted to control Father, but Father refused." Pain shot through Gregory as the spirit wailed. "Torrio or someone working for him had me pushed! One minute I was standing near the station waiting for Johnny the Fox or one of his men. I saw a small, round man with a red face approaching – I thought he was an accountant, so I paid him no mind. The next instant, I was tumbling, tumbling onto the tracks and that oncoming train. I—arggg," and garbled noises erupted from Gregory's throat.

The whole room got colder. Irene screamed then, and dropped Gregory's hand. Teddy patted her shoulder, murmuring "There, there," rather ineffectually.

Around the table, the others froze in various stages of shock.

Gregory reached for his throat. "You were murdered?" he managed to hiss in his own voice.

"Sister, aaa–venge mee–eeee...." Geoff said before slipping away.

Gregory felt the presence go as quickly as it had come, sliding from his consciousness and body like a pair of silk trousers slipping down his legs to the floor before bedtime. He shook his head. Realizing the lady on his right still held his hand, he relinquished his grip. Slowly, heavily, he returned to his seat, not remembering when he had stood up. Wearily, he shouted, "Klein, lights!!" He reached up and stroked his throat which seemed raspier than usual.

A sudden clamor grew in the room.

"I want to talk to my grandmother," put in Mrs. Deneen.

"No, my sister Amaryllis!" shouted Jacob Thomas.

"My departed wife," yelled another man, who stood and shook his fist at Mrs. Deneen.

"Brother!"

Gregory felt completely exhausted, and while under normal circumstances allowed several "spirits" to visit the séance, he was unwilling to do so today. He raised his open palms toward the arguing participants whose pale faces reflected their emotional turmoil, shaking his head "no." Gregory realized that every one of them was as stunned as he had been. He was coming to understand the power his cousin had given him. "Not today," he said. "Come back tomorrow. Go home and return at the usual time. I will take your requests as I am able."

Still bickering, the participants stood and gathered their belongings. They divided into the groups in which they had arrived, continuing to discuss what happened on their way out of the room, down the hallway, and out the front door.

Gregory slowly stood. Irene had found a handkerchief, probably in her clutch bag, and was daubing her eyes and nose with the white lace-edged cotton.

Teddy who had remained behind her, now stood deep in thought. "Your brother must have been one of the casualties of the

Torrio, O'Banion war when it began back in '22. The two bosses attempted a truce, or at least not steal from or kill one another's people." Teddy rubbed his thumb and fifth finger against his eyes. "There never were two men who hated each other as much as those two. Under the guise of cooperation, many of those working for both the North Side and the South Side gangs died when one or the other of the bosses or higher ups became pissed off. The deaths were ugly ones too."

Irene's brother had been murdered – pushed into the oncoming train by Johnny the Fox or on Torrio's orders. Everyone had thought Geoff O'Brien a suicide, but this... this altered everything. He had to tell Harrison. Or should he let Teddy tell Harrison? Yes, O'Banion was dead, but the North Side Gang still vied for power with the Italians. Gregory gulped, suddenly worried. Had this séance put Irene into danger? Had it put *him* in danger?

He looked over at Teddy, raising an eye brow. Teddy shrugged his narrow shoulders, but he also shook his head. Teddy didn't have the answers either.

"I'm going to look into this, don't you worry," Teddy said very quietly, holding Gregory's eyes. "Cousin George should have answers we won't find elsewhere."

"You will see Miss O'Brien home?" Gregory asked with emphasis.

"Of course," Teddy replied smoothly. "I'll be back soon enough. Harrison can take care of the tables in my absence. I want to talk to both of you when I return."

Gregory nodded. He knew it was going to be a late night. He was glad the séance guests made a hasty retreat, gathering their things from Klein, and he did not need to linger in the back parlor. He did not want to think about tomorrow. Promising the others another seance the next day was the only way Gregory could think to get them out of the house now. *Would he be able to call upon another ghost or would the seances return to the performances they had been in the past?* He asked himself, replacing his smoking jacket with the brown suit coat that matched his pants. *How long would Deanie's* ***gift*** *last?*

Harrison was on the floor when Gregory made his way down to the *Hair of the Dog*. Bix Beiderbecke and the small orchestra on stage were playing *Riverboat Shuffle*. Gregory eased his way between the tables of chattering couples, juggling drinks and cigarettes, and the foursomes fingering cards in their hands. Smoke curled up from reddened ash, creating a haze in the room. Passing the Mahjong tables, he could not help but smile when one of the women dressed in a gold satin dress excitedly called out, "Pon!" She squealed and jiggled in her chair, the feather of her headdress swaying like a propeller.

Seeing his approach, Harrison saluted Gregory with two fingers of his right hand. The light brown fedora sat tilted on Harrison's brown hair, pomaded back just like Deanie used to wear. Broader shouldered but shorter, Harrison looked up into Gregory's face.

"Something is worrying you, brother." Harrison gripped Gregory's shoulder through the dark brown silk suit jacket. He steered Gregory toward the office.

Gregory scanned the crowded room, packed with people enjoying themselves. He raised an eyebrow.

"It's safe to leave them for a moment," Harrison confided. Closing the office door behind them, he turned and faced his brother. "Well?"

"Did you know that O'Brien was one of Deanie's?" Gregory cut to the point.

"I suspected." Harrison shook his head. He took one of the leather club chairs and crossed his left leg so the ankle rested on his right knee. "Deanie controlled a great many politicians before he died, just as he had cops on the take covering for him, spreading more than a million dollars a month among them. No sane person would turn his back on that kind of money even honest men like O'Brien."

Gregory nodded. "So why would the South Side go after O'Brien's son?"

"They did?" Harrison's eyes widened. "I thought he had post war trauma, and he took his own life. Geoff was not a stable sort."

So, Gregory leaned back against the wall near the door and launched into the happenings of the séance and how he had somehow channeled Geoff O'Brien. "And he wants his sister to avenge his murder."

Harrison smacked his forehead with his right hand, pushing the fingers up under his hat and into his hair. "My God! Are you serious?" He stared at Gregory then shook his head. "Of course, you are! What a to do! I'll sort it all out."

"Well, Teddy is coming back. I think he knows something. He mentioned his cousin George." Gregory eased himself down to the carpet, sprawling his long legs outward.

"Teddy always said his cousin believed Joliet was safer than Chicago between 1919 and 1922." Harrison chuckled. "Moran never fought off charges that landed him in prison during those years. That was a bloody time with Italians or Sicilians picking off Irish or vice versa."

"I guess we were lucky living out here at the farm," Gregory rubbed his hands together.

"We were, and we still are." Harrison leaned closer to his brother. "I don't know if you have any idea how bad the bloodshed was while Deanie was alive. He hated Torrio and the Italians almost as much as he abhorred the Sicilians. When The Fox tried to implement a truce, Deanie went along – they would have all died if he hadn't, but that didn't mean he liked it."

Gregory knew his cousin could be ruthless to those outside their family, their community. For every story about his soup kitchens or paying off a farm, he had heard stories about the revenge killings and the hijacked milk trucks. But to him they had been terrible stories, nothing more. Geoff O'Brien suddenly brought the reality of the killing spree to life. Gregory suddenly felt cold, and he wasn't certain he'd ever be warm again. He finally asked, "That's why they killed him isn't it?"

Harrison became still. He nodded quickly, as if coming to a decision. "I wasn't ever going to tell you this, but Teddy and I – we were there that day."

"What?" Gregory's eyes widened and a prickle went down his back. He narrowed his eyes, "which day?"

"That horrible day in November," Harrison said, clenching his hands into fists. "We had gone into the florist shop to talk to Deanie. He was in the backroom arranging flowers for some do or another. Teddy and I came in the back, wanting to tell him about our take." Harrison took a deep breath, slowly letting it out. "When the door chimed, Deanie put up his hand."

Harrison's face twisted in pain as he shared the memory.

"Wait here. Don't come out for nothing," Deanie had whispered before he headed into the main room of the shop.

"Teddy and I hunkered down behind the arranging table out of sight, but we had a view of the main room because of the mirror behind the sales counter," Harrison explained.

""Hello, boys," Deanie addressed the newcomers, talking loudly, almost as if in warning. The mirror behind the counter showed us that Frankie Yale, John Scalise, Albert Anselmi, and Frank McErlane had come. Deanie must have thought they were part of the peace contingent because he said, "You from Mike Merlo's?""

"Those were the last words I ever heard him speak." Tears began to trickled down his brother's face, making Gregory's heart shrink painfully in his chest. "Cousin Deanie put his hand out – to shake, ya savvy? Yale just nodded and took Deanie's hand, gripping him so tightly, I could see him flinch." Harrison scrubbed at his face with a handkerchief from his vest pocket. "Then it was Hell. Bullets seemed to come from everywhere, hitting Cousin Deanie in the chest, ripping his cheeks, and exploding through his throat." Harrison broke into a sob. "Teddy and I just clung to each other, while those mooks laughed about what they had just done. Several interminable minutes after the door chime rang, we could see they were gone; so, we went in. Deanie was crumpled up on the floor. Blood was everywhere.

There was nothing we could do, so we ran – out the back—up the street—almost all the way to farm."

Gregory felt the blood drain from his face. He grabbed for his brother, hugging him. A tightness grew in his own eyes, and Gregory felt his tears trailing his jaw. "I never knew."

"I didn't want you to know," Harrison whispered.

"But that could be one reason McErlane shot up our club!" Gregory hissed, a bit of anger competing with the horror of what Harrison had just divulged.

A soft knock came at the office door. Harrison and Gregory jumped apart, straightening their jackets. Teddy eased it open before poking his head in. "I thought I'd find the likes of you holed up in here. I assume Gregory told you what happened?" he asked Harrison as he closed the door behind him and walked over to the other leather club chair. He gave Harrison and Gregory a speaking look before composing himself.

He eased himself into the cushion and produced a gold cigarette case. Almost daintily, he plucked out a smoke. Tapping it against the closed box lid, Teddy eyed first Harrison and then Gregory again speculatively. "Look," he began, slipping one end of the cigarette between his lips and patting his pocket for a light. Harrison tossed his lighter across the room. Teddy caught it single handedly and flicked a flame to life. Cupping the cigarette to the fire, he puffed twice, pulled the smoke away from his lips with his fore and second fingers, and blew a smoke ring into the air. "I don't mind talking to the Sicilians. I have an in. Carlo Anselmo owes me a favor."

He's talking about helping with Geoff, Gregory thought as comprehension struck him.

"Didn't he used to rob grocery department stores?" Harrison asked, as if he hadn't just shared the horror of Deanie's murder.

Teddy's eyes crinkled as he threw his head back and laughed. "Didn't we all?" When he got his serious face back, Teddy shook his head. "Actually, that was Antonio Anselmo. Carlo is twenty-three, but has lived a more protected life, sort of like Gregory here. He was a newsie, but a lot later than when we started." Through his long dark eye lashes, Teddy seemed to glance over at Harrison almost as if seeking approval before returning his cigarette case to his coat pocket.

Gregory had never noticed before. *What was wrong with him?* He thought. Mentally, he gave himself a shake.

"You don't mind consorting with Dagos and Wops?" Harrison asked.

"I know Deanie called them that, but don't do so again. Men like O'Brien fought a war to make us all brothers." Teddy reddened. He put the cigarette between his lips and allowed smoke to curl from his nostrils as he took a deep drag.

"Now, now, Teddy," Harrison sat back against the leather. "I'm just having a bit of fun. I might not have my cousin's prejudices, but we need to be cautious. The South Siders would rather see us dead than see us at all."

After what Harrison had just shared, he knew it to be true. Gregory stopped himself from shuddering.

Teddy accepted this with a nod, blowing out a smoke ring. While he and Harrison started with O'Banion at almost the same time, Teddy had not been an adolescent like Harrison. Six years older, Teddy should have been the boss, but instead he always accepted Harrison as the leader of their band. As always, he backed down, and began smoking in earnest. Every so often, he would send a sidelong glance at Harrison, who never seemed to take notice. "So, you're ok with me meeting with Anselmo?" Teddy finally asked.

Harrison waved his hand. "Yes, yes. Do what you have to. We need to get to the bottom of this business about Geoff."

"I say," Gregory straightened against the wall. "Miss O'Brien might ask her father about the West Point ring and that will cause a terrible dust up."

"Hummm." Teddy tilted his chin downward and rolled his jaw, holding the rapidly burning cigarette between his fingers. "Do I have to sort that out too?"

This question surprised Gregory, who had been certain Irene was

Teddy's latest girl. "I'll go talk to him." Gregory crossed his legs and sat forward.

"No, no," Harrison cut in. "I'm the older brother. I'll do it. O'Brien might feel more comfortable talking to me anyway. I met him on several occasions with Deanie. He'll remember me for sure."

That settled, the three men left the office to oversee the goings on at the club.

5

Teddy shrugged his shoulders, resettling his suit jacket across his back, as he jostled about on the seat of the taxi, he had rented to take him from the North Side down deep into the Loop and the F.W. Woolworth store where he agreed to meet Carlo Anselmo. He felt nervous... anxious about the encounter. In his memory of the young man, Carlo had hauntingly large brown eyes, and shaggy blond hair that seemed to escape the hold of his light pomade. Unlike most of the men Teddy associated with, Carlo had a dusky complexion which gave him an exotic air. Furthermore, he was snorky – an extremely fashionable dresser, tending to wear pin-striped trousers, wide ties, two toned shoes, and flat caps rather than fedoras. Teddy sighed, taking a drag on his cigarette. *Either the meeting would go well or it wouldn't.* Hopefully, the small revolver concealed in his jacket was excessive.

As Teddy left Norwood Park and the farm land behind him, houses stood closer and closer together. He knew when he got nearer to the city itself because houses became tiny bungalows, affordable to the most common folk. The streets, often cobblestone on the outskirts, became brick, and the rumble of the tires against the pavement sounded different also, taking on a whine. Traffic into Chicago increased with the closeness of the houses, controlled by occasional traffic lights. Only a few cars attempted to pass the cab, honking their horns as if they carried more important passengers than he was himself. *Glad I'm not driving,* he thought, and nestled back into the seat cushions. Through the single pane windows of the cab, the smells of the streets encroached, expelling the fresher air of Norwood Park, replacing it with industrial odors of burning metal, rubber or stockyard smells that made Teddy cover his nose with his handkerchief and put out his cigarette. Finally, after ninety minutes, the cabbie slowed the car and craned his head over the front seat.

"We're here, Mack," he said around the short stubby cigar he held in the corner of his mouth.

Teddy gathered up his racoon coat, opened the door, and eased himself out into the street. A car swerved, honking its horn at him. Teddy made a rude gesture. He reached into his coat pocket, drew out his wallet, and pressed the agreed upon amount of money into the cabbie's outstretched hand. "Thank you, Gus. Pick me up in an hour."

Turning away from the street crowded with parked cars, horse drawn wagons of produce or other goods, as well as pedestrians, Teddy looked up at the two story F.W. Woolworth store. The stone building had large windows in front with products advertised in a thematic fashion. Another time, Teddy might have stopped to admire the mannequins and other items, but today he was intent on seeing Carlo. The door clanked with an overhead bell as Teddy entered. Women carrying babies, or walking small children, congested the walkways between merchandise counters offering perfumes, handbags, scarfs, toys, and so many colorful wares. He sauntered over to the soda bar with its chrome backed bar stools, the seats alternating colors between gold and red. On the far side of the bar sat a young mother and her daughter with several stools between where Carlo sat with his elbows on the bar. He wore a subtle plaid suit of blue, green, and brown with a matching waistcoat. The suit jacket was buttoned at the top only, allowing the jacket to fall open over Carlo's broad chest. The high-waisted trousers emphasized his lean, narrow waist.

Teddy let out a breath he hadn't even known he was holding and eased onto the bar stool beside the younger man, slipping his coat over the back of the neighboring stool. "Hello, Carlo," Teddy said, holding out his hand for Carlo to shake. They gripped firmly without squeezing, palms lingering a hairbreadth too long for common curtesy.

"Glad you could come, Teddy," Carlo responded, his Sicilian accent thick, making his voice huskier than it should have been. He looked into Teddy's eyes, blinked, then looked toward the mirror behind the soda fountain. "What'll you have? I heard the phosphate is tolerable," a slow smile spread over Carlo's face, twinkling in his brown eyes.

Teddy's heart quickened. He shook his head, knowing he had to focus on Geoff O'Brien. Still, something fluttered in his stomach, and it wasn't anticipation of a soda. Carlo was continuing to look at him, eyelids with those long blond lashes fluttering slowly, making Teddy's perception of the store close in, until he saw only the man beside him. "Oh, to drink," Teddy said, realizing what the younger man was waiting for. "Chocolate phosphate is fine."

He swallowed hard and leaned forward, placing his elbows on the bar as Carlo had before Teddy arrived. Carlo echoed the gesture, bringing them closer together.

"I'm flattered you wanted to meet with me, but what's this about, Teddy?" Carlo was nothing but to the point. "If it were anyone but you, I wouldn't be here. You know as well as I do that Deanie O'Banion had no use for the likes of us, and Bugs Moran is worse."

Teddy steepled his fingers. "You aren't wrong. My cousin George has hated all South Siders especially after they slaughtered O'Banion. You know what he calls you – I won't dignify it by voicing his words. I don't hold with his sentiment, especially where you're concerned." Teddy glanced sideways at Carlo, causing the younger man to do the same. Their eyes locked. After a long silence, Teddy started over. "Look, Carlo," he cleared his throat. Softly, so no one else in the place could hear, Teddy said, "I need your help."

"My help?" Carlo echoed in his rumbling voice.

"I –" Teddy broke off. *How should he put it so Carlo* would *help rather than be offended?* "A friend of mine is looking into her brother's death," he said, finally. *The truth was best, after all.* "He might have been caught up in that violence in twenty-three slash four. You know, when The Fox was trying to save all of gangland from itself." Teddy knew Carlo would appreciate the idea of Johnny Torrio as a savior of the Chicago gangs. His confidence grew.

Carlo nodded. "I might be able to help you with that. Don't sound like any of Capone's secrets or of the Genna brothers' organization – what's left of them." He was about to say something else when the man behind the soda bar placed two tall sweating glasses in front of them.

"Enjoy! Gents," the man said, flipping his cleaning rag over his left shoulder. Teddy saw the man's reflection in the mirror do the same.

Waiting until they were essentially alone, Carlo said, "You know I'm pretty low in our organization. I might not find out much. Depends whose lips are loose," Carlo's full lips spread upward into another grin before he took the straw standing in his glass into his mouth.

"I trust you, Carlo," Teddy said, taking up his glass with his left hand and stirring the straw around with his right. "I know you'll do right by me," he almost whispered to himself so quietly he wasn't sure the other man even heard until Carlo casually slew his glance over at Teddy, slowly looking him up and down.

"And there you are, looking like John Gilbert," Carlo whispered back. "All alluring dimples and dapper moustache," before he devoted his attention to his chocolate phosphate.

Teddy felt his checks redden. Had he heard Carlo correctly? Had he just described him as the cinema's second most famous lover? *No, no, he was reading too much into something he might not have even heard correctly*. He fumbled a cigarette out of his pocket and used a book of matches from the countertop to light it.

"So, who am I looking into?" Carlo asked, brushing his hair back under his cap.

"Captain Geoff O'Brien." Teddy shot back, puffing out smoke.

"The politician's son?" Carlo gulped.

"You can still help me?" Teddy asked quickly, glancing from Carlo to the flame end of his smoke and back to Carlo again.

"Yes, I'll do it. I just have to be that much more cautious." Carlo looked worried.

"Please do," Teddy urged. "I would hate to see anything happen to you," came out of his mouth before he had time to think how Carlo might take his words.

"So, would I," he responded with a harsh laugh. "Look, I've got to go before I'm missed. I've already been gone too long." Carlo's accent thickened. "Teddy...."

After crushing his butt in a nearby ashtray, Teddy offered his hand. Carlo took it in his firm grip, the palm slightly wet and cold from the Phosphate glass, "Please don't be a stranger, Carlo. And I don't mean just because you're helping me."

Something sparkled in Carlo's eyes before he nodded. Whatever Teddy was sensing, Carlo was sensing it too. The counter felt very lonely after Carlo left. Teddy waved over the man behind the soda bar and paid for the phosphates. He grabbed up his coat and walked out onto the sidewalk, looking up and down the street for Gus and the cab. *What just happened?* He and Carlo had known each other as newsies on competitive corners, but this—this was different. They belonged to rival gangs – worlds apart. *Were they becoming friends?*

Teddy pulled out his pocket watch, flipping open the silver cover embossed with a stag surrounded by trees. Gus wouldn't be back with the cab for another twenty minutes. He went back into Woolworths, planning to walk around aimlessly biding his time. Passing a section with ready-made men's hats, Teddy saw two minor members of Joey Aiello's gang, wearing their signature long black wool coats, huddled in a corner near the dressing rooms at the back of the store. He sidled over as quietly as he could until he could overhear their hushed conversation.

"Picked up five new girls," one of them was saying. "Young ones, not yet broken in. The boss wants them for the *Four Deuces*."

"Wouldn't I love to break 'em in." The other sounded wistful in a learing sort of way.

"Not me. Thirteen is way to fresh," the other replied. "I like my women more mature."

Teddy shuddered. He understood why O'Banion and Moran refused to take a cut from Torrio and Capone's bawdy houses. He almost left when the second man turned the subject to something more interesting.

"Heard the boss is going to deposit more gold in his new bank on Belmont Avenue tomorrow."

"You know how much?"

"Naw, but it's probably a lot." The man laughed, "Business has been good. He's started to make weekly deposits."

Teddy had heard enough. His cousin George would love knowing about the bank and the gold deposits. Over the past two years, his cousin's attacks on the South Side gang had escalated exponentially. *Just the sort of revenge that would really hurt Capone,* he thought, *hitting their bank.* Threading his way through the women and children, Teddy made his way to the front doors and Gus's cab.

About the same time Teddy was leaving F.W. Woolworth's, Harrison was arriving at the swank town home owned by Irene's father, Douglas O'Brien. Facing Belmont Avenue, the brick house had a large porch wrapping three-fourths around its front, reached by three, wide, brick steps, flanked by a short, curved wall. Harrison strode up the steps to the walnut door, with its narrow side windows. He knocked briskly—listened—then knocked again. A tall, skinny butler dressed in black with a white apron finally answered the door.

"Yes?" The man blinked as if the interior was so dark the sunlight proved too bright for him.

"I need to speak to Mr. O'Brien." Harrison stated.

"He is busy," the man replied, attempting to close the door.

Harrison's hand shot out, grabbing the edge and preventing the door from shutting. "Tell him it's a cousin of Deanie O'Banion," he added with importance.

The man faltered, thought a moment, then waved Harrison inside. *Cousin Deanie still had clout,* Harrison thought. *Unbelievable.* Not because Deanie O'Banion hadn't had a long reach – he had, but because his cousin had been dead for five years. Walking through the dark wallpapered hallway, the butler led Harrison past a dining room, and two parlors. He rapped lightly on the open door to an office crowded with books and papers.

"Enter," a deep voice invited.

That was Douglas O'Brien. Harrison recognized the voice. He was about to follow the butler into the office, but the man held out his hand, warding Harrison off. "There is a young man here claiming to be a cousin of Mr. O'Banion's. He seems to have an urgent need to see you, sir."

"Well, let him in, Saunders." O'Brien said, around a cigar. Harrison could smell the faint odor of tobacco.

Harrison worked his way around Saunders and tipped his hat at O'Brien, seated behind a mountain of papers. "Harrison Davenport, sir. We've met."

"Yes, yes," O'Brien said, waving Harrison into the chair facing the desk. "Don't worry, put it anywhere."

Harrison scooped up the newspapers and papers from the seat of the chair and carried them to the nearby sofa, standing against the wall next to a gigantic grandfather clock. Returning, he sat across the desk from Irene's father. "There have been a few developments that might concern you, sir," Harrison began.

"Come to the point, son. I need to get down to the exchange. There is more news about your cousin?"

"Not at all." Harrison shook his head. "It's about your son, Geoff."

"My boy is dead," O'Brien's face hardened.

"Murdered," Harrison returned. "Pushed into an oncoming train."

"He was a troubled young man," O'Brien confessed. "The war..."

"No. It was the Italians," Harrison stressed. "They selected him particularly in order to get to you."

O'Brien wiped his broad face with his handkerchief. "What do you know," he said sarcastically.

Harrison told him about Gregory and the séance, trying to downplay Irene's part in the matter. "He asked for us to inquire about his West Point ring."

O'Brien shot out of the chair, towering over the desk, his shadow wavering against the bookcase behind him. "How dare you!!"

"You have the ring, don't you?" Harrison whispered. His heart hammered in his chest. He never disbelieved Gregory, but the whole idea of a real séance strained things.

"How could I part with it? It reminds me of the injustices done to my son." O'Brien dropped his face into his hands, his cigar—clenched in his teeth-- thrust between them. "My poor, poor Geoff. He never deserved what he got." Slowly, O'Brien eased himself back into his chair. Without looking at Harrison, he tugged at a silver pull attached to the large drawer on the left side of his desk. Fishing around for a second, he palmed a small black box. Reverently, he slid the box across the surface of the baize blotter towards Harrison. In a harsh whisper, he said, "Look for yourself."

Harrison scooted forward on the leather seat of his club chair almost afraid to pick up the box. It was about 3 or 4 inches long and two inches wide, a little like a box jewelry came in. Hesitantly, Harrison eased the lid open and almost wretched. A sour, sweet odor tickled his nose even before he could see the contents. Inside on yellowed cotton wool was a silver ring with a large oval emerald at its center, around the stone Harrison read West Point 1918. On one side, an US American eagle gripping arrows had been embossed, while the other showed an eagle's face hovering over the

US national shield. Through the center of the ring, nestled deeply in the cotton, was a severed ring finger complete with finger nail. The flesh desiccated almost to black somehow made the entire travesty even more macabre. Harrison forced bile back down into his stomach. Slowly, carefully, he replaced the lid on the box and eased it back to O'Brien, who silently returned the box to its hiding place.

"We will avenge him, Sir," Harrison said.

"My poor, poor boy," O'Brien wailed so quietly, Harrison almost didn't hear him.

Harrison reached out his hand to pat the older man's arm, thought better of it, and stood to leave. "We are going to find out who did this."

"Capone." O'Brien smashed his cigar stub in the ash tray next to his left elbow. "I don't see what you can do."

"We will think of something," was all Harrison could offer as he tipped his hat again to O'Brien and left the office, rushing back down the hall, through the front foyer, and out the door into the Chicago sunshine. The memory of that ring, of that *finger* would not leave him for a long, long time.

At the farm, Gregory wondered about Harrison's success with O'Brien, and Teddy–what success the older man might be having in finding out about Irene's brother. He realized with gang business gaining insights into the past was going to bring about results slowly. He sat in a comfortable high-backed wing chair, facing the old Adam's design fireplace in the middle parlor, the wooden floor covered with a lush oriental rug. The room served both as a music room – there was a small spinet piano against the wall near the two ceiling high windows, and an entertainment room – Harrison had purchased the newest RCA radio available. It proudly dominated a walnut folding table on the opposite wall from the piano, closer to the two wing chairs and the small sofa their parents had used while guests visited.

"This RCA has the best sound system of all the units to date,"

Harrison had bragged when he brought the unit home and began setting it up.

The radio set looked very futuristic with bright dials and its tri-scalloped, rounded top. Its two-foot-tall wooden body stood imposing in the short corner of the room between the door and the wall with the fireplace. On its face, to each side, were decorative cut-outs for the sound to filter through cloth panels of deep brown and black swirls. When his brother first turned the radio on, Gregory startled at the crackling and squealing noises. He had almost covered his ears.

Harrison bent over the rounded top of the radio, checking the back, before twisting the dials in the front. "This one controls how loud the sound is," Harrison explained. "This other allows you to select the frequency of the radio signal being beamed into the radio. Each station has its own place on the dial." Harrison seemed transported by the device. "It's a miracle of modern engineering."

"Well," Gregory had scratched his head, having never really been very close to a radio before that time. "I'm impressed with it."

He became even more so when the music that finally came through the set. His brother had been right, of course, the sound quality was excellent. He and Harrison often sat in the two wing chairs, during the early evening after eating and before they had to go to work, listening to radio programs – mostly music, but lately, at 7 pm., *Amos and Andy*—a comedy about two country fellows who moved to Chicago. And enjoying baseball games, especially since the Cubs were doing so well. Although Gregory reminded himself, the last game they had listened to had been quite ground shaking even though the Cubs weren't on the field.

Thinking back, Gregory could almost hear the sports announcer's patter, naming the players in the field, and giving a play-by-play. Cheers of the crowd buzzed in the background. The Yankees were at Cleveland League Field, and they were in the lead.

"It's Babe Ruth at bat," the announcer declared. "He's tapping the bat to the side of each shoe before he sets up. The pitch is thrown. Ball one." The announcer coughed. "It's getting tense here in

Cleveland. The Yankees are ahead, but more exciting – oh, here's the pitch."

Gregory heard a solid crack of wood against leather. The sound thrilled him-- as exciting as when he himself had played stickball with the neighborhood boys. Harrison started pounding his fist against the small table near the chair he always used when listening to the games.

"And there it goes, folks." The announcer started screaming to be heard over the roar of the crowd. "He's done it! He's done it! Babe Ruth has just hit his 500th career homerun!"

"He did it!" Harrison began dancing a jig, grabbing Gregory by his elbow, pulling him to his feet to join him.

"Wowzer!" Gregory exclaimed. "Babe Ruth is a public hero!"

"You said it!" Harrison punched Gregory lightly on the shoulder. "Now they just need to wipe the floor with the other team."

It *had* been a great game. Gregory sighed. He made himself comfortable, allowing the voice over the air waves to soothe his nerves, jangled by yet another séance, with yet another ghost trying to speak to living relatives. There had been eight this last week as if he were becoming famous. He almost missed the light footsteps scuffing against the large floor rug that brought, into his view, a pair of beige pumps, then stockings rolled up at the knees just showing in glimpses through the fringe of a sea-green dress. Quickly, he swiveled around, jumping to his feet.

"Beg your pardon," he said with a grin. "Miss Irene. Good to see you."

She held out her hands, palms facing downward, allowing Gregory to seize her warm fingers with his own hands. A smile twinkled in her eyes. "So, a compromise. Neither Miss O'Brien, but not yet Irene, I see."

Air whooshed from Gregory's lungs. His heart thundered in his ears. He prayed a flush had not spread over his cheeks. "What is the lady's pleasure?" he asked in a choked whisper.

Irene gently ran her forefinger down Gregory's cheek bone. "You may call me Irene, if you please." Their eyes locked for a heartbeat.

Then as quickly as it had come, the moment was gone. Irene flounced about, striding to the other wing chair where Harrison usually sat, plunked herself down, resting her arms heavily on the armrests. "What are we listening to?" Her voice sounded completely nonchalant, almost bored.

"I believe *Amos and Andy* will come on soon. Pepsodent just ran through their advertisement." Gregory eased himself back into the chair. He started to take his pocket watch out but the theme music from *Amos and Andy* began, so he settled back into the cushions to listen.

The two of them laughed as the radio characters discussed the Fresh Air Taxi Cab Company and listened raptly when Amos declared his boss's daughter Ruby to be a sweet woman. Anyone could tell Amos was falling in love with the girl. When the program concluded, the WGN announcer introduced musical numbers to be played next.

"What a fabulous radio set," Irene finally sighed. "Father has one, but it is a much earlier model, so the sound coming out is nowhere near as clear."

"My brother was determined to have the very best," Gregory's smile was wistful.

"Speaking of brothers," Irene began, folding her hands tightly in her lap. "I never thanked you for the other day." Her eyes gleamed with unshed tears.

Gregory shook his head.

"Really," She leaned forward, reaching out and touched his knee. "I never would have guessed you'd actually reach him. No one else ever has."

Gregory, who never had before, also wondered at the miracle wrought by his cousin. He didn't know exactly what to say. *It was nothing?* Because it was something. *It doesn't matter?* Because it very much did. Finally, he decided on, "It was an unusual séance to be certain. I'm just hoping... that is Harrison and I think Teddy might find out more about what happened."

"It would be such a blessing for Father to punish the men who killed Geoff," she whispered. "And for me."

"He must have suffered a lot in the War," Gregory offered.

"Yes. That's exactly why I always thought he took his own life" Irene sat straighter in her chair. "But that's what they wanted us to think...the killers?"

Gregory nodded.

"Father confessed that he showed your brother Geoff's ring."

"Did he?" Gregory knew he had, but he wanted to let her tell it.

"He wasn't happy about it." Irene shrugged. "He has been hiding that secret for years. When I asked about the ring, he refused to show me."

"He must have had a good reason. I can't imagine it a pleasant sight," Gregory offered.

"Will your brother be able to find out who did it?"

"It all depends on Teddy and his connections," Gregory explained.

"Right, Teddy. I was going to tell you something before the séance," Irene said finally. "Teddy came in and – well, that was that," She brushed her hands together as if dusting them off.

Worried, Gregory sat forward in his chair, leaning slightly sideways, toward her. "Are you about to warn me off?"

Irene's serious expression faded into a brilliant smile. She shook her head, her short, bobbed hair shifting from side to side in a silken cascade of dark, reddish blonde. "Oh, not at all!" She raised her two palms up and outward, warding off the idea. "It's about Teddy and me, but it's not at all what *you're* thinking."

Gregory suddenly felt as if he had drunk several glasses of champagne all at once. "You aren't his girl?"

"He wants everyone to think so," Irene confided. "I go along so the men at the Exchange where I work won't get the wrong idea about me."

"Stenographers aren't fast by nature?" Gregory teased.

"Exactly," Irene nodded. "Besides, I am focused on a career. But the bosses seem to think just because the girls in the office aren't TRADITIONAL," she emphasized loudly "the girls aren't as good as they should be."

"What boars!"

"I don't even work for a guy." Irene wrung her hands. "My employer, one of the few female stockbrokers, is Mrs. Eleanor Hall over at S.W. Stearns and Company. She's a pip! But the others there – the men – used to strike up conversations all the time, implying things they shouldn't – that is, until Teddy started coming around."

"I see," Gregory said, and he did.

"He makes a great make-believe beau," Irene admitted.

"On the surface, he seems to like you very, very much," Gregory stroked his chin.

"That's just it," Irene replied. "All surface. No substance." She waved her hands in the air. "Yes, yes, our fathers were close as boys. Our mothers would love to see us married. So, our parents are keen on it. We just are *not* right for one-another."

"I can see the parents' perspective. You make a lovely couple. His dark head—your blonde one. Dancing, you reach his chin." Gregory's gaze became unfocused as he recalled Teddy and Irene doing the Fox Trot just last night. He holding Irene so close that even a piece of paper would not have slipped between them. "Do you mean to say, you have no feelings for him?"

Irene's lips curved upward wickedly at the ends. "Now, I wouldn't go so far as to say that. I like Teddy. Emphasize *like*."

"How does he feel about you?" A cramp gripped at Gregory's stomach.

"That's harder to say." Irene replied airily. "But I believe he looks upon me as a sister."

"He Fox Trots that close with his sister?" Gregory was astounded.

"Let's just say, Teddy remains unaffected by our proximity." Irene hinted.

"Wait—he is immune to your ample charms?" Gregory almost stood up in surprise. His mouth formed an "O".

"Not just mine," Irene confessed. "Any girl's so far as I know."

"But..." Gregory thought back over all the women Teddy had dated, brought to the club or other events he attended with Harrison. There were so many. Not all as attractive as Irene, a few even more stunning, and yet—Teddy never settled on any of them. And then, Gregory recalled the longing looks he occasionally glimpsed Teddy giving Harrison. Looks his brother never seemed to notice. Had Teddy given Harrison the leadership role for more reasons than his brother's natural charisma? "Could he...?" Gregory began, but didn't even want to give the thought voice. He'd have to watch more closely. Listen harder. Gregory shook his head to clear it.

Irene stood and walked over to sit on the arm of his wing chair, swinging her legs above the rug. She smelled of jasmine and heliotrope. Her warmth comforted him as she leaned closer. "I don't think Teddy will mind, say, if you wanted to see a movie with me, even though our parents might believe I was stepping out on him. I really wouldn't be—couldn't be." She reached up and stroked the sleeve of his jacket, then fingered the satin collar. "I think you're swell," she whispered into Gregory's ear before she left.

Later that evening, Harrison called Gregory into the speakeasy's office. The lights on the desk and the chandelier on the ceiling seemed extraordinarily bright. Gregory blinked several times as he strode over to his brother, seated behind the large wooden desk.

"Teddy has been meeting with Carlo Anselmo about Geoff O'Brien." Harrison waved for Gregory to take the empty leather chair across from the desk. "I am glad that I visited O'Brien and saw what I could find out about the West Point ring. Just as you told me, that ring is tangible proof that Geoff was tortured if not murdered."

"I'm so glad that Miss Irene didn't see it." Gregory said.

"Me, too," Harrison agreed, turning slightly green as if bile rose up in his throat. "I wish I never saw it, actually. I promised O'Brien we'd do something. Would you contact Geoff again? Maybe we can learn something more helpful."

Gregory slumped down in his chair. He was not looking forward to making demands of Irene's dead brother, and certainly did not wish to upset his ghost by bringing up its horrible death. "Shouldn't O'Brien be there at that séance?"

"Not a bad idea," Harrison said, tilting his head with a smile.

"Will he be at his home or office?"

"I believe that he might be at the stock exchange. According to Teddy, the man is as devoted to following his stocks as many men are to their religion." Harrison laughed. "Tell you what. We'll go together in a few days. Maybe I can get in on some action in the market."

6

Gregory never heard so much shouting as he heard that day while at the Chicago Stock Exchange. Their cab pulled close to the 12-story stone building that dominated the corner of Washington and La Salle streets, only to enter the pre-existing congestion. Leaving the cab, Harrison and Gregory made their way to the portico entryway decorated with carvings of Celtic knots. The curved shape above the doors was echoed by the arches extending over all 13 windows on the second and third floors combined. Far above them, along the roof line, large flanged cornice work completed the massive presence of the building.

Harrison and Gregory wedged into the elevators with other investors and businessmen going upwards to the trading floor. They were expelled with the others in a burst of sudden movement once the elevator dinged. On an ordinary trading day, the up-lighting and the high ceiling would have made the trading floor seem spacious. As it was, the highly polished wooden floor seemed obscured due to the number of people crowding into the room and even the skylighted stained glass windows in the ceiling could not provide sufficient light.

Men of various ages moved around in the crush of humanity,

yelling, "Sell, sell" or "Buying, buying" followed by the number of shares and of what company they desired to be bought or sold. Across the far wall, near the ceiling, electronic lights showed the symbols for the stocks and their current price. Ticker tape machines rattled like machine guns, spewing out paper by the yard. Brokers, mostly men, but also several women, grabbed at the tape, trying to keep up with the movement of the shares. Gregory tapped Harrison's arm.

"Is it always like this?" Gregory whispered into his brother's ear, hoping no one else could hear him.

"It's always noisy but not usually to this degree." Harrison whispered back. "The architects designed the room so guys like us could whisper and be heard anywhere in the space. Usually this much shouting isn't necessary." Harrison shook his head. "Come to think of it, I've never seen LaSalle street so filled with cars and people. Did you notice the mounted police?"

"Yes. Four of them–no–five. There seems to be negative energy surging all around us," Gregory couldn't help mentioning.

"Brokers are seeming to panic." Harrison suddenly pointed at the big board with the stocks shown. The numbers appeared to be shrinking with each passing moment. "The prices are falling." Harrison's voice seemed to catch. "They are falling much faster and more widespread than I've ever seen!"

Gregory gripped his brother's shoulder. "What does it all mean?"

"If the prices continue to plummet, everyone who has invested will be ruined!" Harrison ran a hand through his hair beneath his fedora. "They will bounce back tomorrow or the next day. It's October. Prices generally surge in December because Christmas has a positive effect on businesses. Can't get distraught because the market has a few bad days."

Gregory noticed that his brother's breathing had quickened. Listening carefully, he could faintly hear Harrison's heartbeat speed up. All around them, other men's heart rates also increased with their breathing–Gregory heard it all. Like his brother, all of the men were concerned, Gregory could tell. *Putting on a brave front,* Gregory thought. He wanted to leave and lock the desperation he sensed behind. He would have panicked, but Gregory recalled that he and Harrison had come to the exchange to find O'Brien.

"Where's O'Brien?" Gregory asked to refocus his brother's attention.

Harrison turned around slowly amid the brokers racing back and forth, waving their hands in the air, as they continued shouting. On the far side of the floor, next to one of the ticker-tape machines, stood O'Brien. He was pulling the tape through his hands, reading the print out, shaking his head with each pull. Harrison tapped Gregory with the back of his hand. "There he is. Poor sap. And we have to take him more bad news. Come on. Might as well get this over with."

Harrison threaded his way through the crowd, Gregory following behind him.

"I've never seen the market so bad," Harrison shouted to O'Brien.

"A bad, bad, business," O'Brien agreed.

"It's sure to bounce back in a few days," Harrison replied. "Happy days are here again and all that."

"Sure, sure." O'Brien stared at the tape again. "RCA just dropped another twenty points."

"Good time to buy," Harrison offered with a wry smile.

"If only you have the money."

"My stocks are on margin; so, I'm out." Harrison shook his head.

"Most of mine are too," confided O'Brien. "Why use your own money, if they give you money to use?"

Gregory never understood the idea of buying on margin – gambling that the prices would go up or down and the buyer or seller would make a profit on the difference between what they said they'd pay and the actual price on a set date. What was worse–banks, brokers, or was it the stock market itself, that allowed investors to buy shares at 10% of the actual cost so the overall market inflated itself like a hot air balloon. Nothing but air served as backing, but banks were going to demand full value sometime. Gregory was afraid that time was rapidly approaching. Harrison and O'Brien pretended not to be gravely concerned, but their breathing and heartrates told Gregory differently.

Harrison stopped O'Brien as the man began to leave. "We wanted to invite you to join us tonight."

"Join you?" O'Brien blinked.

"Yes," Harrison glanced over at Gregory. "My brother here will be conducting another séance. We wanted you to have the opportunity to speak with Geoff."

O'Brien shook off Harrison's hand. "What nonsense is this?" His faced reddened in anger, contrasting with the dark purple of his suitcoat.

"No nonsense, Sir," Harrison hastened to conciliate. "Gregory is an actual medium. It was through him that we found out..." he lowered his voice as much as the surrounding noise allowed, "about the ring, sir."

O'Brien pulled up short. "No one else knew about that. I refused to tell a living soul."

Harrison nodded slipping O'Brien a business card with the address of the *Hair of the Dog Club* embossed on it. "Eight o'clock?"

"Perhaps," O'Brien spluttered, but he snatched up the card before forcing his way through the throng of brokers, who were still shouting and waving their hands in the air.

"We need to go," Gregory said. He was ready to leave the exchange whose atmosphere of increased desperation depressed him.

Harrison took one last glance at the stock board, his features whitening. "Come on, we have things to do," his brother said, grabbing Gregory's arm and pulling him through the crowd.

They exited through the arched stonework over the great doors, where they were almost prevented from getting to the sidewalk because the street was jammed up with cars and a huge mob of businessmen. Some were shouting and waving their fists at the exchange building while others were muttering to themselves.

"Ruined!"

"Out on the street!"

"Broke!"

One young man grabbed Harrison by the arm, trying to drag them toward a jazzy vehicle with white-walled tires. "Do you want to buy a car? Mine's a pip!" His facial features fell. "Can't afford her anymore."

"Sorry," Harrison shook his head.

Gregory glanced around trying to find a cab with no luck.

"Come on," Harrison slung his arm around Gregory's shoulder to steer him to the right. "Let's go down Washington. Maybe we can hail a cab from there or at least from the Bismarck Hotel on Randolph. The further away we get from here the better."

Gregory didn't argue. Throwing one last glance behind him at the chaos in front of the Stock Exchange, he pressed through the crowd behind his brother. He couldn't wait to return to Norwood Park, the farm, and the *Hair of the Dog Club.* The noise seemed to follow them for several blocks beyond the Exchange building. Even on Washington and then on Randolph Streets, horns blared and people shouted. Finally, Harrison was able to hail a cab and they settled inside the tight quarters. Gregory was glad to put the screaming, wailing, and hair pulling behind him, feeling the jangling of his nerves much more than normal.

Once they returned to the house, Gregory did not have much time to prepare for the séance. He once again checked the bells and knockers around the room and under the table. Within the armoire in the corner, the lantern that glowed through the tiny pin-prick holes in the wood worked smoothly. The chairs around the large round table each had their small apparatus that could cause the chair to vibrate slightly. Nothing was amiss. Still Gregory fretted. *Would Geoff return?*

Eight O'clock arrived much faster than Gregory wanted. Klein ushered the guests into the parlor, assigning seating so that O'Brien, when he came, would be seated at Gregory's left. The large man looked skeptical, but his discomfiture increased when Irene and Teddy joined the group, Irene sitting at her father's other side.

"What are you doing here?" O'Brien asked quietly, shrugging his dark navy suit jacket back over his shoulders.

"The same as you Father," Irene replied, slipping out of her woolen coat, revealing a silver lame gown, dotted with seed pearls.

"I heard about the last time," her father hissed. "I can't believe you are here for more."

Irene eased into her seat, composing herself, primly. "Well, you believe wrong," she whispered.

Gregory understood the father and daughter's discomfort, but there was little *he* could do about that. He cleared his throat. Looking out at the guests seated around the table, he saw O'Brien and Irene, of course, with Teddy, cigarette dangling from his lips, remaining standing as he had before behind Irene's chair. Heavy-set and balding Darryl Kempt, head of the Poultry Union, and his wife came next. Mrs. Kempt was a plump woman with her greying hair twisted into a bun, half covered by a smart yellow hat. Lanky red-haired Ned and Nancy Thompson, cousins to the Chicago mayor sat beside the Kempts. Mrs. Thompson, willowy thin, contrasted starkly with Mrs. Kempt. Furthermore, her thin plucked eyebrows, lightly rouged cheeks, and bee stung red lips showed her sense of style reminiscent of her recent years at Vassar. Her gold beaded dress and short, bobbed hair seemed even more haute fashion than Irene's ensemble. Finally, Clarice – in her man's suit, and Letty, dressed in red, along with a young couple Gregory did not recognize made up the final participants. Everyone was chatting quietly with the person seated next to them. Gregory cleared his throat again, then clapped his hands for silence when that did not work.

"Ladies and gentlemen, quiet please while we attempt to contact the spirits." He raised his hands and took up O'Brien's and Letty's, demonstrating. "Clasp hands to unite our group. Klein – lights, if you please." Gregory waited several heart beats. He could not see much difference between when the lights were on and when they were off – something he felt was strange, but shrugged it off.

Several of the guests coughed while others shuffled their feet beneath the table. When they settled, Gregory intoned, "Spirits, we seek you. We need your counsel. Please come to us."

Someone far from him stifled a cough. Gregory started to reach his knee toward the button that cause the knockers under the table to clack when the room chilled.

"Geoff O'Brien? Is that you, returned to speak with your sister? Your father –" but his voice cracked. Gregory shook his head fiercely, only he had not directed the movement. His chest tightened, and he felt as if he had shrunk in his chair.

"I am not he whom you seek." A childlike voice emanated from Gregory's throat. It was a high-pitched soprano. Young and female.

"Who?" was all Gregory could rasp before he became a passenger in his own body.

"I am Melody—Marietta Anselmo, cousin to the Genna brothers. At thirteen I died from wounds inflicted by men at the *Four Deuces Club*." Gregory sobbed, the girl's tears running down his cheeks.

Deep inside he was able to remember the club separately from Melody. At 2222 Wabash Avenue, the club was a principle holding of Capone inherited from Big Jim Colosimo; a place for gambling, drinking, and loose women; a place neither he nor his brother frequented.

Melody wailed. "Men vied for the honor from Big Al Capone to instruct me in the ways of the club." Her voice cracked. "Never have I suffered such pain. Or humiliation."

Around the table, Gregory heard a collective gasp as if from far, far away. He noted that every face had gone white with shock. The mouths of the women, especially, rounded into "O"s.

"What can we do for you child?" It was Clarice, her alto voice which so resembled Greta Garbo seemed strong in the strange silence.

"I would ask for revenge," Melody began, "But my need is much greater."

"Greater?" O'Brien asked aghast.

"I have a sister – Margaretta."

"No!" The women wailed, anticipating what came next.

"When the men stole us away with promises of sweets and fine dresses, she was only five. I fear that she is old enough now to suffer my fate." The scream curdling from Gregory's throat burned. "Save her. Pleeeasse saaave her!"

Gregory's head fell forward against the table as the presence of Melody Anselmo retreated away like the tide on a beach. He heard gasps from the guests around the table. O'Brien slid a protective arm around his daughter's shoulders. Teddy sucked in air. As his eyelids rolled shut, Gregory sensed rather than saw Clarice leaping to her feet, anger bristling off her like charged lightening.

"We must save that girl! What was her name?" Clarice snapped her fingers.

"Margaretta," Letty finished for Clarice.

Klein must have turned the lights back on. Gregory could detect their warmth. He wanted to open his eyes, but the lids still felt too heavy.

"Why don't you notify the mayor that underage girls have been stolen away to service patrons at the *Four Deuces*," O'Brien told Thompson gruffly. "Bill is your cousin, after all. He will be able to do something."

"Capital idea," agreed Kempt who was readying himself and his wife to join friends at *Hair of The Dog*. Mrs. Kempt nodded furiously.

"My cousin is controlled by Capone," Thompson muttered. "The very man who doesn't give a damn what girls work in his places. Some patrons want 'em young."

Thompson's wife, Nancy, smacked her husband on the back with her beaded bag. "It's unconscionable, Ned. That's what I say, evil. You will speak up on that girl's behalf."

Ned took his wife by the elbow and escorted her towards the door. "I'll do what I can," he shot over one shoulder. "No promises."

Clarice turned to Letty. "We will mount a rescue ourselves. If we wait for them," Clarice gestured toward the others, "that other girl will die the same horrible death as her sister."

Gregory agreed. As a good Catholic, he hated the idea of bawdy houses because they went against so many commandments. Cousin Deanie and his gang might have been racketeers, thieves, and mobsters, but they never trafficked in unwilling women.

Teddy left Irene to her father and appeared at Gregory's elbow. Flipping a new cigarette into his mouth, he said, "I want to help rescue that girl." His face had taken on a pallor like a hotel bedsheet, the skin over his cheekbones tight. Flicking a cigarette lighter from his pocket, he lit the tip and took several long drags. Smoke circled around his dark, pomaded head.

Gregory could read that thoughts were whirling around in Teddy's brain. He just didn't have a guess what they were about. *Wait a minute.* Anselmo. Anselmo, that was the girls' last name and ... the last name of Teddy's South Side Gang contact. *Same family? It was possible.*

"You know the family, don't you, Teddy?" he finally asked, softly because his throat was still a bit raw.

Teddy flushed, blood rushing up his cheeks. He nodded, perhaps not trusting himself to speak. Glancing back toward the armoire at the O'Briens, noting they were busy donning coats and hats, not paying him any mind, Teddy seemed to relax.

"Carlo?" Gregory pressed.

"Yes." Teddy hissed, allowing smoke to trickle through his teeth. "Margaretta might be his cousin, too."

"You know," Gregory said slowly. "We could do with his help. An in at the club would do wonders. The doormen must know all of us on sight being part of O'Banion's crew so to speak."

"Hatred runs deep." Teddy agreed, taking another long draw.

"It's Capone." Gregory shrugged. "Man despises all Irishmen."

"Cousin George hates all Italians, even if some are Sicilian," Teddy shot back, stabbing the air with the cigarette between his two fingers. "It's pretty much even as far as that goes."

"Can you blame him?" Gregory asked. "Man had cousin Deanie brutally offed."

Teddy merely shook his head as if he didn't know what the world was coming to. "I'll help get the girl out, is all."

"Will you talk to Carlo?"

"Yes. Yes, of course," Teddy said, giving a wave over his shoulder as he walked away and out of the house. Gregory heard the thud of the front door, closing behind his brother's friend.

Teddy strode swiftly to the lean-to where he had hidden the Ford cousin George had lent him. He cranked the engine, pulled out the choke, and cranked again, urging the car into life. It sputtered and puttered loudly in the quiet of the night air. Wanting to find Carlo as quickly as possible, Teddy ran through the places his friend might be at this time of night. Not the *Four Deuces,* that was certain. There was a bar, just outside the Loop which tended to cater to *his* sort of crowd and that of Clarice and Letty. The joint was called *Parisian Gaiety*. He could try there first, but Teddy would not be able to risk checking into too many places if that failed. An Irishman looking for a Sicilian – not a safe proposition in this town.

Teddy's heart clenched as he drove along the dark roads toward Chicago. At the same time, butterflies fluttered in his stomach in anticipation of seeing Carlo again. The younger man's deep brown eyes, chiseled cheekbones, and handsome, swarthy complexion haunted Teddy as no one else ever had. He pressed the accelerator harder, bouncing and jolting on the brick road.

Finally, Teddy saw the overhead trains of the El with the miles and miles of tracks. Unlike Norwood Park, the Loop was almost as bright as daylight. Crowds of people milled on the sidewalks and cars clustered between traffic lights on the streets. Teddy ultimately found a place to park the Ford, five blocks away from the small, exclusive jazz club located on Pine Street near East Pearson. The front doors of *Parisian Gaiety* were concealed by two flights of stone steps leading down into a basement beneath a building constructed of large, limestone blocks. Teddy could hear a clarinet squeal as a bass and piano thumped away accompaniment. His shoes made scuffing noises on the brick and then on the stone sidewalks as he edged his way through the press of well-dressed Chicagoans some sporting racoon coats over evening wear, while others had on silk.

Teddy knocked at the door, praying that he would not need a password. He patted down his coat pockets, looking for a smoke and, finding one, lit up. The sharp taste of the tobacco soothed his nerves.

A short, balding man with bad teeth answered his knock. "What'd ya want?"

"A drink, my good man," Teddy said with a nervous laugh and a small puff of smoke. The club was fairly dark inside with low ceilings, the up-lighting not contributing to more than atmosphere. Beyond the man and his cloud of cigar smoke, Teddy saw couples dancing, men with men; women with women. At the few tables he could glimpse through the partially opened doors, Teddy spotted men in expensive suits or women in flapper dresses curling a hand around tumblers of dark liquid, with most free hands holding cigarettes.

The doorman looked Teddy up and down before finally deciding that Teddy might be harmless. "Ya look too much like John Gilbert to be a pig," the man rasped out in a deep smoker's voice.

"Not a copper," Teddy shook his head and laughed again. He wanted to ask if Carlo were there, but that would cause too much trouble later-- call too much attention to them. He edged his way past the doorman and worked his way toward the bar. Surreptitiously, his eyes roved around the room, through the thick smoke, looking for Carlo.

"Hey, Mack, what'll it be?" asked the bar man, who shouldered his cleaning cloth.

Teddy turned his attention forward to the large bartender, who stood between the mahogany bar and the floor to ceiling mirror behind him. The man had hams for arms and a barrel sized neck. Not a man to make angry, Teddy decided, putting his cigarette down in a nearby ashtray. "How about a beer?"

The man pulled on one of the taps, pouring a frothy liquid out into a glass mug. With a clunk, he put the mug in front of Teddy. "Two bits."

Teddy fished around in his pocket for change, leaving the cost of the beer and a nickel for a tip. Sipping at the lager, he slowly turned, leaning his back against the rounded edge of the bar. About to give up, he sighed thinking: *Finding him here would have been too easy.* Then, just as he began to turn back and place his mug on the bar, Teddy spotted Carlo. He huddled against the wall at a small table in the farthest corner of the room, about twelve feet from the stage where the musicians performed. Teddy snatched up his smoke. Propelling himself forward, Teddy worked his way through the foxtrotting couples, the rapid beat of the music now pulsing through him on his way to his goal. When he reached Carlo, he pulled out the empty chair.

"May I join you?" he asked quietly, forcing Carlo to look up at him.

Shock ran across Carlo's features, but when he recognized Teddy, his generous mouth turned up into a smile that reached his eyes. "I didn't expect to see anyone I knew here, least of all you."

Teddy turned the chair around one handed, so he could straddle it, facing the table. Resting his forearms against the chair, he relaxed, mug in one hand and cigarette in the other. Taking his time, Teddy inhaled deeply then held the cigarette away from his face. "Disappointed?" he asked, blowing the smoke sideways away from their table.

"Oh, no, no, no," Carlo said, his accent thickening. "Not at *all*."

When Teddy set his mug on the table, Carlo reached across the short distance, stretching the suit jacket across his flat chest, and covered Teddy's hand with his own. The warmth sent a tingle up Teddy's arm causing him to smile wryly. Carlo's thumb made small circles across Teddy's hand, and Teddy's throat threatened to close up. He ground out his cigarette in the ashtray, wanting to focus on the man across from him.

"I have been thinking about our last meeting," Carlo said in low hushed tones. "I don't have news yet on that favor you asked, but I haven't been preoccupied by that. It's you, my old friend."

Teddy swallowed. He closed his fingers over Carlo's, but allowed the other man's thumb freedom to continue its stroking. He ran his tongue over his lips to moisten them.

"Is there any possibility you have been thinking about me?" Carlo raised his gaze to Teddy's. There was hope in that look, the moist brown eyes glittering in the flickering light of the candle set near the wall. Here in this secretive and safe haven for couples like them, Teddy felt he could finally be truthful.

The hissed "Yes," came out of Teddy like a deflating balloon. "Despite all the reasons not to, I can't stop." He wanted to speak of his feelings, the budding rose growing in his heart, but he was on a mission, a rescue mission, not one of romance and love. How could he just blurt it all out? He did not want Carlo to stop looking at him as if he were the hero of the story, as if he truly *were* John Gilbert, handsome, suave, winning the love of his life.

While those thoughts ran through Teddy's head, Carlo had taken the hand previously holding the mug and folded it between his own two hands, bringing Teddy's closer to his face. Carlo opened Teddy's hand, exposing the palm, and grazed the open tender flesh with his lips. "I want us to be dear friends," Carlo said, concealing a plea.

"I—," Teddy knew he had to tell Carlo about his cousin. He had to do it now before Carlo interpreted his actions as a rejection. Quickly, he said in a low-pitched whisper. "Carlo, you are the most attractive person I know. I want desperately to explore your proposal, but there's something I need to tell you. Please understand."

Carlo's face hardened. He slid his hands away and hid them under the table. "You love Irene O'Brien." He said flatly. The expression on his face made him look like a five-year-old boy whose ice cream had fallen into the street.

"Nothing of the sort!" Teddy practically yelled. "I suspect I'm falling in love with you. There, I said it." He ran his hands through his hair. "Carlo, oh my God, man. Don't twist this around." Teddy wanted a smoke so badly, but he couldn't take his attention off Carlo.

Carlo held up a hand, palm out. Shadows from the candle on the table danced across his face. "You are falling in love with me?" a light laugh escaped him.

"Isn't that what you wanted?" Teddy's stomach fell. *Had he made a total ass of himself?*

"Oh, yes," Carlo's big smile was back. He relaxed against his chair, taking a cigarette out of a silver box in his vest pocket, offering a smoke to Teddy, before sliding the box back into his pocket. Lighting up using the candle flame, he took a puff, allowing the smoke to drift out through his nostrils. "So long as we agree on that, I am willing to hear you out about any *thing* you wish."

Teddy let out a huge breath in relief. Lighting his cigarette from the same candle – it felt so *appropriate,* he stood, turned the chair around to sit properly, moving it to the same side of the table where Carlo sat. The chairs were so close, in fact, Teddy's leg pressed against Carlo's, making the Sicilian's eyes glitter. Teddy allowed himself a slow smile, smoke escaping from between his lips. "I'm glad that's settled."

Instead of creating distance, Carlo seemed to move even closer.

"Do you remember a Melody Anselmo?" Teddy began cautiously before launching into an explanation of the Séance, and what the ghost had revealed. "She mentioned being related to the Genna brothers." Teddy crushed his cigarette in the ashtray and looked intently at the man next to him.

Carlo nodded. He passed his own cigarette off to Teddy, who took a puff, before handing the smoke back. They shared a searching look before Teddy continued his rendition of the evening's events. The cigarette went back and forth between them as Teddy spoke. When Teddy finally finished, Carlo put out the cigarette, pensively.

"So potentially the *Four Deuces* is holding one of my cousins and planning to use her as a whore?" Carlo asked, anger underlying his words.

"Unfortunately." Teddy said. "But we have a plan—I hope there is now a plan—to rescue her before anything worse can befall her. Will you help us?"

"Why didn't you say that in the first place?" Carlo asked, humor lacing his words. "You can count on me."

7

"BLACK TUESDAY, STOCK MARKET CRASHES."

Gregory read the headlines in all the Chicago papers, and they were all the same. The companies selling on the exchange all saw plummeting prices on their stocks in a downturn never before seen on Wall Street. The panic Gregory sensed while he and Harrison were on La Salle Street was real and wide spread across all of the United States, not localized in Chicago. Sitting across from Harrison at the kitchen table, Gregory noticed the cool air of the lower floor provided no comfort.

Harrison, red faced from anger, pounded his fist on the table, rocking the spoon in his oatmeal. He rattled the newspaper and shouted, "Idiots! The reporters are going to make matters worse with this garbage." He thwacked the table again, then pointed at the headline. "Just look!"

Running his free hand through his brown hair, creating a wave effect in the pomaded coif, Harrison shook his head.

"Are they wrong?" Gregory asked quietly.

"They might well be," Harrison retorted. "The market has been strong these past ten years. Yes, yes, there have been small downturns, but the market has rallied. The economy of our great nation is strong, healthy. President Hoover has even said so many times."

"So," Gregory shifted in his chair. "You think it will get better."

"Of course, it's going to get better. Just give it a few weeks. But these stupid reporters will create an uproar to be sure." Harrison's face clouded over.

"What will you do?" Gregory leaned forward. He remembered the young man trying to sell his new car; others who looked distraught enough to do themselves harm.

"I'll have to sell the short call stocks," Harrison said glumly. "The broker has already asked for the funds. But, the others..." his brother held his open hands up spreading them wide, palms out, "I'd like to hang onto them until they recoup." Under his breath he muttered "if they recover. I hope they recover," thinking, Gregory suspected, that Harrison believed he could not hear the words of despair.

Gregory nodded. He didn't know what else to say to Harrison. After all, he himself knew little about the stock market, or trading shares.

Harrison brightened. "I could buy up a few solid companies' shares like General Electric to make up the difference." He seemed able to put a better face on things with that thought.

Teddy came in then. "I couldn't help overhearing your conversation." He pulled out a chair, folded his overcoat over the ladder back, before flipping his suit jacket away so he could sit. Reaching for an apple in the bowl at the table's center, he said, "I have an idea of what to do while we are riding out the stocks." He took a bite of apple, placing his cigarette in an ashtray next to the fruit bowl.

Harrison sat forward, tossing the folded newspaper aside. "Do tell." Harrison forced a grin.

Teddy leaned in closer to Harrison and motioned Gregory nearer even though no one else was close by. He ate some more of the apple, crunching its juicy flesh, wiping a drip with his handkerchief. "It's an idea I have to run by cousin George, but would definitely help O'Brien get revenge for the murder of his son."

Harrison's eyes widened. "Oh?"

"When I was at Woolworth's the other day, I chanced to hear two of Capone's gang talking about a large gold and silver deposit Capone regularly makes at the Belmont-Sheffield Trust and Savings Bank on 1001 West Belmont Avenue." Teddy finished up the apple then crushed out his stub against the glass ashtray.

"That's a new bank," Harrison said. "The second and third floors have offices, and there may be hotel rooms on the upper two floors. If I follow your train of thinking, we might run into lots of difficulties due to heavy foot traffic."

"Yes, the Montfield Hotel does occupy floors four through six, Clarice mentioned a friend moving in there last year when the building opened," Gregory pointed out.

Teddy waved a dismissive hand then patted his pocket for a cigarette. "Look, I bet cousin George will offer us any help we need. My idea is to take an office on the second floor for a month. The first two weeks, we can scout out the security at the bank and the last two weeks finalize plans for the job. We take that gold and silver and we will be set no matter what the stock market does. Revenge for Geoff's murder will be gravy on the mashed potatoes." Teddy stroked his pencil thin moustache, stuck the unlit smoke between his teeth, and stared at Harrison.

Harrison's lips curled into a tentative smile. "I like it," he nodded, "but Teddy, let's give it a week or two to boil in that noggin of yours. If the market rallies as I suspect it will, then we will let your cousin and his gang do the job, getting revenge for O'Brien. We run a lot smaller operation here."

"A safe operation," Gregory murmured. He didn't like the idea of Harrison participating in a dangerous bank robbery where he might get maimed or killed. "Besides," Gregory said aloud so Harrison and Teddy could hear, "We need to focus on rescuing Margaretta Anselmo."

Harrison nodded in agreement. "I think Clarice and Letty may have some ideas about how to get the girl out, but someone needs to visit the *Four Deuces* and figure out where Capone and his men are keeping her."

"Carlo might do that for us," Teddy offered, lighting his smoke. "I can't see any way any of us could go into the *Four Deuces* as a patron and come out alive. I believe that all of us are recognizable as members of the North Side Gang."

Harrison pushed back on his chair and stood. He held out a hand, inviting Teddy to do the same. "Come on. Let's find Clarice and Letty, and see what they have come up with."

"Give me a moment," Teddy said, talking around the cigarette. He went over to the telephone, cranking it, then saying, "I want to place a call to Brunswick 8-793 please."

Gregory heard the squawking of the operator in return. The call went through. Teddy gave Clarice's address. "Two hours," he said before ringing off. He turned to Harrison. "I'm ready now."

The three men grabbed over coats for the wind, jumped into the Model T, and headed for Chicago's North Side and Towertown, connected to The Loop by a newly constructed bridge. Clarise and Letty had leased an apartment not far from where cousin Deanie had his floral shop. The bungalows closer to Norwood Park gave way to taller, stone buildings with arched porticos, and tall windows on the lower stories, short ones higher up. The brick road had fewer and fewer pot holes, but became more and more congested the closer in they drove. Horse drawn vehicles competed with various types of cars and trucks. Klaxons sounded, startling Harrison, who had taken the driver's seat, forcing Teddy to squeeze between the brothers. Cars and other traffic thickened around Clarise and Letty's brownstone.

"We'll get out here," Harrison said as they finally made the near corner of the building. "Gregory, you park the car, then meet us upstairs."

Harrison and Gregory jumped out, exchanging places. Teddy slid out after Gregory, slammed the door shut, and caught up with Harrison on the sidewalk side of the car. He gave Gregory a little salute before he and Harrison headed for the steps leading to the double doors of the apartment. Gregory shifted the Ford from park to drive and inched forward into traffic. He would make the block, looking for a safe parking spot. When he saw nothing on the first block, he moved two blocks away, finding a small park, surrounded by the houses on the street. After he parked the car, Gregory noticed that Irene—of all people—was sitting on the green bench in the park, under a tall American Elm tree.

"Irene," he called lightly, jogging over to the bench.

She looked up, eyes wide, surprised to see him. Her cheeks pinked with pleasure. Up close, her light weight jacket and peach, short sleeved dress with its low waisted, pleated skirt gave her a professional air she did not carry while at the *Hair of the Dog*. "Why hello, Gregory."

Gregory took up one of her hands, wanting to kiss the back, but shook it instead. "What brings you here; albeit, the weather is quite fine." Nearby a few birds chirped in agreement.

"I live not far." She glanced down the tree lined street in the near distance.

"I should have thought you would be at work today." Gregory sat beside her, not waiting for an invitation. He flicked back his dark brown suit jacket beneath his overcoat, protecting the suit from wrinkling.

Irene wrinkled her nose adorably—at least in Gregory's opinion. "I should have been." She stretched her arms out in front of her, fingers locked and palms forward. "My boss gave all us girls the day off. I suppose you heard the news?"

"Heard it?" Gregory straightened. "Harrison and I were at the exchange yesterday. Chaos."

"It was bad enough at our office. Mrs. Hall couldn't say which way the market will go." Irene nodded. "I can't imagine how horrible it must have been on LaSalle Street."

"Bad," Gregory whispered. "But Harrison is certain the market will rally. He's waiting – waiting and praying."

"If it doesn't, I will be out of a job," Irene confessed, staring down at her beige, heeled pumps and the flagstones under the bench. She shook her head, her blonde wisps of hair sticking out along the rim of her yellow felt hat fluttering in the breeze. Gregory could smell the jasmine and heliotrope scent of her, knowing he would never breathe in the fragrance of those flowers without thinking of Irene.

"Say," he began, then hesitated before committing, "I would love to see *Broadway Melody.*"

"With Bessie Love and Anita Paige?" She glanced sideways at him, through her long dark brown lashes, a slight smile curving on her lips.

"Yes. That's the one." Gregory looked longingly at her. "Would you consider going with me a week from Friday?"

A giggle bubbled up from her throat. She nodded gleefully, her two fists up near her chin. "Yes, yes, of course," she finally said. "I'd love too."

"It's playing at The Oriental. I could pick you up for dinner at five and that would give us plenty of time to make the 7:00 start." Emboldened, Gregory took up one of her hands in his. Her fingers were so dainty and pale against his own larger hand. "I have to go, but look forward to our date."

Irene turned, pouting, and looked at him, "What's so pressing?"

"Harrison and Teddy are at Clarice's planning a way to help Margaretta Anselmo." Gregory grew serious, leaning back against the wooden slats of the bench.

"I want to help that poor child. I heard what her sister said," Irene replied, standing up, flouncing her skirt. "I'm going with you."

What would O'Brien think? But it really didn't matter. If Irene wanted to help, Gregory was not going to stop her. "All right," he said, getting to his feet. "Come on. I think we are late." He tugged on her hand, and they left the park at a quick march, their shoes clacking on the flagstone.

They wound their way through the press of people on the sidewalks, making their way to the brownstone where Clarice and Letty shared an apartment. The neighborhood was genteel, but slightly shabby, being closer to the North Side and Towertown. The small gardens in front of the buildings were well tended, but the buildings themselves were older, the stone worn and sometimes blackened by the pollutants carried in the air. Unlike South Chicago where the stockyards and huge industrial plants were, the North Side was fortunate the air was clearer and more breathable. Clouds billowed high above in the blue sky and the wind gusted, pulling at Irene's skirts and at Gregory's coats. Slightly breathless, Gregory and Irene ran up the steps to Clarice and Letty's apartment, and had the doorman ring them up. Rather than wait for the brass grill-doored elevator to return, they climbed the steps to the third floor, Gregory knocking on the door of 3B.

Letty swung the door open, revealing a living room in art deco style with a large peacock screen in front of the fireplace across the room from the door. The wooden floor of the room was mostly covered by a Persian carpet woven in yellows and blues. To the right was a hallway lighted with up-lighting, most likely to the bathroom and bedroom, while to the left was a small dining area and a kitchen beyond it. Letty did not look surprised to see either Gregory or Irene.

"Come in, come in," she said in her light, high voice. She flounced her cream pleated skirt as she sauntered back to the cream colored, sloped back sofa where she had apparently been sitting next to Clarice. Harrison and Teddy had taken up the arm chairs facing the sofa. Another man about Gregory's age dressed in a deep purple plaid suit with a purple waistcoat sat on the upholstered arm of Teddy's chair with his arm loosely resting along the wooden rail running along the chair's back, behind Teddy. All three of the men—Harrison, Teddy, and the stranger looked at Gregory and Irene, eye brows raised in a similar gesture of inquiry.

"Look who I ran into parking the Ford," Gregory offered sheepishly, indicating Irene with a wave of one hand.

"I am determined to help," Irene said, stepping further into the room. "I won't take no for an answer."

"Pull up dining chairs, and we will fill you in on the plan," Clarice said, waving them to join the group. "I think you know everyone, Irene. Except Carlo Anselmo."

Gregory collected a heavy oak and walnut chair with an embroidered cushion placing it for Irene before getting the second seat for himself. Irene slipped out of her yellow wool coat, folded it lengthwise, then hung it behind her, covering the dark walnut inlay on the back of the chair. Gregory did the same with his overcoat, then flicked back his suit jacket before sitting beside her. Teddy watched much more dispassionately than Gregory feared he would. He was, instead, captivated by the man perched beside him. *Carlo Anselmo. That's who Teddy had called before they left.*

"Please bring them up to speed, Clarice," Harrison said, folding his arms across his chest.

Teddy – his long legs stretched out on the carpet–crossed his ankles. A cigarette dangled from his lips. He leaned his weight on one elbow to better see Gregory's reaction to the plan, or to move closer to the young man beside him.

"The *Four Deuces* is in a four-story building at 2222 Wabash Avenue in the Levee," Clarice began, placing her hands on her knees and leaning forward. "Capone took over management from Jonny Torrio who had it from Big Jim Colosimo. That you probably knew." She looked at the faces around the room.

Gregory nodded. He settled back into his chair, trying to get comfortable, noticing that Irene did the same.

Clarice warmed to her subject, her voice becoming deeper and more seductive. "They had a saloon on the first floor until 1920 when Torrio turned it into a gambling joint. With booze illegal, the saloon was a liability. Girls used to be on the third floor, but were moved up to the fourth floor at that time." She unfolded her long legs and stood in a whisper of silk. Striding back and forth on the rug, Clarice explained further, "A madam watches the gals, making certain the men are happy customers, make quick selections, and pay."

"But surely Margaretta isn't already on the fourth floor," Irene said, her face whitened in horror. Her hands gripped at the scrolled wooden arms of her chair.

"We think she is being held in the building next door – 2220 Wabash. It's an apartment with 20 flats," Harrison said. "She is most likely in one of those since 2224 is a front for Capone."

"An antique furniture store," Teddy chimed in. "He most likely has a capper stay there to watch over the *Four Deuces*. Keep the peace if the guy is always on the premises."

"I'll go in and investigate." Carlo Anselmo said in a husky voice thick with a Sicilian accent.

"You?" Gregory and Irene asked as one.

Carlo laughed. His deep brown eyes twinkled. "They won't question me. I'll dress like one of the boys from the neighborhood, and no one will ever suspect."

"All right then," Gregory replied with a laugh. He liked Carlo. The man had a sense of humor.

"Carlo will be able to locate his cousin for us." Teddy glanced up at Carlo with admiration.

"Then we," said Clarice, "will be able to get into the apartment and smuggle the girl out."

"How, pray tell?" Irene asked.

"Yes," Gregory added. "They won't be letting her walk out."

"Letty has a very large trunk—we are hoping the girl will fit inside long enough for us to get her into a waiting truck or cab." Clarice looked at Letty.

"Yes. We will pretend to be moving in or out of the building. Hopefully, no one will pay much attention to us." Letty smiled and smoothed down the green material of her skirt.

"I'm afraid of starting a bar fight because Capone's men would rather kill me than boot me out," said Harrison, "but I bet we could get Louis Two-Gun Alterie to go into the gambling area dressed in his ten-gallon hat and cowboy boots in order to make a ruckus like he used to for cousin Deanie. I'll talk to him."

"Now you're on the trolley!" Gregory slapped his knee. "If the capper is busy with Alterie, he and the rest won't care if two women move a trunk or two out of the building next door to the *Four Deuces*."

"Carlo just needs to fill out locations for us, and the plan will be jake," Clarice said. She turned to look at Irene. "You can act as look out for Letty and me. I'd feel a lot safer with another set of peepers."

"Oh, certainly." Irene bounced a little in excitement. "I can help with the trunk, too. It's bound to be very heavy with that poor child inside."

"It's settled then." Clarice smiled. She placed her fists on her hips and rocked back on her heels.

Harrison got to his feet and shook hands with Clarice. "I'll let you know when I get Two-Gun on board." He slipped into his overcoat and headed for the door.

Gregory rose, offering his hand to Irene, who took it and pulled herself to her feet. With her free hand, she grabbed her coat from the back of the chair. Leading Irene out after Harrison, Gregory turned back and said, "Thank you, Clarice. It's a solid plan."

Once the door closed on the apartment, Gregory asked, "So how is Teddy getting back, or should I ask?"

"I believe," Harrison, clapped his fedora onto his head and tilted it to the left with two fingers, "he has an alternative ride." His brother chuckled, then a broad smile spread across his face.

"I'll walk Irene home. The Ford is really close to her building." Gregory casually looped an arm around Irene's waist to guide her down the brightly lit hallway. He was pleased when she remained pliant under his arm instead of pulling away. "Come with us," he told Harrison.

After turning the keys to the Ford over to Harrison, Gregory led Irene to her brownstone. The walk felt too short, but he would see her again soon. He took both of her hands in his keeping them low and near their sides. Squeezing her hands gently, he told her softly, "I can't wait to see you."

Irene smiled radiantly. Dipping her chin, she breathed, "Likewise," before she pulled from his grasp and dashed up the steps. At the doors, she peeked back over her shoulder at him and winked, her lower right foot kicking up a heel.

Gregory felt a warmth blossoming within his chest. Joy bubbled through him like the old-style Champagne that they could not get anymore. If he hadn't been schooled in patience all his life, he would *not* have been able to wait. As it was, he had to tolerate Harrison's teasing the entire drive back to the farm.

Gregory turned in the worn leather seat of the car toward his brother, "What astonishes me is Carlo Anselmo."

"Teddy seems to like him," Harrison replied with a shrug.

"I think we can trust him." Gregory said, facing forward again, watching the Chicago skyline retreating behind them. The road seemed much less congested now than earlier. There was still traffic, but it wasn't as constant. Stars were starting to come out, and the moon hung large over the tops of the buildings. "I know the girl is his cousin, but there is more to him than that. He seems genuinely a good fellow."

"Bushwa!" Harrison laughed. "You don't even know him."

Gregory stretched out as best he could in the confines of the Ford. "Not yet. But I'm betting we will."

Harrison jogged the wheel to avoid a small hole in the road. The car bounced and jerked, sending them jostling against the doors. The tires whined against the bricks.

"Better let you drive," Gregory laughed. He wouldn't mind being alone with his thoughts, recalling the scent of jasmine and heliotrope. *Irene is the bee's knees,* he thought with a sigh, *the leopard's spots.* Propping his elbow up on the "C" shaped opening above the door, he rested his cheek on his palm, not caring how the car's motion jolted up his arm.

8

Harrison was unable to find Two-Gun as quickly as he had hoped, delaying the rescue of Margaretta. To make matters worse, the stock market prices continued to fall. Harrison took the car every day and haunted LaSalle Street in hopes that his frequent visits would force the market to recover. The few times Gregory accompanied him, he noticed that more and more men and women, dressed in older clothing, had begun first to sell pencils and now apples. Somewhere in one of the Chicago Dailies, Gregory had read how an orchard company supplied the fruit for almost nothing so that the poor souls without jobs could resell the apples for a nickel. Chicago was becoming a bastion for the jobless and homeless with parkland sprouting cardboard villages, soup kitchens occupying once empty buildings down town, and sidewalks transforming into open air markets.

"Harrison," Gregory began over his coffee one morning as he took a seat in the kitchen, "should we offer our own apples to the apple sellers?"

Harrison, seated opposite the kitchen table, rattled his newspaper, then slowly looked at Gregory over the top edge. "We'd better keep 'em. *We* might be selling apples as early as next month the rate the stocks keep plummeting."

Gregory shook his head. He had nothing he could say.

Fortunately, Teddy bounded down the stairs and entered the kitchen beaming. "Cousin George is all agog about hitting the Belmont-Sheffield Bank. Capone opened a soup kitchen on 9th and State Street. The mug goes in and actually serves up soup himself. The papers are calling Capone a hero. Cousin George is furious because all the food comes from extorted market owners. He thinks it's all bushwa! Wants Capone's head even more than ever before. So, Cousin George is hot to hurt Capone any way we can." Teddy took a wooden chair, spun it around, and straddled the seat, facing Harrison and Gregory, with his arms crossed and propped along the chair's back. He popped a cigarette into his mouth and lit it. "Are you still against it, Harrison?"

Harrison made a face but quickly concealed his feelings. "I am inclined to want in at this moment. I wish I could say we are flush enough to avoid it, but with the stock market --." Harrison shrugged, laying down the newspaper. "I hate to admit it, but I believe that we are behind the eight ball." He held up a hand like a stop sign. "Yes, we have the farm and the club, but no way to pay bills if the property doesn't continue to make a profit. My fear is that as our patrons become more and more penniless, the less custom we will have."

Teddy nodded, blowing out smoke. Gregory agreed the downward spiral seemed especially bleak. "If we steal the gold and silver in the bank, we will not only get the reserves, we will also be hitting Capone and the South Siders hard," Teddy suggested, putting the cigarette back into his mouth.

"He's certainly not hurting badly," Gregory added. "According to the last report, he owns most of Cicero."

"That's going to be most of Chicago before he's through," Teddy pointed out, resting his elbows on the table. Smoke gathered around his head like a turban.

"Ok, ok," Harrison said, sitting up in his chair. "You've convinced me. Let me in on the onions – but later. Can we rescue the Anselmo girl first?"

"Absolutely," Teddy nodded.

Gregory finished his coffee, rose, and rinsed the china cup in the sink with water from the small pump. "I'm going to do some things in the parlor for the seances," he told them, excusing himself. He had reached the door to the parlor, when he heard soft footsteps behind him. Gregory turned and saw Teddy coming down the hallway toward him.

"Let's talk a moment," Teddy said, gently griping Gregory's elbow and leading him into the parlor. He smelled of smoke, bergamot, and pine.

They walked past the tall, narrow wooden armoire, and past the fireplace to stand near the tall floor to ceiling window, whose curtains had been thrown open to allow daylight into the room. Teddy released his hold on Gregory and looked at him intently.

Gregory dropped his gaze to the thick green carpet beneath their polished shoes. "What?"

Before Gregory could ask more, Teddy said around his cigarette, "I can tell you are very taken with Irene O'Brien. She seems to admire you as well."

"You aren't hurt, are you?" Gregory asked, quickly looking up to read Teddy's expression.

"Oh Lord no!" Teddy laughed, his eyes twinkling. He removed the cigarette from his lips, letting smoke out through his teeth. "She is a swell girl. Just fine for someone like you."

"Just what do you mean by that?" Gregory retorted.

Teddy leaned his hip against the window pane and took another draw. "Oh, don't get all huffy. You know exactly what I mean. Irene and I – we are *not* meant to be no matter how much our parents might dream of a match between us." He noticed the stub between his fingers and crushed the end, blowing on it before putting it into a pocket. "*You,* on the other hand, are exactly the sort of man they would like, if only they would think about it."

Gregory straightened with some pride. *He would be good for – with – Irene.* "How will you tell them?"

Teddy shook his head and took out another cigarette from his silver case. Lighting the tip, he returned the box to his vest pocket. "I don't have a clue." He drew in a deep drag before blowing the smoke out in little circular puffs. "But I am more concerned how the North Siders or worse the South Siders will see her defection."

"You are not." Gregory crossed his arms over his chest and leaned back against the nearby wall, raising his left foot to brace himself. "Be honest, Teddy. You're worried that they will find out about you and Carlo Anselmo."

Teddy stiffened. His hazel eyes hardened, making his features look wild. He blew out a smoke ring.

"Don't act that way with me," Gregory held up a hand. "You are my brother's best friend. I won't do anything to harm you or endanger your friendship. Besides, Harrison likes Carlo – for you." Gregory smiled.

"If we go out, no one can know," Teddy said quietly. "The North Side gang can't know about it, and especially the other gang leaders. Being in a same gender relationship is hard enough given my profession, but Carlo belongs to North Side's worst rival—Capone's crew-- at least, the fringes of it. I don't want him to be tortured like O'Brien's son."

Gregory thought, *When the gangs find out, they will destroy him. Teddy's Cousin George Moran had been killing off important South Siders since Capone killed Deanie O'Banion in 1924.* "If you care about him as much as Harrison and I think you do, we'll help think of something." *You can't let your cousin know – he'd torture you both before taking you for a ride.*

"I need to break off with Irene." Teddy stroked his chin. "Perhaps walk around with two or three gals at once so none of them will think I'm serious."

"Now you're on the trolley, Teddy! It will enhance that lady killer reputation, too."

"Do you really think so?" he asked, twirling the tip of his thin, black moustache. He struck a pose, his hand with the cigarette out away from his face.

Gregory laughed aloud. "Oh, absolutely." He reached out and clapped Teddy on the shoulder, the deep navy silk of Teddy's suit jacket smooth under Gregory's touch.

Teddy was wiry rather than extremely muscular, but he was an extremely agile fighter. Harrison had taken Gregory to the street boxing gym the newsies worked out in long ago where he watched Teddy box. *Would that be enough to protect him?* Gregory didn't know. Now he worried about Teddy for different reasons.

While they waited to rescue Margaretta, life at *Hair of the Dog* continued as normally as Harrison with his constant worry over stocks would allow. The séances over the next weeks were almost unremarkable. Yes, there had been ghosts, but not terrible ones. Mrs. Streed got to tell her beloved, departed husband she missed and loved him. The Haymersmyths talked to their daughter, discovering she had an illness that caused her death, and they were not to blame. "I love you both," she had said before fading from Gregory's body.

Mr. and Mrs. Boeker found out a servant had stolen the family silver and not her sister as they had suspected.

"I'm *not* sorry I took it," Embergine said stiffly, forcing Gregory to lean forward across the table towards the Boekers. "You certainly didn't need an extra set of silver, and my poor family," she whined. "It put bread in their mouths, it did."

"But you made us think Ellen had taken it," Mrs. Boeker sobbed. "She is my only sister, and now we haven't talked in ten years all because I accused her."

Embergine cackled, twisting Gregory's features into a grimace. "That Ellen always did admire those rosebuds carved into the handles."

"You evil woman!" Mr. Boeker said with crisp emphasis. He squeezed his wife's hand tightly and looked over at her with concern.

"Sort it all out as you will," Embergine finished, cackling even harder than before. "I surely don't care."

"Ooooo," Mrs. Boeker exhaled angrily. Before she could stand up, Embergine was gone, leaving Gregory exhausted. The Boekers promised to reconcile with the sister, Ellen, immediately. They had hoped to recover the silver, but at least the family had been reunited. Gregory was able to sleep with a clear conscience, and he dreamt of Irene.

Gregory tossed and turned on his four-poster bed that night. His mattress wasn't any less comfortable, he was just excited about his date with Irene. At three in the afternoon, he drew a hot bath, soaked for ten minutes, washing his hair with extra care. He put on his favorite dark gray silk suit, with the red waistcoat underneath. His highly polished Italian leather shoes finished off the ensemble with Harrison lending a hand to tie Gregory's grey paisley bow tie. A matching handkerchief peeked out of his front suit pocket. Gregory did a spin before the full- length mirror in the hallway between the bedrooms and Harrison applauded.

"Very dapper," his brother pronounced, clapping. "She can't help but fall in love."

"Don't joke about that," Gregory retorted. "Love is a serious matter," his smile softened his words.

"Best luck," Harrison nodded in agreement. "Don't worry about me tonight. I'm going to catch the game. Pat Malone is pitching today," he said, adding with a wink, "See you later, Alligator."

"In a while," Gregory responded, a slow smile spreading over his generous mouth. "Crocodile."

When he drove up to Irene's brownstone, he couldn't help but notice the beginnings of a cardboard village in the little park they had conversed in several weeks before. Men in heavy overcoats clustered in around a large tin cannister, holding their hands out as if over a fire. While Gregory could not see smoke, he could smell the odor of burnt wood. The cool evening breeze whistled through the buildings, pushing pedestrians on the street. As he parked the car against the stone curb, Gregory saw several men selling newspapers, rather than boys, and yet another man offering to sell his car. This one was a hotsy-totsy, fancy Isotta, complete with white walled-tires and a covered passenger compartment. The man was telling a prospective buyer about the eight-cylinder engine and the brakes on each wheel. *Poor slob.*

Gregory rushed up the stone steps and announced himself to Irene's doorman, who touched the brim of his red uniform's hat. The man rang Irene's flat.

"She'll be right down, sir," the man told Gregory.

Gregory clasped his hands behind his back and paced the lobby. The marble floor tiles clacked under his shoes. His reflection in the mirrored wall on the far side of the entryway copied his every turn. He saw a well-dressed man in a dark gray silk suit, with stylish pomaded hair -parted on the right, a dapper overcoat folded over his left arm, and a dark brown fedora jauntily sitting on the side of his head.

Soon, she was there before him. Dressed in a blush pink chiffon drop-waisted evening frock with a layered skirt, Irene took his breath away. Her eyes outlined on top with kohl, and a dark green color on the lids that matched her bright eyes drew his gaze before his vision rested on her reddened lips. *Wowzers. He did want to kiss her.* Instead, he said, "I'm so glad to see you."

Unable to resist, he gathered her close for a hug, surrounding himself with her special scent. He breathed in deeply and nuzzled her neck before grasping her upper arms and putting her a few inches away from him.

"I'm looking forward to our evening," she said, raising one hand to cup his cheek. Gregory tilted his head, pressing his lips to her palm.

"Me, too," he said, smiling. He helped her on with her pale yellow, wool coat, then guided her to the door with a gentle hand on the center of her back. "I have heard that the music in this film is outstanding." He wanted to tell her how lovely she looked, but *was it too soon?*

"I also think Bessie Love is supposed to be wonderful in her part. I do so enjoy watching her films." Irene allowed herself to be steered to the car, and once he opened the door for her, eased herself up onto the seat. "So, where are you taking me to dine?" she asked, stifling a giggle.

Gregory cranked the Ford after opening the clutch, returning to the vibrating and chuffing vehicle. He grabbed the wheel and pulled himself into the driver's seat. "Daley's in Englewood. They have the best crab cakes in town, unless you'd rather have the stew?" He glanced over at Irene, who sat poised in the passenger seat, her hands primly in her lap around a small beaded bag decorated with tiny Scottie dogs.

She glanced over at him, shyly. "Crab cakes sound wonderful." She made it sound so musical when she said `wonderful,' as if the word were four syllables rather than only three.

Gregory mentioned how Harrison was struggling over the plunging stocks.

"Well, Mrs. Hall has closed her brokerage at S.W. Stearns – at least for a while. I'm... I'm out of work." She wrung her hands. "I suppose I'm not the only one, but if feels worse because its me."

"It is worse because it's you," Gregory said softly. "Unlike those who have bought stocks and on margin, too, you have been working."

"Those other people were working, too," Irene looked down again. "They have families, many of them. It's an awful thing. So many people at S.W. Stearns are very frightened. It's been only a few weeks, but what will happen if it continues?"

"More and more people will live in cardboard boxes in parks or under the bridges," Gregory responded. "I don't like it any more than you do. There was a Depression in the late 1800s – Mom and Dad used to talk about it, but these times seem much, much worse."

The atmosphere in the car became sad and quiet. The taller buildings of the city closed in around them, lights flickering in many of the upper story windows. Their tires rumbled over the bricks with a high whine as Gregory headed toward the restaurant. Irene's heart rate sped up, and Gregory did not fully know why. He dropped one hand from the steering wheel to cover Irene's hands with his. "Don't despair," he said gently.

"What if I can't stay in my flat? I so don't want to move back in with Father and my younger brother. It would just show my family what a failure I am – that I can't make it on my own." Irene's eyes grew bright with unshed tears.

"Look," Gregory said. "I know we can give you an honest job at *Hair of the Dog* and a suite of rooms at the farm if you get desperate. With that as a fall back, you can face whatever the future brings."

Irene beamed up at him. "That is the kindest offer I have ever heard."

"Let's don't think about that anymore tonight. Let's just have the time of our lives."

With both of her hands, Irene raised Gregory's hand to her lips, brushing a soft kiss there. "Swell. Let's do that."

While Gregory and Irene ordered crab cakes and beers at Daley's, Teddy escorted Carlo to the *Dill Pickle Club* on Tooker Alley. Teddy, dressed up in his double-breasted black silk suit with a bottle green waistcoat and green and black striped tie, had driven them into Towertown.

Earlier, Teddy had phoned Carlo, just catching him at his flat. "We have to talk," Teddy had said.

"Do we?" Carlo joked. His voice husky over the phone line – something Teddy had trouble understanding because the telephone always made people sound so tinny.

"I'm coming for you," Teddy said before ringing off. He did not want the party line or the operator to know their business.

Swinging by the flat, Teddy found Carlo waiting outside on the street, wearing a loud plaid three-piece suit that could never be mistaken for understated. The man wore his signature black newsboy cap slanted over one eye brow looking for all the world like the cat's meow.

Teddy popped the door to the model T open for Carlo, "Get in," he ordered.

Carlo jumped into the seat. "23 Skidoo?"

"You are full of baloney," Teddy couldn't stop himself from remarking, his cigarette clenched between his teeth. "I am taking you to the *Dill Pickle Club* so we can see a show and maybe go dancing."

Carlo reached over with his left hand, squeezing Teddy's right forearm. "Darling, you are sooo good to me." His brown eyes danced. Under the evening stars, Carlo's handsomeness almost took Teddy's breath away.

"Be serious for just one minute," Teddy pleaded. "Please?"

"For you – any *thing*."

They were close to Towertown, the bridge linking the Loop and the Bohemian district was up ahead. Unlike before when most of the people wandering the streets were artistic types in flamboyant clothing, tonight most of the people seemed to be businessmen all down on their luck from the glum expressions they wore. It was this downturn in the market, Teddy knew, but he didn't want the circumstances of the rest of Chicago dampen his buoyant mood at being with Carlo. They had enough going against them.

Knowing it had to be said, Teddy began, "You know our gangs despise one another."

"Your cousin has killed off most of the Sicilian bosses, including the Gennas," Carlo countered.

"Cousin George isn't the only one to hate the Gennas." Teddy retorted. "Capone..."

"Has hated them enough to gun them down." Carlo rested his elbow on the edge of the door where a window might have been, then leaned his head against his fist. "Aiello and the Anselmos are also on Capone's hit list. He'd take a bean-shooter to us all."

"I'm just saying there is animosity on all sides and we're – we're in the middle." Teddy's voice softened, a curl of smoke escaping from the side of his mouth. He did *not* want to fight with Carlo.

"We just have to be careful," Carlo said. "So, they don't find out." He turned around and looked squarely at Teddy. "I'm not giving you up, if that's what you are fishing for."

"Baby," Teddy sighed like a plea. He stopped the car before pulling into a parking spot along State Street. Cars lined both sides, and crowds of people packed sidewalks. "I can't lose you," he said, finally, turning to face the younger man.

"Ok, then. We're good." Carlo offered seriously. He leaned in and placed a soft kiss against Teddy's well-shaven cheek. "Let's go see the show."

Teddy nodded, set the clutch and brake, before jumping out of the car. Carlo jumped out also, and they met at the car's hood. Teddy placed his right hand on Carlo's back and gently steered him toward the alley. Well concealed, the club's orange door lit by an odd green light had *Danger* with an arrow pointing toward it.

Carlo stepped toward the door. "Step high, stoop low," he read, "leave your dignity outside. Sounds fun."

They entered the club, hearing the plaintive strains of jazz from inside. The large main room had a stage at the far end where the musicians played. Four men dressed in cancan dresses were dancing with their arms slung over each other's shoulders, kicking their legs first right then left high into the air, flipping the skirts in a flurry of red and black stripped fabric. The colorful chairs around the room were filled with couples who were eating or had drinks on the small surrounding counters. Teddy guessed over two hundred people were crowding the space.

Carlo leaned close and whispered in Teddy's ear. "Now this is a great place."

"I could get used to it," Teddy whispered back. "Come on. There's some open seats over there." Teddy guided Carlo over toward the vacant seats.

They ordered sandwiches and drinks, sharing bites of each

other's fries and roast beef. When they had finished eating, Carlo asked Teddy to dance, and they joined the foxtrotting couples pressed cheek-to-cheek. Teddy never felt so content.

Across town, Gregory and Irene had completed their crab cakes and dessert. They left Daley's for the Oriental Theatre where *Broadway Melody* was playing. The streets surrounding the theatre were crowded with people and cars. Horns sounded when pedestrians, not paying attention, wandered into the street. The marquee above the movie theatre was ablaze with the title of the film. Beneath *Broadway Melody* were the names Bessie Love, Anita Paige, and Charles King. In smaller print were the times the feature was showing. Posters near the box office advertised coming attractions. Chatter and excitement bubbling from those close by seemed to surround Gregory and Irene as they waited in line for tickets. Some of the women wore stylish low-waisted frocks, stockings, and pumps, while their male counterparts had double or single-breasted three-piece suits, overcoats and hats. Mixed into the crowds were older couples dressed in older fashions popular in the past. Their clothing looked shabbier, but the faces and joy these people showed were the same as Gregory and Irene's own.

"Two please," Gregory told the man in the ticket booth.

"First or second balcony? Mezzanine is sold out." The man chewed on a tooth pick and his small black eyes bore into Gregory's soul.

"First balcony – toward the front. If you have it."

The man checked his tickets and handed two through the rounded opening in the glass. "That'll be 70 cents."

Gregory took a dollar bill, one of his silver certificates, out of his leather wallet and passed it through the glass to the ticket taker. The man counted out change which Gregory scooped up. He guided Irene to the side and toward the large ornate gold painted doors of the theatre. They could see the lobby beyond with its red velvet and gold trimmed walls. Everything inside was plush and ornate, including the thick red carpet on the floor. As Gregory opened the heavy door, the smells of popcorn, candy, coffee, and sweet rolls engulfed them.

"Popcorn?" He asked in Irene's ear, her large earrings decorated with a bumble bee on honeycomb brushing his chin.

"Please. And perhaps soda water," She smiled shyly up at him, her blue eyes sparkling. Beneath her felt hat, her reddish blonde curls had been set into waves which framed her oval shaped face. Irene toyed with the two long ropes of pearls that hung around her neck. As he ordered their treats, Irene continued to gaze at the tall ceiling overhead where an artist had painted a blue sky with thick, fluffy clouds.

Once at their balcony seats, Gregory helped Irene with her coat, gripping the bags of popcorn in one hand. Their soda waters rested on the floor, guarded between his feet. When she had made herself comfortable, Gregory handed her a bag of popped corn, still warm from the popper, and one of the waxed paper cups of soda water, with a straw. He busied himself with arranging his own overcoat over the back of his seat before settling in beside her. The noise of the hundreds of audience members was almost deafening, as patrons excitedly awaited the newsreels, short, and the feature film. Because of the length of this movie, the theatre announced there would be no vaudeville act accompanying the show. Gregory didn't care. He enjoyed watching Irene's wide-eyed expression as she took in the huge gilded proscenium arch over the movie screen.

"I'm so glad Mezzanine was sold out," she confided. "It makes one uncomfortable when Bessie Love's eye is larger than we are tall."

Gregory laughed. "I agree. So much more fun to sit up here where we can also see who's below."

"You mean," Irene moved in closer to Gregory, almost leaning against his shoulder, "like that oddly powerful looking little man with the terrible scars on the left side of his face," she whispered, pointing gingerly at a thickset man below, three rows ahead and to the right.

Gregory instinctively gripped her arm. "Do *not* look at him. That's Al Capone with his newest tomato."

"What's *he* doing here?" She asked, scrunching up her nose.

"Enjoying the movie like the rest of us, I suppose."

"Horse feathers!"

"Really. I have heard he likes movies as well as the next man," Gregory hissed.

"Quiet you in front," a woman in a large feathered hat complained from behind them. "The newsreel is about to start." As if the projectionist had heard her, the lights dimmed and the audience began to settle.

Gregory could feel the warmth of the bodies packed into the seats around him. Even if the performance wasn't a sellout, there were easily 800 people in the auditorium tonight. He was relieved when the music for the newsreel began, distracting them from Capone and other dangers in their day to day lives. The newsreel focused instead on Europe and the rebuilding of the old world after the war. Germany had yet to recover its pre-war industrial glory. People in Berlin stood in bread lines with wheel barrels filled with Deutsch Marks.

"Those poor souls," Irene murmured, placing her free hand on Gregory's arm. "Will that be what will happen to us?"

"Surely not. President Hoover—"

Before Gregory could finish, "Sh—shhhh!" came again from the lady behind them.

Broadway Melody was wonderful, thought Gregory. Charles King's tenor and the dancing had Gregory's feet tapping. Irene, also, seemed to find the same dialog funny, laughing at the same time as Gregory. The humor in the film seemed to unite the audience, and everyone wanted the main characters to succeed in their endeavor to launch a Broadway show. When the film came to an end and the lights came up, Gregory was not ready to return Irene to her flat.

"Are you tired?" He asked, his voice expressing hope that she was not.

Irene giggled, dimpling her rosy cheeks. "Not at all."

"Good," Gregory said, taking her elbow after helping her slip into her coat. "I know just the place." Filing out with the huge crowd took more time than Gregory expected, but at least the Ford was parked relatively close. He wanted to take her dancing at a small club he knew about outside the Loop. Chances were that they would even have one of those marathon competitions where he and Irene could show off their Charleston, Fox-Trot, and Black Bottom. His blood raced at the thought of holding Irene tight against his body while they glided, kicked, or shimmied to the music. She seemed as hungry for him as he was for her, making joy bubble up from deep inside him. Once at the club, he and Irene joined the dancers on the floor, moving to the beat of the drums and the muted "whaaaa, whaaaa," of the trumpets. Neither of them considered conditions outside the dance hall, the danger faced by Margaretta Anselmo, nor what Teddy or Harrison were doing. Gregory stared down into Irene's joyous face, both of them laughing as they became absorbed in the newness of their feelings for one another and the fast, ever-changing music.

9

While Harrison continued to track down Two-Gun, Clarice and Letty oversaw the repainting of a truck Teddy had borrowed from his cousin George Moran. Instead of a floral sign, they had designed a bakery motif with a large loaf of bread. "Quick Rise Dough," they stenciled in black block letters above the bread with "Bakery Goods," below.

"That's right," Clarice said. "That will have them fooled. No one will suspect a girl inside a bakery truck." She jumped up and through the back doors into the van, and began placing a few guns along the gunwales on the walls. Next, she and Gregory hoisted the empty trunk up and in, before she slammed the two doors shut.

"You are so clever, darling," Letty said. Her sparkly dress was covered by painters' overalls which had smudges of brown and yellow paint.

"I'm still unclear how the trunk is getting inside unseen." Gregory said, swiping his hands against one another to remove the dust from the trunk.

"Carlo will be on watch," Irene answered. She was working on the right side of the truck, while Letty painted the left.

"When you're finished, all we'll need is Two-Gun," Clarice said with a throaty laugh.

Harrison finally found Two-Gun on the street a block down from Deanie's floral shop – even though Deanie had been long gone, they all thought of the shop as his even though Moran ran it now. He approached the extremely tall cowboy, who had so admired cousin Deanie. "Alterie. Good to run into you." Harrison stuck his hand out for Two-Gun to shake.

Two-Gun pumped Harrison's hand and said, "Not a chance thing. I heard you have been looking for me." Pedestrians flowed around them on the sidewalk. Harrison studied the man's serious clean-shaven face, bushy eyebrows, wide set eyes, and pointed chin. A dimple appeared near his chin, on the right side of his face.

"Yes, well," Harrison smiled sheepishly. "Let's go talk in Deanie's old office." He indicated the shop down the block. "More private that way."

Two-Gun nodded, tipping his white cowboy hat back on his reddish-brown hair. His boots clanked against the flagstones. The wind whipped his large overcoat's flaps in the wind. Two-Gun had been in a bar fight or two in his day and should be willing to help them when he explained the circumstances, Harrison thought.

The bell over the door at the flower shop jangled as the men entered. Harrison nodded to the brunette in her low waisted dress, standing behind the counter. She inclined her head toward the office. "It's empty. The boss is out for a few minutes."

"Good." Harrison nodded. "Thanks." He gestured toward the door of the office, following Alterie into the small room filled with a large desk, two chairs, several file cabinets, and a small window on the back wall, that allowed light in from the alley.

"So, what's this all about?" Two-Gun turned to face Harrison, not bothering to take a seat.

"There's a girl," Harrison began.

Two-Gun threw his head back and laughed. "Ah-ah," he said, wagging two fingers of his right hand at Harrison.

"Now don't go getting the wrong idea," Harrison started, stiffening.

"Baloney," Two-Gun sniffed.

"It's a girl about eleven years old," Harrison corrected him. "She's being held by Capone for the *Four Deuces.*"

Now it was Two-Gun's turn to get angry. "Why didn't ya say so?"

"I am, saying so." Harrison retorted. "We want to get her out, but we need your help. She's being held on the top floor of the building next door to the *Four Deuces* in one of the upstairs flats. My crew will get her out and back to her family, but we need you to make a ruckus in the *Four Deuces* so no one will suspect what they are doing."

"You mean like I used to for Deanie?" Two-Gun looked speculative.

"Exactly!" Harrison felt relieved.

"Sure thing," Two-Gun agreed. "I miss those days." A grin spread over his face. "Just let me know when to be there." He strode over to the desk, picked up a pen and paper, scribbling down some numbers and a street name. "Here's my address. Just give me the onions when it's a go."

After slipping the paper with the address into his suit coat pocket, Harrison pumped Two-Gun's hand while clapping him on the arm. He couldn't wait to get back to the *Hair of the Dog* and tell the others. "It will most likely be in two nights, but I will let you know."

Harrison returned to the farm, wondering what Carlo will have discovered when he visited the *Four Deuces* tonight. The Sicilian will also have to skulk around the apartment building to find the girl's location. *Clarice and Letty will not have enough time to check out a bunch of flats.*

Teddy wanted to go with Carlo when the Sicilian investigated the apartment building at 2220 Wabash, but Carlo refused. "What good will it do, if we are discovered?" Carlo asked him. "I can be inconspicuous but *you* certainly can't. Everyone knows you're George Moran's cousin."

"I'd just feel better having your back." Teddy offered, lighting up a cigarette.

"Back or front?" Carlo teased, cupping Teddy's chin tenderly. He glanced up into Teddy's hazel eyes, smiling shyly. "Don't worry, darling boy – I shall be Jake."

That had been several hours earlier and now the evening waxed cloudy with rumbles of thunder overhead. Rain began to drizzle then opened to a full downpour before Carlo could make it into the *Four Deuces*. Teddy nursed a drink at the *Parisian*, wishing Carlo would hurry up and appear. Another set sung by the torch singer went by with no Carlo. Teddy began to worry. She was about to go into her third rendition of "More Than You Know," when he saw movement toward his table. He casually took a drag. Trying not to seem eager, Teddy glanced sideways at the man coming toward him. Gone were the snorky clothes, replaced by slightly shabby dark gray three-piece suit and a black fedora.

Teddy stood, taking Carlo by the hand, which he rose in the air in order to twirl the Sicilian around. "What have you done with my stylish boyfriend?" Teddy chuckled, exhaling a puff of smoke.

"I am offended," Carlo replied, laughter in his brown eyes. "This is a perfectly serviceable outfit."

"You hate it," Teddy laughed louder. "You know you do."

"Yes, yes. But sit. I have lots to tell," Carlo bubbled. They took the empty chairs at the table, and Teddy signaled for another round. Teddy took a cigarette from his case, lit it from his own and handed it to Carlo.

"So?" Teddy raised an eyebrow.

"She's definitely on the top floor, most likely in 4 "E" or "F" because they are at the back of the building where fewer people might see." Carlo looked down at his hands. Smoke from his cigarette circling upwards. "I couldn't get in so I don't know for certain."

"So, should they wait? I mean for you to know more before we go in?" Teddy asked softly. He took his cigarette away from his mouth, blowing a smoke ring. The waiter came over then with their drinks, placing napkins down before setting a glass in front of each of them. Carlo waited until the man had gone before continuing.

Carlo shook his head. "No. Not necessary. When I was at the *Four Deuces*, I heard rumors about them breaking in a new girl next week. We'd better hurry or Margaretta will suffer the same fate as Melody. Those men are extremely rough. I, personally, wouldn't want to be touched by any of them."

Teddy nodded. "Let's go tell Clarice and the others. They'll be at *The Hair of the Dog*." He took the check stub out of his pocket, then crushed his cigarette in the glass ashtray on their table. "Wait here, I'll just get my coat."

"So, you aren't certain, but you think she's in 4 "E" or "F,"" Clarice clarified after Carlo had shared everything with all of them in the back parlor.

Letty draped herself dramatically over Clarice's shoulder, her long cigarette holder containing a burning ash of a smoke. Her black dress was scalloped with ecru, and her dyed bob was encircled by a black sequin headband, sporting a large matching plume. Harrison stood by the curtains, peeking out every few minutes. Irene sat in one of the séance chairs with Gregory beside her. Teddy leaned an elbow against the fireplace while Carlo paced. Teddy could tell he was uncomfortable.

"Yes, I told you. I couldn't poke around too long," Carlo stopped and looked at Clarice. "We don't want them getting suspicious."

"No. That is definitely true." Clarice took a deep breath. "How would you feel about narrowing it down tomorrow night before we make the grab? That would mean less time in the building for Letty and me."

"Ok. Ok," Carlo agreed, raising his hands palms out. "And then I'll head over to the *Four Deuces*. Remember the signal to call it all off?"

"The bobwhite whistle once and then a second time after five seconds," Letty said. "Just how many bob whites are there in Chicago, anyway?"

Harrison looked lost in thought for a moment. "We don't know if any of them are bird lovers. Let's come up with something more inventive."

"Like what?" Carlo asked, slightly offended. "Too loud and it will bring everyone running out to the street."

Gregory snapped his fingers. "How about whistling "Stairway to Paradise" or "Happy Days Are Here Again"?"

"I can do that," Carlo agreed. "A guy can whistle. It's a free country. I'll revisit the apartments. There are five to a floor, but she's gotta be on the top where she couldn't easily escape. I'll find out which one and let you know on my way to the *Four Deuces.* I can salute you gals with one finger for "E" and two for "F". You already know top floor."

"I'll have Two-Gun in the wings at seven when it will be dark enough to conceal ourselves in a stoop across the street. Good thing construction is over," Harrison put in.

They all agreed to turn in early. "Tomorrow is going to be an eventful day," Clarice said, ushering them all out of the parlor.

The next afternoon in their cramped flat in South Chicago, Carlo once again donned his older brother's bland gray suit and black fedora. He looked in the mirror over the cracked sink, shared by the eight people living with him, and decided to brush his hair to the left, pomading it very lightly to keep the curl. Carlo didn't want anyone to recognize him when he went into the apartment building or recall seeing him there later.

Taking the street car, he headed to South Wabash Avenue. People flowed on and off the car, most looking more forlorn than Carlo had ever seen them. Apple sellers sold fruit for a nickel on every street corner. He also saw men in long coats huddling together around ash cans with fires in them. Some of them were adding newspaper as extra padding against the cold wind. Most had their hats clamped down as far on their ears as they could. It was too early to snow, but the weather had definitely turned cold. Carlo was glad to be crammed into the street car where body heat ran high, keeping them all warm. His own wool overcoat was actually too thin to protect him from the lake effect. He really missed his raccoon coat. *Now that was a warm wrap.*

As he jostled back and forth, holding on the overhead handle, Carlo thought of Teddy and sighed. Joy bubbled through him at how protective and caring Teddy was. *He does look a lot like John Gilbert.* Carlo mused. *My own movie star.* A chuckled escaped him. Through his half-closed eyelids, Carlo saw the suspicion and disapproval on the faces of two older women seated on the sides of the car. He wanted to challenge them, demand to know why they felt so superior as to judge him, but recalling Teddy's smile, Carlo just ignored them. He would be at his stop soon enough and he'd never see them again. Wabash appeared as the car rounded an intersection. Two more blocks.

"South Wabash next stop," the driver called. "South Wabash."

Carlo forced his way to the doors along with others getting off. He wanted to investigate the apartments during the daylight when the South Siders would most likely be away, then he'd hide out somewhere nearby until it was time to launch the rescue. Carlo's shoes tapped along the flagstones as he wove his way from the Lexington Hotel, working his way down Wabash toward the *Four Deuces.* The stone buildings lining both sides of the street were all four or six stories tall – no skyscrapers like downtown. Cars, trucks, and pedestrians made their way up and down the street. Carlo even saw a few horse-drawn vehicles. Horns blared occasionally as drivers became impatient. Carlo tilted his fedora forward, shadowing his features as he approached 2222 Wabash. He didn't want the capper who worked the club to see him approach. There were always guys passing out cards and hawking, "Girls, girls, girls! What's your pleasure gents?"

Quickly, Carlo strode purposefully past the *Four Deuces* walking around to the street side of the walkway. When he reached the apartment building, he stepped under the large stone archway to the double door entry. The building had an odd design, he had thought, with two bow type windows on the outer edges of the second floor, creating an overhang. The third and fourth floors had bow windows pushing the center two windows outwards. The small tiles of the entryway floor gave way to cheap, fraying carpet in the stairwell. Carlo hurried up the steps, his heart thumping. Glancing over his shoulder and around the fourth-floor landing, he checked for people. Luckily, he was alone in the dingy vestibule with its yellowing carpet.

"Why do I have to?" whined a young girl with a Sicilian accent. Rustling sounds. A thump. More rustling.

"Do you want the good man or the bad man to come talk to you?" replied an Italian woman.

"The good man," the girl whimpered. "The good one."

Carlo crept closer. *Was that "E"?* He heard sounds of movement deep inside the apartment. Definitely, "E" not "F." Poor chicky. She seemed terrified. His own heart clenched for his cousin.

Before anyone might enter the vestibule and find him, Carlo stealthily returned down the stairs, exiting to the street. He headed back toward the Lexington Hotel. It was as safe as anywhere else. They even had a public phone—he would call Teddy and tell him 4 "E." Then he wouldn't have to give a signal to Clarice. Once clear of the building by several blocks, Carlo already felt better. He just wished he could change out of his brother's horrible suit and that Teddy could have joined him in the long wait until evening.

Clarise commandeered one of the waiters to drive the bakery truck and assigned Irene shotgun. She had reasoned an independent driver would permit the truck engine to remain running while she and Letty rescued the girl. Clarice huddled with Letty in the now more cramped space in the back of the truck, stabilizing the large trunk so that it didn't squash them as the vehicle rounded corners.

"We'll get that poor, girl out, won't we?" Letty asked. For once, she was dressed in a more sensible frock more appropriate for an office than a club. It's light wool pleats, flattened bust line all took away from her looks, making Letty unremarkable. While Letty didn't like the idea of being invisible, Clarice painstakingly explained that their safety demanded it.

"Yes. I have some skeleton keys we can use to get through the door. If they don't work, I'll give it the old boot." Clarice lifted her leg, thrusting the flat of her foot back in a horse kick. "We've got our guns, too, if we need them." She seriously hoped they would not require any shooting because they would call too much attention to them and what they were doing.

The truck finally parked just past the *Four Deuces*, close to the doors of 2220 Wabash. Clarice and Letty got out. Irene joined them.

"Ready?" Irene asked, rubbing her hands together.

Letty nodded.

"We wait for Carlo to go into the club. Give him a few minutes to look around. Then Two-Gun will go in and that's when we get the girl." Clarice ran through the plan again.

A lithe man in a dark gray three-piece suit and overcoat strode by, touching the rim of his black fedora as he passed them. It was Carlo. While his clothing was understated, no one moved with quite his grace. He entered the *Four Deuces* by the old saloon entrance, forcing him to walk past the wooden phone booth, through the gambling parlor before passing through to the back area with the stairs leading up to the brothel. Carlo hadn't been gone very long when he hastily reappeared and began whistling "Happy days are here again," as he made a quick retreat back towards the Lexington. Two-Gun, who had been waiting across the street beneath an awning where he wouldn't be seen, followed him.

"Well, gals," Clarice said, "It's a no go for tonight. We'll find out what spooked Carlo soon enough." She ushered Letty back into the rear of the truck before hopping in after her; Irene jumping in with the driver. "Head for the Lexington. We'll meet up with Carlo there," she told the driver.

The women left the truck in a hurry, scurrying into the hotel lobby and then upstairs to the dining room with its pale blue walls and white wooden trim. They found Carlo seated at a corner table, joined by Two-Gun. The three women by-passed the maître D, with a quick, "Oh. There's our party," before he could even object.

"What happened?" Clarice asked as she sat down in the plush dining room chair. The chatter around them was so noisy, she had no fear of eavesdroppers.

"Capone's men – Frank Rio and John Scalise were there," Carlo said quietly. "I didn't want to risk Two-Gun going in and getting shot."

"What's gonna keep 'em away tomorrow night?" Two-Gun wondered.

"They haven't been there the last times I checked the club out for us. We'll just have to trust our luck," Carlo offered with a shrug. "Look let's just try again tomorrow night. If its another no go, then we'll come up with another plan."

"Letty and I are willing to do that," Clarice said. "How about you, Two-Gun?"

"More fun than I've had in a long while. Count me in. I'll be back at the same time."

"Ok, then." Carlo stood. "Look for me again tomorrow night." He saluted the others before departing. They all rose from their seats. Weariness seemed to fold over them like a blanket.

"Tomorrow will be better," Clarice commented as she escorted Letty toward the front door.

The weather, at least, was better the next night with cloud cover, but no rain or freezing wind. Clarice, Letty, and Irene pulled up in the bakery truck just after dark. They got out, looking around cautiously. While they knew Two-Gun stood under the awning across the street, they couldn't see him. Once again, Carlo strode by in the grey three-piece suit, black fedora tilted forward over his face. He saluted the ladies before entering the *Four Deuces*. This time they saw him wave from the upper window, giving the go ahead.

As Two-Gun briskly walked across the street avoiding traffic, Letty and Clarice dragged their trunk out of the truck and into the apartment building. They concealed the trunk as best they could behind potted plants at the back of the first-floor staircase, then made their way to the fourth floor. Once near the door of 4 "E," Clarice raised a finger to her lips. Gingerly, she removed the skeleton keys, running through them to open the door.

Whimpering noises came from inside. There was a slap. A girl began sobbing.

The very last key opened the lock. Clarice twisted the knob, inching the door open. Letty had eased her small pearl handled pistol out of her overcoat pocket. Clarice nodded approval. The shabby one-room kitchen-living space was cluttered with cheap furniture – a kitchen table and four chairs, a radio stood on a small end table beside a sofa with its stuffing popping out at the seams. A tiny bathroom stood between two closed doors which must have been bedrooms. Sobbing clearly came out of the room on the left.

Clarice motioned for Letty to follow behind. She reached out and opened the door in such a way that the door itself shielded them from being seen by the occupants of the room.

"Who's there!" demanded a woman with a thick Italian accent. "What do you want?"

Clarice looked into the room beyond through the crack between the door and the wall, the woman was not armed. She charged in with Letty behind her. Letty aimed the pistol at the woman.

"Don't make a sound." Letty said. "Or do, and it'll get you shot."

Clarice hastened to the eleven-year-old Margaretta, tied to the bed by one wrist, her right cheek bright red where her keeper had just slapped her. "Your sister Melody sent us. We are getting you out of here."

The girl began to cry. "Please. Oh, please." Tears ran down her heart shaped face and down her neck where her thick dark curls met her shoulders. She was a tiny slip of a girl, under nourished, and pale, rarely seeing the sun.

Clarice took a blade from her coat pocket and sliced the ropes holding Margaretta captive. "Quickly grab any sort of wrapper you can."

"I've nothing but this night dress," the girl sobbed. Her narrow shoulders shook.

"Then we will take *her* coat." Clarice went into the other bedroom, opened the narrow armoire, and pulled out an old ratty coat. She returned to the girl. "Here wrap this around you," she said, helping the girl with the sleeves and pulling the large coat tight around her waist. Clarice then took the scraps of rope and shoved the woman into the only chair in the room, tying her wrists to the wooden arms. Leading Margaretta out of the apartment, Letty waved the gun menacingly before backing out after Clarice. They shut the outside door to the apartment and raced Margaretta down the four flights of stairs to where they had hidden the trunk.

"It's going to be a tight fit, but just long enough to get you into the truck to freedom," Clarice explained, beckoning the girl toward the trunk.

Margaretta understood at once, folding herself inside the trunk as best she could. The lid would not close completely, but it was close enough that no one would see her inside. Clarice and Letty slid the trunk along the floor, not lifting it until they absolutely had to. By the time they neared the front door of the apartment building, Irene ran forward to help them carry the trunk to the rear of the truck. Suddenly, Carlo was also there helping lift the trunk, and slamming the rear doors from the inside of the truck where he joined Clarice and Letty. Irene climbed up into the passenger seat and closed the door. Carlo signaled the driver to take off by banging twice on the roof. Loud retorts and shouting were still coming from the *Four Deuces* as the truck pulled out into traffic.

Suddenly, they heard more shouting and gun shots.

"Get that truck!!!" Men were yelling.

"They're getting away!"

"It's the bakery truck!"

"After them!" More gun shots. A bullet careened off the rear doors, startling the driver to swerve, the truck shifting its weight more on the right wheels, before bouncing back with a jolt.

Clarice held on as tightly as she could. Their driver pushed the truck to its fastest speed in traffic, gears grinding. They turned off on Michigan Avenue, and then left onto a smaller street, before a quick right, to lose the men trying to follow them. Ultimately, they were free of traffic, the close set, taller buildings of the central city, and headed to Norwood Park.

"I think we've lost them," Carlo said, easing the lid of the trunk open so his cousin could sit up. "But they suspect Bugs Moran is behind this. We weren't as careful as we could have been. Capone will be watching."

"What about Two-Gun?" Clarice asked, wrapping one arm around the girl, comforting her, smoothing her dark hair back out of her face.

"You should have seen him." Carlo laughed. "He danced around with his cowboy boots and made a royal ruckus. No one took their eyes off him. It was when he threatened to start shooting pips out of cards that they asked him to leave. He started a brawl and the midst of it all, made his escape. They don't make em' like him anymore." Carlo wiped at his eyes.

Despite her fear, Margaretta brightened hearing Carlo talk. As her newly won freedom became more real, her trembling subsiding. "What's to become of me?" she asked quietly.

"Ideally, we would return you to your parents, but Capone would guess that. With the current economy, your parents might sell you back to him." Carlo stroked his chin.

"We are *not* doing that," Clarice said, shaking her head vigorously. "It's too great of a risk."

"She's living with us," Letty stated firmly in a no-nonsense way.

"It's decided then," Clarice added. "No one would dare harm the chick now. For tonight, she can have a room at the farm, next to ours."

"She needs clothing," Letty tapped her chin with her forefinger. "I'll get her something then take her shopping in Norwood Park. There's no reason to let anyone see her who might tell Capone."

"I'll teach her how to shoot," Clarice chuckled. "That would serve them right. She needs to be able to protect herself."

Margaretta looked back and forth between the women, uncertain who to focus on. Her relief at her safety transformed her features from pinched, sharp angles, to a rounded girlishness.

"Did you say, Melody had sent you?"

"Ah, yes," Carlo nodded. "I knew that would come into it. We had a séance – they hold them consistently where we are headed – and your sister came, begging us to rescue you."

"But why would you care?" The little girl asked, her eyes wide.

"You and your sister are my cousins," Carlo admitted softly. "I too am an Anselmo. And we had to right an injustice."

"Exactly," Clarice and Letty agreed. "We weren't going to allow another girl suffer Melody's fate."

The truck had been jolting over pitted roads for over ten minutes and had come to a complete stop. Irene threw open the back doors. "Come on! We're here."

Gregory raced out to greet them, clasping Irene's hands in his own. "Did you have any difficulty?" he asked.

Irene and Letty answered him simultaneously. They chattered about getting the trunk out of the house and being able to hide Margaretta in the bread van. "But Carlo almost didn't make it out of the *Four Deuces*," Irene finished. "He just closed the door behind him so we could drive away..."

"And all Hell broke loose," Letty concluded. "The men at the *Four Deuces* had started to fight with Two-Gun, but some must have seen Carlo run outside. They followed and started shooting."

Clarice brought Margaretta out of the van, her arm around the little girl's shoulders. Margaretta looked tiny wrapped in the shabby overcoat, three sizes too big. "But she's safe now." Clarice grinned down at the girl, who smiled shyly up at her.

10

Since they couldn't participate in Margaretta's rescue, Teddy, Harrison, and three others from the North Side Gang had met in Harrison's office to discuss Belmont—Sheffield Trust and Savings at 1001 West Belmont. Harrison had finally conceded that he needed the financial boost from the robbery—he was behind the eight ball. His stocks had all dropped, their certificates were merely worthless pieces of paper, but the brokers were demanding money – more money than the Club could possibly provide. The five men peered down at a map of downtown, tracing out potential escape routes and talking about what steps they would have to take in order to steal the gold and silver from the basement vault.

"The bank is on the first floor," said Tippy O'Connell. "The top floors, four to six are a hotel – so lots of people come and go. As banks are concerned, it's very secure.

"The entryway and lobby curve around an open atrium where they have some plants and benches," Charlie Ward, added. "It lets in lots of light.

"That's gonna be a problem, see," Charlie's brother Frank said.

"We have to figure out how to get into the bank and out again with the least amount of fanfare."

"So, what if I go and open a safety deposit box?" Harrison sat up in his desk chair. "Then several of us could go, as if we were accessing the box, but instead break into the vault and steal the gold and silver."

"Not bad," Teddy remarked around his cigarette, stroking his chin. "If the vault looks too difficult, then we could hide inside and do the job after closing."

"Exactly," Harrison stood with renewed energy. "We can look things over tomorrow and finalize the plans. Duck soup, boys. Duck soup."

Teddy could not believe how rapidly things developed. The day before, the gang had visited the Belmont-Sheffield and determined the vault would cause no difficulties. Tippy O'Connell was an expert safe cracker. "Berries!" he'd said with a smile. "Easy as pie."

This afternoon, Teddy was in the bread van on Belmont Street, nervously watching pedestrians access the bank building and cars pass by in the street. His truck vibrated violently around him as he sat, tapping his fingers impatiently against the steering wheel. He smoked constantly to calm his nerves, but it wasn't working. Every few minutes, he'd reach into his vest pocket for his pocket watch. Shaking his head, he realized it had only been fifteen minutes, but each minute dragged on as if it were an hour.

Harrison came running out the door of the bank, gripping his hat on his head with one hand and a bag in the other. He slapped on the door of the car. "Here," Harrison said, shoving a heavy bag into Teddy's lap. "I need to open up the back for the others."

As Harrison walked around to the back door of the truck, O'Connell and the Ward brothers speed walked out of the bank and headed for the bread truck. Teddy saw that people on the street were beginning to notice the unusual flurry of movement. A little girl tapped her mother's sleeve and pointed toward Harrison.

"Hurry!" Teddy hissed, wishing they were all inside the truck, and they could leave.

Harrison moved to help O'Connell and the Wards with the heavy valise when three armed men in navy blue uniforms raced out of the bank.

"Drop those bags and put your hands in the air!" one of the men yelled. He could have been a bank guard, or he could have been one of Capone's men – there was no way to tell.

Harrison merely shoved at O'Connell. The Ward brothers pulled guns out from their coats instead of getting into the truck. To make matters worse, they began firing on the three uniformed men. The shots echoed loudly in the busy street. Pedestrians scattered.

Teddy screamed, "Get in, get in!!"

O'Connell and the valise were already deep inside the back of the truck. Harrison was attempting to jump in behind O'Connell when he shrieked in pain. The Ward brothers shoved him the rest of the way into the back of the truck and slammed the door, yelling, "Go! Go!"

Teddy didn't hesitate. Heart racing, he put the truck into gear and gunned the engine, taking off as fast as he could. In his rearview mirror, he could see the Ward brothers shooting at the men, dodging cars in the street, and creating a safe passage for Teddy to escape. *Not according to plan.* From the back, he could hear Harrison moaning.

"Harrison has been hit badly," O'Connell said. "He needs a doctor – right away."

"We can't risk going now in this truck," Teddy explained heading back to the *Hair of the Dog*. "Gregory will have to take him. We can hide the loot in with the alky in the root cellar under the club office while they go to the hospital." The drive seemed interminable. Finally, the turn off to the farm became visible just ahead. "Hang on Harrison. We're almost there."

Gregory, Clarice, and Letty raced out the front door of the farm house as Teddy pulled up to the house. Gregory could see the bullet holes in the side panel and the rear door; his heart sinking. He reached the rear door before the others, yanking it open as Teddy careened to a halt. "What happened?" Gregory demanded. "I thought no one was supposed to get hurt." He was furious, heart pounding.

"Some guards or Capone's men came out after us," O'Connell said. "We were almost clear, but the Wards started firing on them and they shot back. I'm sorry, Gregory, but Harrison took a bullet in his back. He needs to see a doctor right away."

Clarice and Letty crowded in behind Gregory, trying to see. "I'll get a blanket we can use as a stretcher," Clarice said. "He needs to be moved as little as possible, but he can't go to Mercy Hospital in this truck." She and Letty ran back into the house ostensibly for a blanket. When they returned, the women each carried a thick blanket.

Carefully, they eased Harrison onto one blanket. While they did so, Klein ran around the back and drove up in the Ford. O'Connell, Clarice, Letty, and Gregory eased the blanket up off the floor of the bakery van, levitating Harrison into the seat of the Ford. Gregory wrapped his brother up in the second blanket, to help prevent shock. Clarice took the keys from Klein. "I'll drive. Gregory, hold Harrison up, and prevent him from moving. Come on!" she urged. "Let's go."

Gregory slid into the seat with Harrison practically on his lap. Clarice eased the Ford into gear and drove off. She leaned out the window, "We will let you know something as soon as we can."

Clarice drove as carefully as possible to avoid pot holes in the streets or uneven bricks. Still, the ride to Mercy Hospital on 26th and Calumet took much longer than they wanted. Harrison's breathing had become reedy and his heartbeat faint. Gregory shook with terror for his brother. His own breathing was shallow while his heart raced. The interns and sisters dashed out to greet the car when Clarice ran in to have Harrison admitted. It was an Irish hospital – they didn't ask questions, merely prepped Harrison for immediate surgery. Before wheeling Harrison into the operating room, the doctor turned to Gregory, "The bullet may be lodged in his spine. I'll do what I can for him."

Gregory took up one of the uncomfortable chairs in the

emergency waiting room with Clarice sitting slumped next to him. "I didn't want him to do that job," Gregory began, staring at his hands in his lap. *I'm furious with him for almost getting killed,* Gregory thought. *What will I do without him?*

"You can't blame yourself. He's a grown man and makes his own decisions." Clarice folded her hands over her knee. "I think O'Connell blames the Ward brothers. They started shooting."

"No one knows what happened to them?"

"They might be in tomorrow's obituaries." Clarice studied the shiny marble floor tiles, and Gregory fell silent.

Four hours and twelve terrible cups of coffee later, Dr. Flannery came out from behind the doors to the operating rooms. He strode over to Gregory. "Your brother is going to pull through, but I'm afraid he is going to be in a wheelchair for the rest of his life."

Gregory reached to shake the doctor's hand. "What happened?"

"The bullet bounced around inside his back – but I was able to remove it. The bad news is that some bone splinters lodged in his spinal column, cutting the chord, causing paralysis." The doctor shook his head. "I'm sorry."

"Don't be, Dr. Flannery. At least you were able to save his life." Gregory thought about the future and the years ahead. Behind him, he could hear some of the hospital machines beeping and dinging. He felt numb inside.

"His recovery will be slow. Don't rush him. He's going to be in intensive care for at least several weeks." Dr. Flannery looked over at Clarice, who shook her head. "You'll be needing a nurse then?"

"Yes." Gregory said. *Anything to make him comfortable.* "One of the Sisters?"

"Of course. I'll make arrangements."

"When can I see him?" Gregory asked.

"He's being moved to intensive care. You can visit him then," Dr. Flannery said.

An hour later, Gregory pulled aside the pleated white curtain that surrounded Harrison's hospital bed. Machines whirred, beeped, clicked, and pumped oxygen into the clear tent covering Harrison from chest to head. His brother seemed to be resting quietly, several tubes coming from his nose and mouth. Gregory wanted to hold Harrison's hand, to tell him everything was going to be Jake – but it wasn't true. So, instead, Gregory dragged a heavy metal chair closer to the bed and sat vigil. Thoughts jumbled in his head and his heart felt like lead.

"Is this chair taken?" a soft voice whispered into his ear.

Gregory startled. He must have fallen asleep. Smiling up into her sweet face, Gregory urged Irene to come and sit beside him on the metal chair. "He's comfortable."

"That drip," Irene pointed to the hanging bag near the other side of the bed, "must have opium. He won't be in pain."

"He won't be able to walk," Gregory explained. "The doctor says bone fragments from the shooting have partially cut his spinal cord. Harrison has always been so independent. He will hate being an invalid."

"You will be there for him," Irene said, running her hand up and down Gregory's sleeve. "That's all you can do."

With Harrison in the hospital, the atmosphere at the *Hair of the Dog* was subdued. Every day, Gregory visited his brother. The streets became more and more crowded with bread lines and apple sellers, forcing Gregory to jostle through them. In the small corner groceries, people started to hoard canned goods. Gregory noticed a shift in mood from the gaiety of the earlier part of 1929 and now when desperation boiled beneath the surface of Chicago. Gregory was glad when Clarice bought chickens for eggs and that the farm had a large garden for fresh vegetables. Food prices were rising almost as rapidly as the number of jobless.

Harrison needed one more week in the hospital, and Gregory visited every day, urging Harrison to recover as fully as possible. Teddy and Carlo, also had been in to visit, attempting to cheer

Harrison with their banter. But December 2 was Carlo's birthday. Teddy wanted very much to celebrate and have their friends with them. Without discussing things with Carlo, Teddy pulled Gregory aside.

"It's Carlo's birthday in two days. I know Harrison won't be home from the hospital, but I would really like to do something special for Carlo."

Gregory nodded. "Of course. We'll do whatever you want. Count Irene and me in. Clarice and Letty, too." *They needed something joyous.*

"I was thinking *Kelly's Stables*. They always have great shows, good drinks, and food," Teddy offered.

"Fine," Gregory agreed. "Set it up. I'll make certain the club is covered so we won't be missed."

That evening, they took the street car to Rush Street, all six of them crowding into a single car, chatting and joking amiably. Riders around them pulled their coats tighter and avoided eye contact. Carlo was looking especially snorky, as he deserved on the occasion of his birthday, dressed in his racoon overcoat and a lavender plaid three-piece suit. He tilted his newsboy cap at a rakish angle and continuously glanced over at Teddy through his long brown eyelashes. Teddy and Clarice adopted a more severe look with their black three-piece silk suits, white handkerchief stuffed in the coat pocket, and their pomaded hair. Like Gregory, Teddy and Clarice wore fedoras. Gregory decided on a dark gray suit, complimenting the deep garnet drop- waisted sleeveless dress Irene wore. A beaded head band replaced the cloche hat on Irene's blond head, and Letty wore a similar one on her dark curls. Her silver dress contrasted with Clarice's black suit. When they exited the street car and walked down Rush Street towards Kelley's Stables, they looked like party goers on the town for the evening.

Gregory guided Irene toward the club with a gentle hand on her back. He watched Teddy do the same for Carlo and smiled to himself at how happy the two men were. The door to the club seemed heavy and the multi-colored brick walls held the cool air inside despite the large number of people inside. A low beat reverberated through the space that Gregory felt through the floor. A clarinet wailed as Johnny Dodds accompanied his brother's drums. A sax joined in while a bass viol continued to play the moving bass.

"Right this way please," a dark-haired waiter said, escorting them to a table for six. He pulled out chairs for Irene and Letty, allowing Teddy to seat Carlo. Gregory and Clarice each sat in the open places by their girlfriends. "Drinks?"

They gave their orders, also selecting appetizers off the menu. After the drinks arrived, Irene lifted her glass. "A toast to Carlo. Happy birthday and many returns."

"Here, here." The rest of the group responded. They relaxed into their seats, Letty, Clarice, and Teddy lighting up cigarettes, letting the smoke drift towards the high ceiling where the modern chandeliers gave off yellow light. Even though he and Irene were having a good time, Gregory felt guilty that Harrison could not be there. He allowed his attention to wander away from their table of friends, glimpsing a dark-haired Italian out of the corner of his eye.

"Teddy," Gregory said quietly, as the other man finally looked away from Carlo. "Who is that?" Gregory tilted his champagne flute toward the man who sat four tables away from them.

Teddy gasped. "Jack McGurn."

Carlo glanced over his shoulder. "Machine Gun Jack?"

Next to him sat a wide-eyed man with protruding ears, most likely John Scalise, and beyond him sat a rotund man with tiny round spectacles. The more the man drank, the redder his face became. Carlo scooted down in his chair, making himself less visible.

"Teddy," Carlo said plaintively. "I think we need to go."

Teddy and Carlo stood quietly, gathering their things and headed for the back door to the club. The others dropped a few bills on the table to cover the drinks and food before accompanying the two women toward the back. Gregory noticed as he followed Clarice, Letty, and Irene that McGurn, Scalise, and the third man had also readied themselves to leave. His heart sped up in his chest.

"Irene, hurry," Gregory hissed, the heavy rear door closing behind them. Once in the alley, Teddy and Carlo climbed the fire escape ladder and headed for the roof.

"We'll meet back at Clarice and Letty's," Teddy said, reaching for Carlo's hand and yanking the younger man up onto the roof. They took off at a run, sending pebbles skittering to the street below.

Gregory and Irene, Clarice and Letty cleared the alley and walked rapidly down Rush Street. From behind them, they heard an Italian accented voice shout, "There they go"

Gregory saw Scalise pointing upwards toward the skyline where he could barely make out Carlo and Teddy.

Scalise took off running, shoving his way between Gregory and Clarice, who had been protecting Irene and Letty. McGurn followed in pursuit. "Capone wants those two," McGurn shouted, pulling his pistol out from inside his jacket. Luckily, his machine gun would not fit under his suit coat. The third man had disappeared from sight.

Several blocks ahead, Scalise stopped and spun around, looking along the roof tops.

McGurn caught up. "You lost them?" he asked.

"We'll find em," Scalise said, gun in hand. "They can't get too far."

Gregory led Irene, Clarice, and Letty away from Capone's men and headed north towards Clarice's flat. Luckily the Italians didn't know where they were all headed. Clarice and Letty ran on ahead, leaving Gregory and Irene to walk more leisurely. Gregory was certain that McGurn and Scalise had given up, returning toward *Kelley's Stables. But where had that balding, fat man gone? Maybe he lost them too?*

Gregory drew Irene closer to his side. His heart still hammered in his chest,

"Have they gone away?" Irene asked.

"Hope so," Gregory said. He looked up and down the street. Clarice's flat was mere blocks away. Beyond the block where Clarice's building stood, he thought he saw Teddy and Carlo reappear. About to raise his hand in greeting, Gregory caught a flash of light out of the corner of his eye. From behind them, a large car had entered the street and was heading toward Teddy and Carlo, it slowed, and Gregory noticed the black muzzle of a machine gun poke out of the passenger window.

"Get down," He shouted at Teddy and Carlo, starting to run toward them. "Get down!"

Instinctively, Gregory folded Irene tighter into his side, curving his arm around her head and eyes. "Don't look," he whispered as the powerful retort of the machine gun sending bullets against the sidewalk filled the air. The horrible noise, at once so familiar, resonated inside Gregory.

"Take that you traitorous whores!!" A man's face became visible under the street light. It was the small, fat man with the glasses and red face. He started shooting again.

Gregory could not look away as the bullets ripped into his two friends, destroying their bodies beyond recognition. He wanted to throw up, to rage and scream. Gregory led Irene on into Clarice's building, needing to get out of the street and as far away from the tragedy as possible. Tears wet his cheeks and Irene's hair. Gregory knew that he could not do anything to save them, but he blamed himself. He finally realized who the third man had been – Jack McErlane.

"Teddy and Carlo were just gunned down in a drive by shooting," Gregory cried when Clarice buzzed them up. He held Irene tightly by his side. She sobbed hysterically against his shoulder.

"I don't believe that." Clarice said. Her face pasty. "It must be someone else."

"No," Irene hiccupped. "I saw them before Gregory hid my eyes. I heard the shots, the screaming. It was horrible." She began sobbing again. Gregory led her over to Clarice's sofa, sat beside her and rubbed her back soothingly.

"If only there were something we could do." Gregory said. "Jack McErlane was sitting with Scalise and McGurn. I should have recognized him. If we had left earlier... or never gone at all." Gregory felt so guilty. He had so much he wanted to change.

11

Bullets screamed by, and the thunk, thunk, of metal hitting, splintering wood made Gregory cringe. He coughed and coughed, the dust and the smell of machine gun smoke surrounding him. Darkness began to take him. He had put his head down. Now he returned to consciousness. The silence around him was deafening. Pain lanced through his shoulder and burned across his left temple. A hand clamped on his right arm, and someone was shaking him. "Gregory, Gregory, can you hear me?"

He must be dreaming. Of course, he was dreaming. He hadn't been able to get the machine gun fire out of his mind. *That had to be it.* Gregory tried to lift his head, thinking he would see his bedroom at the farm. Instead, glass shards and wood chips scattered from his hair. He wasn't in his bed at all. He was on the floor of the *Hair of the Dog,* near the footrail of the mahogany bar that he and Harrison had hand polished so lovingly. Beneath him, the oriental carpet was covered in dust, wood fragments, and broken glass. The décor was Chinese, not Art Deco, the Chinese design they had originally installed back in 1921. The black lacquer tables, upended and riddled with bullets, were scattered over the floor. *What was happening? Had the past eight months been but a fever dream? Or was it something else entirely? What had Deanie done? It had to be Deanie!*

Whoever it was continued to jostle his arm. Gregory tried to brush the hand away. "No," he muttered, squeezing his eyes shut. "Leave me be. I can't face it."

The man knelt closer, cradling Gregory's head. "Can't face what? Come on, man." A gentle patting on his cheeks, forced Gregory to crack one eye. Harrison's tousled brown hair swam into view. *Harrison?*

"Harrison?" Gregory tried to get up, but couldn't. His brother shook him again, clearing Gregory's head.

He sat upright, resting wobbly on one arm. "Harrison?" He was so shocked he could not think of what to say. Then, Gregory grabbed his brother in a big hug. Harrison struggled slightly against him. "You are all right!" Joy flooded Gregory.

"Of course, I'm all right." Harrison grinned down at Gregory, gripping his shoulders firmly. Gregory winced at the shooting pain in his left shoulder. "But you? I leave you for one day to get the alky, and I come back to this—" he used his chin to encompass the mess of the club. "What the hell happened?"

Gregory sat back, stunned. More glass and wood fell from his hair. He raised a hand toward his left temple, where blood seemed to drip into his eye. A bullet had grazed his head along the hairline and also clipped his shoulder. "We were hit by Capone—no, by McErlane," Gregory finally told Harrison, remembering what had happened back in April. "He sent men to destroy the place with machine guns, just like the Valentine's Day massacre. Fortunately, the patrons got out in time, and it's just cosmetic damage. We'll rebuild. I'm thinking along the lines of Art Deco," Gregory offered, and his brother nodded, a bemused look on his face.

"It's April, right?" Gregory asked, just to be certain. Then he recalled Deanie's last enigmatic words – *"Death has taught me time is not as it seems." A second chance...* His heart raced. *This must be what Deanie had given him. The real gift-- a second chance.* Hope exploded inside him.

"Yes. Of course, it is," Harrison looked at Gregory as if he had grown a horn rather than been grazed by a bullet. He tilted Gregory's chin, looking at the wound. "That might scar," he mused.

Scar! Horse feathers! Joy bubbled in Gregory's chest. He wanted to leap up and dance a seaman's jig, shout to the heavens. He didn't know how, but he had Harrison back. Harrison who could walk and retained independence. No hospital, no wheel chair, no doctors! "It's a miracle," he whispered. "I have a chance to change it all." A burden he hadn't realized he felt lifted from his heart. *It doesn't matter how Deanie did this, just that he did it.*

"What's that?" Harrison said, scratching his head.

Gregory merely smiled and shook his head. "You wouldn't believe me if I told you. I don't believe me right now. But you will." He'd go to O'Brien. That's where he would start. He would get that ring to show everyone he actually could predict the future, and they would have to believe him. But he'd do it tomorrow; no wait, they had to rebuild the club first. He'd go after that. Gregory sat back down, his head and shoulder throbbing. *Owww. Where were Clarice and Letty? They would help him, but wait – it was April.* There was so much to do.

Harrison began the renovations and the Art Deco version of the club Gregory knew for the past seven months started to take shape; meanwhile, the time allowed his head and shoulder to heal, and after two weeks, he felt almost back to normal. New cut-glass chandeliers in layered octagon shapes were delivered, and the waiters helped Harrison hang them. Carpenters put up the etched glass and removed the old wall decorations. They added the triangular wall sconces that increased the light coming into the club. Wood workers patched over the bullet holes and added mirrors, making the club more elegant, while creating the appearance of an even larger space. After four weeks, *Hair of the Dog* looked much more the way Gregory had recently become accustomed.

Teddy had stopped by several times to talk with Harrison, but Gregory had been too busy overseeing the back parlor for his seances to do more than salute. Seeing the men together caused Gregory's heart to clench. *What he had experienced had to be real, had to have some purpose. He had to be able to change things.* So far, Gregory wasn't even certain he believed in what he had lived in the past eight months, but he just couldn't let it go either. He just didn't know where to begin proving it – first to himself, and then he could deal with the others.

Harrison sat at his desk in his office. "The renovations are Jake," he said.

"Yes. We can reopen soon." Gregory said, rolling his slightly stiff shoulder. The bullet wound on his head was also healing nicely. "Have you hired the people for the front door, yet?"

"No," Harrison chuckled. "Some of the applicants are arriving this morning. I was going to meet with them in my office." Hammering and sawing still made hearing difficult. The workers should be done in a few more days, but the waiters and capers needed to be ready to work when the doors reopened. The club had been almost completely transformed into its sleeker, familiar mirrored, silvery Art Deco look that Gregory had come to love.

"Send them to the front parlor upstairs." Gregory said in a no-nonsense tone. "I'm thinking of something specific." *And extra protection, like body guards.*

"Give me a minute to finish up with these books," Harrison waved over the ledger on his desk. "Klein will see to it that the applicants know where to go." He picked up the telephone and punched in the single number that connected with Klein in the other part of the house.

Gregory gave Harrison a two fingered salute, ducking out of the office and heading up the stair case leading to the ground floor of the farm house. He headed for the front parlor – a large airy room that the family had used to gather in the evenings, or meet guests. Klein had indeed shown the potential workers into the cream and gray walled room. Several men stood, milling around near the fireplace or near the two long sofas which faced one another across the open floor. As Gregory began to look over the prospects, Harrison joined him, saying, "Well, at least there are choices."

Gregory gave their applicants a quick once over and was about to dismiss them all, when Clarice Daniel strode in, her long overcoat flapping loosely behind her, and a fedora tilted on her pomaded dark, auburn hair. She had a hand on Letty's back, directing her girlfriend toward the small curved sofa placed in front of the floor to ceiling window. Letty perched on the edge of the cream fabric, one languid arm along the wooden rail at the back edge of the sofa. She twisted the long rope of pearls which hung around her neck with her other hand.

The moment he saw them, Gregory left Harrison mid-conversation with one of the male candidates, a lanky boy with stringy hair. "There they are," Gregory said. "At last."

Gregory didn't give Clarice a chance to sit beside Letty. He held out his hand which Clarice took and shook firmly as he expected. Gregory's mouth curved slowly into a welcoming smile. "Glad you finally made it," he couldn't help remarking, relief in his voice.

Clarice raised a well-groomed eyebrow at his words. If her features appeared more severe than he remembered, perhaps Clarice had softened her look over the long months of their acquaintance, or familiarity had done so. She still feathered her brows with a reddish-brown pencil, and applied light rouge on her cheeks. Her three-piece suit of dark, dark burgundy appeared almost black, wasn't one Gregory recalled, but the familiar tilted fedora on her head encouraged Gregory to continue the interview, as if these were the women he knew so well.

"Let's just say, your reputation precedes you, ladies." Gregory indicated for Clarice to sit beside Letty. He flicked his coat tails up behind him as he took the Queen Anne chair beside the sofa. "As far as I'm concerned you both are hired."

Clarice gave a throaty laugh. "Just like that?" She crossed one leg over the other, ankle at her knee.

"I know you and Letty, here, better than you realize," Gregory offered, deciding to go all in. "When my brother sees how you can hit five pips on a playing card from fifty feet, he'll be convinced too."

Letty's gray eyes widened, and her fingers stopped toying with the long strand of pearls around her neck. "How the devil did you know that?" She glanced nervously at Clarice.

Gregory coughed. He used the time to study them. The chatter of the men in the room, receded to a dull hum.

"You aren't going to say, `lucky guess,' are you?" Clarice slid the raised leg over the other, the silk of her trousers whispering in the sudden quiet of the room.

"I wouldn't dare." Gregory patted his heart and tried to look as innocent as possible. He had to persuade them. Leaning toward them, he added, "But, I know you can, so there's no debate. I want the sort of protection you ladies can offer for my brother and myself, and for the club."

Clarice nodded. "I appreciate directness," she said, slipping an arm over Letty's shoulders and pressing back into the sofa. Letty took her cigarette holder from her beaded bag, rolled tobacco into the thin paper before inserting it in the holder.

Gregory reached across, offering her a light from the lighter in his pocket. She took several languid puffs, her kohl outlined eyes narrowed in pleasure.

"And, you wouldn't just be watching the door," Gregory became excited, warming to his subject.

"We won't be flirting with customers or worse," Clarice cut in. Beside her, Letty's face hardened.

Gregory startled. "Nothing of the sort." *My God! He never even considered...* "We want you to sing, Clarice. And Letty. We want *you* to be one of our regular headliners."

Clarice sat up. Her eyes brightened. She really had not expected any of what Gregory had just told her. She raised a palm. "Let me get this straight. You're offering us jobs as cappers, and you want us to sing at the club?"

"Exactly," Gregory was nodding excitedly. "I just love your renditions of `Sugar,' and `Someone to Watch Over Me'." He rose and beckoned them over to the upright piano against the wall furthest from the French doors leading into the parlor from the hall. Gregory sat down and began to play, "Stairway to Paradise."

The music and Gregory nodding at her, overcame her reluctance. Clarice leaned against the piano and began singing in her deep alto voice. At the chorus, Letty joined in as did Gregory in three-part harmony, as if they did it all the time. The rest of the room stopped talking, listening to the performance.

Harrison applauded when they were done, staring at his brother a little quizzically. "Marvelous," he said, "just marvelous." Harrison came over and whispered, "I didn't know you could play that," then he went quickly to talk with two other applicants.

"There's a lot about me you don't know," Gregory chuckled, thinking about the skills he had acquired in what he had spent as the last eight months.

Clarice and Letty glanced around the room at the applicants who came and went as they remained at the piano and spoke to Gregory about the details relating to their new jobs. Some of those others would serve as waiters, getting hired on, but Harrison hadn't successfully found what he was looking for in a capper. Gregory knew without his intervention the search would have taken a lot longer. Ultimately, Harrison would have realized he needed Clarice and Letty – he had before, but Gregory wanted to hasten the process. *He* needed the women on his side right away as soon as the club reopened.

"So, what do you say?" Gregory stood up from the piano bench and held out his hand toward Clarice. She stood from where she had been leaning against the top of the upright, took his hand, and shook it vigorously.

"Berries!" Clarice said in her deep Garbo voice. A broad smile twinkled up into her eyes – and there she was, the Clarice he knew.

"Thrilled," Letty said, beaming, shaking Gregory's hand.

"Welcome aboard!" Gregory said, guiding the women over to Harrison, introducing them.

Harrison looked suspicious. Gregory had never taken charge like this before. "Are you certain, little brother?"

"Wait until you see their card trick," Gregory confided. "You'll be amazed. They are exactly what we need, I promise." He wasn't going to let Harrison interfere.

Later after they had all gone and the brothers returned to Harrison's office deep inside the club, Gregory explained. "You would have hired them, eventually." It would have taken Harrison another few months. He had taken them on in July last time, after the club had opened, not before.

Harrison shook his head, a broad grin on his boyish features. "So, you get shot and suddenly, you're going to take charge."

"Be more involved in the business end," Gregory nodded. "I'm still going to play sax and piano, but I will help with more decisions." His voice took on some urgency. "There are some things that we need to do."

Harrison sat up in his desk chair. He looked Gregory up and down. "Who are you? And what have you done with my brother?"

Gregory ran his hand through his brown hair. He laughed softly. "I know you've been buying stocks on margin."

"Woah!" Harrison put out his hands. "Club decisions are joint ones, but finance – that's been strictly my ballywack."

"I get it, Harrison. But diversify," Gregory suggested. "I had a tip, the other day," he lied. "Gold and silver—that's the true path to riches, brother, not stocks."

Harrison lit a cigar. "Gold and silver? Now there's an idea. I'll consider it."

Gregory knew Harrison might, but probably not. There was time to change his mind on stocks later. "Look, I've got the séance tonight," he said, getting up from the club chair opposite the desk. Gregory had decided that they needed the income from the seances and since the farm house didn't require any repairs, there was no reason not to start those up prior to the club's official reopening in a few weeks.

"Go, go" Harrison waved a hand, fingers down, dismissing him and picking up some papers lying on his blotter.

They would talk later. Gregory knew he had to prepare the table. He headed up the stairs and towards the back parlor where he held the seances. Would he contact a ghost or was that merely part of whatever it was that happened to him?

The room needed dusting even though he had most likely conducted a séance there only last week in his own timeline. However, the attack on the club had stirred up dust everywhere, even though it was several floors beneath the house. Therefore, he took out a rag and some lemon wax. He was busy polishing the table when soft foot falls behind him alerted him that someone had entered the room. Gregory hastily looked over into the mirror that hung over the fireplace.

"Irene!" He exclaimed softly. His heart swelled in his chest and his tongue grew slightly swollen with emotion.

"You know me?" she asked good humoredly, blue eyes sparkling. The brown mascara on her lashes made them seem extremely long and feathery. "You have me at an advantage, sir." She ran a gloved finger over the back of one of the chairs set around the table. Her pale blue felt cap fit snugly over her reddish blonde curls, cut into a stylish bob.

Oh, no. Gregory thought. *Our first meeting. What do I say?* "No advantage, I assure you," he said, but he wasn't at all certain it was true. *He had met her on August 9th in the alternate timeline,* he thought. *She's early. But they had so much to do, perhaps meeting her early was a key component to changing everything.* "Are you here alone?" *Where was Teddy?*

She spun and faced him, laughing and more at ease. "No, but I seem to have lost my escort."

"Not well done of him," Gregory said, easily, remembering that Irene actually saw Teddy as a brother and cover rather than as a romantic interest.

"It wasn't his fault, entirely, because he headed downstairs, while I came in here; but, I interrupt your work." Her features fell.

Gregory hid the rag behind his back. "There's a séance in here at eight tonight if you'd like to come."

"I would," she confided. Coming closer, she lowered her voice. "I would love to say good bye to my brother Geoff." She glanced down at her beige pumps, allowing Gregory to watch her lashes fan out along the top of her cheeks.

He could not help himself, and took up one of her gloved hands, bringing the kid-covered fingers to his lips. "By all means, attend," he whispered. "Were you close? To your brother, I mean."

"I was." She looked up at him, but the adoration he was used to seeing, was not yet there. Nodding, she moved away, and took her hand, released from his clasp, away as she went to study the armoire between the doorway and the fireplace.

Gregory's heart sunk, but they had time. He knew he could win her back. He just had to be patient. Behind them, someone cleared his throat.

"Teddy." Irene said, spinning around.

"Ah, there you are darling." Teddy carried his brown overcoat over one arm. He swooped over and kissed Irene on the cheek. She moved away quickly, not allowing him to put an arm around her waist.

"I want to see the séance," Irene said to him.

"What? No dancing?" Teddy raised an eyebrow at Gregory, his hand holding the cigarette poised in the air. His energy and vivaciousness acted like balm on Gregory's sore heart.

Gregory dropped the cleaning rag onto the table top and shook Teddy's hand. "Good to see you, Teddy."

"Harrison said you'd changed." Teddy's dark eyes glittered. "I thought it was horse feathers, but he was right." He glanced over at

Irene. Holding out a hand, he said, "Darling, come get a drink – we'll come back at eight with everyone else."

She allowed him to take her hand and guide her away. At the last second, as they walked through the doorway, Irene glanced back over her shoulder and winked at Gregory. "Later," she said with a giggle.

Gregory sat down hard in his chair at the head of the séance table. He dropped his head into his hands, wondering whatever was going to happen next. *If Geoff appeared again – then he'd know he hadn't merely fabricated the entire past eight months no one else had lived through yet.* If Geoff did not appear, he could still go to O'Brien and talk to him about the ring. He needed to tell someone about the ring before tonight so that at least that person might believe him and his – gift? Gregory's thoughts raced. He wanted to confide in Harrison as he always had as a boy, but he needed Harrison to believe in him from the start in order to prevent those terrible things – paralysis, bankruptcy – from happening to his brother. Teddy was even more complicated, but almost a better choice. But as he sat there, thinking, Clarice poked her head inside the parlor.

"Gregory," she said, sliding her hand along the door frame.

He looked up. *Had God answered his prayer?* "Yes?" he replied.

"Might we chat?" Clarice asked.

"Absolutely. In fact, I have a few things to share, myself," Gregory straightened in his chair, bracing himself.

"Berries!" Clarice strode in and pulled the chair at Gregory's left out from the table, flicked her coat back, and sat. "You first," she offered crossing her arms and leaning on the table.

"You remember the first day when you and Letty arrived?" Gregory began.

"Y-e-s. And you seemed to know us extremely well. I have been wondering about that for the past four weeks, and that was what I had wanted to talk to you about next." A slow smile pulled at her mouth.

"Well, I do know you." Gregory put up a hand. "I didn't make inquiries. I know you because – now please listen first –"

"What?" Clarice stared intently at him, making her nose look particularly hawkish.

Gregory looked away and just dove in. "Somehow after the bullet grazed my head in the shootout, I awoke and lived here for eight months, all the way until January 1930. Those events are now beginning to repeat. Hiring you and Letty, for instance, Harrison did hire you, first as a capper and later as a singer. You and Letty had become my friends – I wanted you aboard faster, so I didn't wait for Harrison."

"So, when we arrived four weeks ago, you met us." Clarice's green eyes were bright with her concealed laughter.

"Yes, exactly. I offered you the jobs I knew you were going to perform – and perform so excellently. I wanted my friends back." Gregory spread his hands out as if asking "what could I do?"

"Before – the first time, we showed you the card trick?" Clarice asked.

"Yes." Gregory nodded. "You wanted to prove to Harrison that you and Letty were crack shots. Took out the five pips easily at fifty feet, could have been fifty yards—would not have mattered. When you came, I knew mentioning the shooting might hook your interest. It has not been a widely known fact how good you both are with those small guns of yours."

Clarice smiled now and nodded. "You do know us," she chuckled. "And that song at the piano – well that was brilliant. When you played with us, it felt as if we had performed that song many times with you even though we could not have."

"Yes," Gregory nodded. "It is one of the many our patrons ask for. I can't tell you how many times we performed it, but it would never have been so polished without our practice."

"Which we don't need because you've already done it?"

"Exactly."

"Swell," Clarice seemed to beam. "I'm going to find this friendship of ours very easy."

"Berries!" Gregory said, giving one of her favorite phrases back to her. They laughed. "But," Gregory held up a hand, "Tonight is one of the nights where an event might happen. I want to tell you about it. That way, no matter how things fall out, you will believe me."

"I believe you," Clarice jumped in.

"I see that," Gregory said. "But I need you as an ally; so, you have to accept certain things I say even if they –" he broke off.

"Sound like bushwa?" Clarice finished.

Gregory nodded. "Tonight, I may or may not actually channel a ghost. Before the raid, the seances here were elaborate but no real spirits appeared. After the raid—during the first time I lived through to January of next year – I began actually bringing real spiritual connections into this very room. I can't say if that will still happen, but I wanted to tell you about Geoff O'Brien and his ring now."

"Then if it comes out tonight, I will know you already knew about it," Clarice rubbed her chin. "It would prove part of what you have been telling me."

"The ring – his West Point ring was sent with his finger to his father because O'Brien would not support Capone over Deanie O'Banion. Everyone thought, thinks, Geoff took his own life because he could not live with the war atrocities, but he was murdered and he wanted his sister to know."

"And, that will come out in tonight's séance?" Clarice seemed fascinated.

"It sounds fantastic of course, but I think I have been given a chance to change so many horrible events for my family and friends—our friends." He looked over at Clarice who had placed an ankle up to her knee and folded her hands.

Clarice slid her foot to the ground and stood. She came over to where Gregory sat and placed a hand on his shoulder. "I definitely want to be here for that," she said. "You can count on me and my discretion."

"You can tell Letty, of course," Gregory laughed. "I know you two very well. I shall be grateful for your support, especially as all the things begin to play out."

"If this ghost thing happens, we will believe you completely."

"Horse feathers!" Gregory laughed, but he felt better having taken this step. "But at least, you'll question me less and less as I demonstrate I'm telling the truth."

Clarice clapped him on the back. "We'd best get ready for the séance. It's going to be quite an event, I hear."

Gregory stood and gave her a salute. Clarice left, and the grandfather clock down the hallway rang out 7:30. He only had a half hour to get ready. His hands turned slightly clammy and his heart beat sped up. Once the séance took place, he'd know. But Clarice and Letty would know as well, and they had already promised to help him. He raced off down the hall and upstairs to his rooms where he prepared for the séance, washing then changing into his séance suit—the loose fitting, dark green and purple jacquard smoking jacket and his dark gray trousers. He just wished he already knew for certain whether or not he'd be needing the extra pockets or the buttons and levers under the table.

When he took his chair—the larger one nearest the window and armoire, Gregory knew there would be nine at the séance tonight – eleven because he had invited Clarice and Letty. The cousins to Senator Deneen—Mr. and Mrs. Steven Deneen would be there, Jacob Thomas and his wife, Irene and possibly Teddy, widower Efflehower, and the Blake sisters – Gregory remembered because they had all returned on later nights with requests to speak to their own departed, except for Irene and Teddy. Taking a deep breath, Gregory nodded to Mr. Klein, who began to escort the participants into the room. Teddy led Irene around the table to seat her at Gregory's left so that she would be in the most direct line with the spirits.

He had forgotten how breath taking she had been in that green seafoam colored scarf which she had used as a coverup over her ice green, low waisted dress. Her dark green cloche hat covered her reddish blonde curls, but complimented her creamy complexion. Irene sat demurely beside him, while Teddy remained standing behind her chair as if for moral support. After the others had taken their seats, Gregory cleared his throat.

"Please clasp hands so that we can invite the spirits," he began, offering his left hand to Irene. Her fingers felt slightly cool and very fragile in his own, but she griped his hand firmly. Gregory nodded at her with a slight smile before checking on Clarice who held his right hand on his other side and Letty who sat just beyond her. "Mr. Klein, lights please."

Mr. Klein dimmed the lights using the switch nearest the door. He would remain there, standing in the way of anyone who might disrupt the proceeding.

Gregory repeated the prayer he had taken to using prior to the proceedings, asking for God's help in communicating with those who were lost or needing to speak. Then he took three calming breaths, praying he would not need to use the foot pedal under the table.

A deep knock resounded throughout the room. "Spirit, will you identify yourself and speak to us?" Gregory asked, his heart racing.

"I... I have come... to speak with my dear sister," the spirit began, using Gregory's voice hesitantly as if he were long unused to talking. *Praise the Lord!* Gregory thought. *It's Geoff O'Brien.*

Beside him, Irene squeezed Gregory's hand tighter. "Geoff? Geoff is that you?"

"It is, dearest Irene," Geoff replied sounding more and more like himself rather than Gregory.

He hadn't lost his ability to speak with the dead! Gregory thought, that would go a long way helping him to prove his last eight months had really happened. *Was his brush with death the reason the spirits talked through him? Or was that Deanie, too?* But, Geoff was telling Irene how Torrio or Capone had ordered his murder, and Gregory needed to focus on the séance.

"Ask Father about my West Point academy ring, then you'll believe me," Geoff was telling her.

Some of the men had gone green, while the Blake sisters blanched under their face powder. Mrs. Steven Deneen, two persons down the table, muttered something about O'Brien and the Pineapple Primary. "As straight as a crooked cucumber," she added with a hrruumph.

Geoff was fading, Gregory could feel the grip on his vocal cords loosening. "Avenge meeee," he said.

Last time, Gregory had been shocked at his own ability and tired, but tonight he wanted to invite someone else to speak, someone whom he passed over because *he* hadn't felt up to it. Instead of asking Mr. Klein to bring up the lights, Gregory said in a raspy, albeit his own voice, "Amaryllis Thomas, can you hear us? Please come forward, kind spirit."

Jacob Thomas sobbed. "Please sister. If you are here, please Amaryllis."

"Don't cry, brother," lisped a young girl's voice from Gregory's throat. He sighed. "Please, Jacob. I am in a better place."

"Father and mother had said you were. The influenza had been so very bad," Jacob said, blowing his nose into his handkerchief.

"The fever burned me clean," replied the little girl. "I am sitting with our Grandmothers and Grandfathers, who tell me stories."

Jacob laughed. "My heart gladdens to hear it, little one."

"Remember me in your prayers, dear brother," Amaryllis said, "and I will continue to protect you and yours."

"Thank you, Gregory Davenport," Jacob Thomas said. "Thank you."

"Lights, Mr. Klein." Now Gregory was weary, but he also felt glad he could put Jacob Thomas at ease. The best thing was that Geoff O'Brien had talked to Irene. She sat so quietly at his left, digesting the news of what she had heard. Teddy held her shoulders, as if he feared she could not hold herself upright.

As the lights came up, the patrons sitting around the table began a clamor for attention. Gregory released Clarice's hand and held up his own for silence. "We did indeed speak with departed spirits tonight," Gregory began. "At subsequent seances, I will try to communicate with more of the departed. Those with the greatest need will come through me to speak with their loved ones. Be assured, I will make as many connections as I'm able at each séance. You may tell your friends and family." Everyone attempted to speak at once. Clarice shared a speaking look with Letty then Gregory, and he knew they would talk later.

"We will return Sunday night, won't we, Mr. Deneen?" Mrs. Steven said with conviction. Her husband nodded, folding his racoon coat over his arm.

"I want to speak with Mrs. Efflehower," the widower said, sliding an arm through the sleeve of his heavy, overcoat. "I'll be back next Friday."

The Blake sisters tittered. They shared a look, then flounced off toward *The Hair of the Dog*. While not officially reopened, regular patrons had been coming for the past two weeks to buy their alky and to gamble.

"There will be opportunities for you all, but tonight, we are finished." Gregory and Irene slowly let go, allowing Gregory to place his hands on the table in order to rise. "Thank you, everyone."

Teddy came closer, and Gregory could smell the bergamot he used as an after shave and the cloud of smoke that always accompanied him. "O'Brien must have been one of the victims in the O'Banion—Torrio beer war."

Gregory grabbed Teddy's arm and directed him quickly from the room with Irene trailing them, her fox collar coat quickly retrieved from the armoire. "You're correct, of course, Teddy," Gregory said, trying to mollify his brother's friend, "but the rest of them don't need to hear the tale."

Looking over his shoulder, Gregory saw Irene lagging behind. "Let's all go to the kitchen for some tea, shall we?"

12

Gregory led Teddy and Irene down the stairs to the kitchen. He released Teddy and toggled the lights on, brightening up the white washed walls, glistening white china on its shelves behind the glass-doored cupboard. Irene walked in, blinking and slightly disoriented after her séance experience.

"Sit, sit," Gregory urged them, waving his hands in the direction of the wooden, high-backed kitchen chairs around a small oak table. He strode over to the large white, enameled gas stove and lit a burner. From the sideboard by the sink, he collected the kettle, pumped some water into it from the sink, then set the kettle on to boil. From the dishes, he collected three tea cups, with saucers, which he set before Teddy, Irene, and his own empty spot at the table.

Taking out his cigarette case, Teddy cleared his throat, watching Gregory, who scurried over to the pie safe. "As I tried to tell you earlier, Geoff O'Brien must have been killed as a result of the Torrio–O'Banion violence back when Torrio had offered that white flag of cooperation."

"Yes, I quite agree," Gregory said, finally finding the lemon bread cook had put up earlier that evening. Irene was particularly fond of it

– or she would be. Gregory shook his head, grabbed the plate of lemon bread, and brought it to the table. "There are still many very bad people involved in that fight, resulting in violence."

"Are you accusing my cousin?" Teddy sniffed. Searching his pockets for his cigarette lighter.

"No, but he's not called Bugsy Moran for nothing, I'll have you know," Gregory retorted, pulling three dessert plates from the cupboard, then three forks and a knife from the silverware drawer. Slicing three pieces off the end of the lemon bread, Gregory used the knife and his fork to lift a piece to Irene's plate. "You are going to love this," he told her softly, passing her a fork, which she took with careful fingers.

He scooped a piece onto Teddy's plate, then handed the plate and fork to his brother's friend. "Here's one for you." Gregory looked hard at Teddy. "The bad blood between the Irish and Italians has escalated. I have four words for you – St. Valentine's Day Massacre."

Teddy nodded, but busied himself with his cake. He had set his cigarette case and lighter beside his plate.

Taking his own piece, Gregory edged into his chair at the head of the table. The kettle began to boil, giving him a moment to relax. Gregory glanced over at Irene. "The killing has just gotten worse and worse over the years. When Torrio ran the South Side, he seemed to understand a truce would be necessary."

"But Father is a politician," Irene said, forking off another bite. "What could they really expect him to do?"

"Capone wants all the politicians in his organization." Gregory explained, "Then he can do whatever he wants."

"He does that already, doesn't he?" Irene asked.

"Maybe so, but it's all about control," Gregory said, but he was watching Irene close her lips around her bite of lemon bread and close her eyes in pleasure as the lemon—tart and sweet, exploded inside her mouth. She moaned softly, making Gregory's heart flutter and his breath catch.

Teddy took a bite of the cake, then waved his empty fork toward

Gregory. "I can ask around and find out more about what O'Brien said. Find out who actually did the deed."

"A good idea," Gregory said, still watching Irene enjoy her lemon bread.

Teddy took another forkful and warmed to his subject. "I have a contact in the South Side gang."

Gregory tore his eyes away from Irene. "Carlo Anselmo," he breathed. Memories of Carlo with his snorky outfits and generous smile, especially when he looked at Teddy, flooded Gregory's thoughts.

Teddy sat back in sudden surprise. "How do you know?"

"We can talk about that later," Gregory coughed into his hand. Irene stared at him her blue eyes wide with curiosity. "Just be extremely cautious. Your cousin hates the Italians." He put up a hand, "hates the Sicilians even more. You can't let either North or South Siders know you are talking to Anselmo."

Teddy frowned and pressed his thin moustache with his thumb and forefinger, smoothing the short, dark hairs. "Agreed." He straightened and studied Gregory intently. "I like this forceful, new Gregory," Teddy said with a slow smile.

"Don't flirt with me," Gregory chided, shaking a forefinger at Teddy, and sending a look toward Irene. "I'm not your type."

"Oh, I know," Teddy teased, grabbed a napkin from the center of the table before dabbing his mouth. He grabbed his cigarette case, picked out a smoke, replaced the case in his pocket, and lit up. After taking a few long drags, he slid the lighter into his vest.

"Harrison's never going to feel the way you want him to either," Gregory pointed out, knowing Irene already protected Teddy's secret.

Teddy blew out smoke and placed his left hand over his heart. "I'm wounded."

Gregory laughed softly. "Look. I know someone who sees you as his John Gilbert."

"Who?" Teddy glanced down and his eyelashes fluttered. Smoke rose from the cigarette between his lips.

"Carlo Anselmo," Gregory said, quietly. "Which is why I want you to be especially careful for both your sakes." The kettle whistled shrilly into the silence of the room. Irene licked her fork completely clean before placing it across her empty plate.

Teddy's face took on a cat who ate the cream expression. "Carlo?"

"Yes," Gregory nodded, starting to rise. "The very one."

"I take it, then, you won't be needing me?" Irene finally commented, pushing her plate toward the center of the table.

"No," said Teddy. "Might be needing you even more than ever."

"Except, that wouldn't be fair to Irene, Teddy," Gregory cut in. He could *not* have Irene tied to Teddy and court her as he wanted to. "She might have met the love of her life."

Both Teddy and Irene turned to stare at him. Gregory held up his hands and laughed. He left the table, and prepared the tea in the kettle before bringing it over and pouring the amber liquid into the porcelain cups where steam rose in spirals into the air.

"Go see Anselmo, Teddy." Gregory said once he returned to his seat and held the china cup in his hands. "I want to visit O'Brien. I will ask about the West Point ring."

"I could talk to Father," Irene volunteered.

Gregory shook his head. "He will not be happy that we have discovered this secret he has been hiding from everyone for the past seven or eight years."

"I suppose," Irene said, carefully taking a sip from her steaming cup, "he meant for Mother never to find out. Still, I want to accompany you."

"That has to be true," Teddy offered, "Your father would not like your mother knowing."

"What should we do, then?" Irene asked, looking from Gregory to Teddy and back again.

"Like I said, I'll visit with your father. You may join me if you truly wish it."

"I insist," Irene replied.

"I will also look into your brother's death – quietly," Gregory said.

"And you promise to tell me everything you discover?" Irene asked, her cheeks flushed.

"Always," Gregory swore, pressing a hand over his heart.

"Then we are agreed," Teddy said, rising and crushing his cigarette stub in the ashtray. "I'll plan on visiting Carlo in the next day or two, while you two will see O'Brien. We will get to the bottom of this."

Gregory and Irene nodded. Teddy came around the table and offered his hand to Irene. She set the tea cup down, pushed up and out of her chair, and accepted Teddy's hand.

"For tonight, at least, dancing?" Irene asked. She snatched up her fox collared coat from the seat next to where she sat.

"Whatever the lady wishes," Teddy replied with a chuckle, crooking his arm for her to take. Gregory wondered who might play at the *Hair of the Dog* tonight, or if Teddy would take Irene to another club. The official opening of their club was next week, but Harrison managed to jump start things.

Irene glanced longingly at Gregory. He rose to his feet and bowed to her. "We will talk. I promise," he told her, knowing he would see her even sooner in his dreams. "Teddy," he called after them, "please don't forget what I told you."

Teddy's face grew serious for a moment as he nodded. Then he was smiling again and they were gone.

Gregory finished his tea in silence before collecting the dessert dishes and putting the porcelain into the sink. He pumped out water to clean the plates, cups, and the silverware, thinking the entire time he worked about Irene and their visit to her Father. He left everything in the drying rack on the counter beside the sink. *Now I need to find Clarice.*

She was standing, leaning one arm against the piano with Letty seated on the stage step beside Clarice's feet. George, the regular pianist, began the opening bars of "Lady Be Good," and Clarice sang in her deep alto. In the background, the small band consisting of a bass, a clarinet, two horns, and a sax accompanied her. Couples covered the dance floor, moving in complex patterns, as the music surrounded them. The newly redone tables were filled with couples drinking, playing cards, Maj Jong, dice, and betting on the roulette wheel. Laughter and calls of delight hit Gregory's ears, bringing a sense of joy. This was what *The Hair of the Dog Club* was all about. In the far corner, Harrison stood, arms folded across his chest, surveying the club like its monarch. When he saw Gregory, he beckoned with one hand.

Gregory made his way through the press of people, finally arriving at his brother's side.

"Teddy tells me Geoff O'Brien was murdered," Harrison began.

"Yes. I plan to see O'Brien tomorrow. If it was Capone, I think we should encourage him to seek the authorities, maybe the Prohibition Bureau, and not try revenge on his own." Gregory frowned. "He is a good man and as honest a politician as we can find here in Chicago."

Harrison chuckled. "That's the damn truth. I certainly don't need any more trouble with the South Side Gang."

"We just got the club back on its feet," Gregory added, thinking *we don't need another run in with Jack McErlane.*

"That's all Jake," Harrison said. He took the cigar from his vest pocket and lit it with his silver lighter. Puffing, he said, "I am not up for risks right now."

"Really?" Gregory cornered his brother, sheltering them from prying eyes. "Would you consider exchanging half your stocks for gold and silver? I'm telling you, right now they are the better investment."

Harrison grabbed Gregory's arm. "You are gonna keep after me about this aren't you?"

Gregory nodded. "I want what's best for us."

"I promise to think about it," Harrison nodded.

"Don't think too long?" Gregory warned.

"What's that supposed to mean?" Harrison reddened and tightened his arms across his chest.

"October is a very bad month. Please don't have stocks then," Gregory told his brother. He wanted to explain about the Crash and how he *knew*, but right now Harrison wouldn't believe him. He just needed to keep poking at the idea of selling and buying up gold or silver. Hopefully, he would have enough proof of other things that Harrison would just listen. He clapped his brother on the arm. Clarice was finishing up her set, and he needed to talk with her. She might be instrumental in getting Harrison on board with his efforts.

Harrison shook his right hand in the air, the way he did when he indicated he would consider something. Then he shooed Gregory away as Lysette came strolling over with her hip rolling walk Harrison just seemed to adore. Just before he got away, Gregory saw Lysette stretch on her tip-toes to kiss Harrison on both cheeks in that French way of hers.

Gregory pushed through the crowd again. Clarice had moved to stand near the doors to the club. She was now in capper mode. He might be able to speak with her alone. Letty, he knew, was off watching over the dice tables because she was not needed by the door once the Club had been open for a few hours. As Gregory approached the door to the club, a group of three well-dressed young couples had just finished Clarice's inspection.

"Clarice, aren't you the cat's meow," Gregory said with a smile in his voice. "Just the person I wanted to see."

She beamed at him, patting the side of her auburn hair, pomaded into a helmet on her head. Her deep navy-blue suit made her look imposing as well as important. Shooting the cuffs on her jacket, Clarice turned towards Gregory and stepped down onto the club's carpeted floor. "Happy to see you, too. What a swell guy you are."

"What'd I do?" Gregory asked, pressing an open palm against his chest.

"Channeled ghosts! Magnificent. And," she really beamed now, "O'Brien came through with that ring."

Gregory raised an eyebrow and leaned closer to Clarice so that the nearby patrons might not overhear. "He did at that."

"You're no ringer and that's not baloney," Clarice told him, her eyes wide with admiration. "Letty and me – We talked and talked after the séance. Those voices coming from inside you – talk about the heebie jeebies. What you did can't be faked. We believe you, believe in you."

"Be—rr—ies," Gregory said slowly with relief, convincing them might not have been easy.

"Do you think," Clarice lowered her voice, "that your gunshot wounds have anything to do with your special abilities? Letty suggested it."

"It's possible." He stroked his chin. "I haven't really figured it all out."

"Hmmm." Clarice studied him closely.

"We have so much to do," Gregory hastened to say.

"Ok, then. Give us the scoop, and we'll help all we can," Clarice offered.

Gregory nodded. "Let me mull over what we need to take care of."

"I'm thinking that ring," Clarice said.

"Yes. Irene and I will see her father about it tomorrow sometime."

"You need back-up?" She patted her coat pocket.

Gregory held up a hand. "Naw. It's *her* father. We should be fine." He chuckled. Thinking about the rescue of Margaretta and some of the other things they needed to do, tomorrow's meeting with O'Brien should be a cakewalk.

Clarice clucked her tongue. "That Irene seems like a pretty together tomato."

Gregory dropped his voice even lower. "To tell you the truth, she's the bee's knees."

Clarice clapped a firm hand on Gregory's arm. "You need

anything, just say the word." She laughed before turning back toward the doors. A new group of patrons had arrived and wanted a table. Gregory saluted her and faded into the crowd.

Fats Waller came into the *Hair of the Dog Club* that night, his coat flaring out behind him, waving his too small derby hat at patrons shouting out his name. Walking through the couples on the small dance floor in front of it, he jumped up on the stage. When he saw Gregory, he tipped his hat, smiled broadly, and said, "Get me a glass of the good stuff."

Gregory signaled to the red-haired waiter nearby, "Bring out a glass of our best Canadian."

The teenager nodded and scurried off toward Harrison's office and the secret stash.

While he waited, Waller played his famous "Handful of Keys." The chubby, young man with his pencil thin moustache and round face was a favorite of Gregory's. He loved watching Waller's fingers fly over the keys, his hands rolling to palm chords over an octave wide. Gregory, himself, took up the glass of amber liquid, three ice cubes bobbing and clinking against the crystal. With a flourish, he presented the whiskey to Waller.

Winking, Waller plucked the glass from Gregory's hand, tilted it back into his mouth and sighed. Smacking his lips, he said, "Just as good as I remembered. Best hooch in nine states." Waller laughed and so did Gregory.

"It should be. We still bring it in from Canada," Gregory confided, leaning closer to the pianist.

"Just keep those glasses coming, and I'll play all night." Waller turned to the piano and tickled a few keys before pivoting back to Gregory with a wide grin. "Why don't you go get that sax of yours? We'll do some numbers."

Gregory went to the corner behind the stage where he stored his clarinet and his sax. Grabbing his saxophone, he tuned it quickly, while Waller lit a cigarette. He returned to the small orchestra on stage, tapping the shoulder of the sax player to relieve him. When he was ready, Gregory signaled Waller. The pianist stomped his foot for a few beats then started in with *Muscle Shoals Blues*. Swinging the sax, swaying, and tapping his foot, Gregory closed his eyes blissfully and played. They ran through a medley of songs – *Henderson Stomp, Please Take Me Out of Jail, Everybody Loves My Baby,* and *Sheik of Araby* as well as renditions of other famous composers' songs. Waller included his fast patter even as he sang the lyrics, making those patrons sitting at the tables surrounding the dance floor laugh loudly. Leaning against the upright piano, Clarice joined in for several songs before she had to return to the door.

Every time Waller's glass emptied, Gregory would signal the red-haired waiter to bring another, inclining his head towards Waller, who had no trouble downing each one. Afterwards, he would insist, "Best hooch in nine states," with a smack of his lips. For Gregory, it was a night he'd never forget.

"Wowzer!" Clarice said, after Waller left. "Didn't know you could play a mean sax."

"Fats Waller is one of my favorite pianists. Playing with him makes it easy," Gregory laughed. "His hands can stretch an octave and a half! He's the cat's meow, and that's no baloney!"

Letty tossed her black, bobbed hair and chuckled. Her silver and black hip-waisted gown made her look androgynous, but the kohl on her eyes, rouge on her cheeks, and her bee stung lips – an affect created by her red lipstick, gave her a waifish look that was completely feminine. She seemed glad to see Gregory, and her gray eyes twinkled up at him. "You, yourself, are the bee's knees, the leopard's spots. I mean to say –," she pressed an opened hand against her bare throat where the gown dipped low, revealing the upper curve of her bosom. Letty glanced over at Clarice, who placed an arm around her waist, drawing the smaller woman close.

"You gals are too kind," Gregory said, blushing. They had never been this effusive with their praise, making him feel embarrassed. He began to wonder if the relationship he had with them was now irreversibly altered, and the old camaraderie he had shared with Clarice and Letty was gone forever.

Letty and Clarice shared a look. They both gave a subtle nod. Clarice cleared her throat. "Admiration party over," she said gruffly, as if she too were embarrassed.

"Berries!" Gregory said, because he could think of nothing else.

They all three laughed, and the cloud of discomfort dispelled. He left Clarice and Letty at their post by the door and headed upstairs to his rooms. He knew Harrison would be entertaining Lysette long into the morning. No need to bother his brother.

Stripping off his suit, Gregory slipped into his striped, gray silk pajamas and fell into his bed, exhausted. The next day held out promise for beginning the changes he wanted desperately. If O'Brien could be convinced to speak with the Treasury Department or the Bureau of Prohibition, then so many more deaths could be prevented. Plumping up his pillow, Gregory turned on his side and closed his eyes.

13

Robins and finches chirped outside Gregory's bedroom window as the sun came up over the tips of the trees in their orchard. He pulled the pillow over his head, attempting to fall back asleep. In his dreams, Irene adored him and he wanted to go back there. He missed her sweet smile and the shy glances she would give him, when she thought he was not looking. What will it take, he wondered, to regain her love?

Talking to her father, for one thing. Gregory shot upright in bed. He had to ready himself for that interview with O'Brien over the ring. *Too bad Harrison can't help.* If only his brother could remember where the ring had been and exactly what O'Brien had told him as he would in that alternative time, then Harrison could have saved the day for him. That time though, they had promised revenge on the South Side mob. *He would not do that.*

Gregory washed, dressed, and hurried down to the kitchen for breakfast. Harrison sat at the table with his newspaper in one hand and a steaming cup of coffee in the other. He glanced over the top of the newsprint, "Morning."

"To you, too, brother," Gregory replied. He went over to the stove after collecting a coffee cup, and poured some of the hot beverage. "You want eggs or toast?"

"Whatever you are having will be swell," Harrison answered. "By the way, the market is down today. It has been slightly unstable these past two weeks."

"Un-huh," Gregory lit the stove, took a bowl of eggs from the ice box, and cracked them into an iron skillet. With a fork, he beat the eggs then let them bubble as they cooked. Taking a salt shaker from the rail on the wall above the stove, Gregory first salted then used the pepper grinder to season the eggs.

"I'm going to look into gold prices this morning," Harrison mumbled.

"If they're too high, check out silver," Gregory tossed over his shoulder. He strode over to the cupboard and pulled out two plates, and freed two forks from the silverware drawer. He placed the dishes on the table, then hurried back to the eggs. Turning off the heat, he shook the pan, flipping the eggs over once before returning to serve Harrison half and pouring the rest out onto his own plate.

Absently, Harrison picked up the fork. "So, what are you doing today?"

Gregory sat down at his place, grabbed a napkin, then took up his own fork. "Irene O'Brien and I are going to visit her father."

"Old man O'Brien, the politician?"

"The very one," Gregory nodded. His eggs were fluffy and perfectly salted. The coffee Harrison had brewed wasn't bad either. "Did you know that her brother Geoff was murdered?"

Harrison lowered the newspaper, opened to the baseball scores. "No. I thought his was a suicide due to the horrors of the Great War."

"So did everyone else," Gregory agreed.

"Well?" Harrison raised a sandy brown eye brow.

Gregory cleared his throat, took a sip of coffee, then said, "You missed the excitement at the séance last night. Geoff actually came to speak with his sister Irene. It seems there is a West Point ring that will prove he was tortured by the South Side mob right before he was killed. His death was no accident."

Harrison slapped the paper down on the table and sat upright. "You actually talked to his ghost?"

Gregory managed to conceal a smile. "I did."

"Swell! That's gonna bring in the crowds." Harrison held out his hand to shake Gregory's. "You will put *The Hair of the Dog* back on the map!"

"Don't you care about Geoff O'Brien?" Gregory asked, surprised.

"Of course, I do." Harrison sat back down and grabbed up his newspaper with a shake to straighten it out. "We'll get even with those South Siders, just wait 'til George Moran finds out."

Gregory held up a hand, palm open. "Could we not do that, yet? At least give us time to talk with O'Brien?"

"Sure, sure," Harrison responded, intently reading a new article on the page before him. Gregory could see the headlines on the backside of the paper, declaring Babe Ruth the hero of the New York Yankees, and another asking, "Cubs Headed for the Series?"

Gregory hastened to finish his eggs and coffee. He checked his pocket watch. It was 9:00 am. He could drive over to collect Irene and then they would be able to drive over to her Father's together. "Gotta fly. I'm going to take the Ford."

Harrison merely waved his hand in a shooing motion Gregory recognized as his brother's dismissal.

The Ford bucked and spluttered as Gregory drove into North Chicago. Irene had a flat over near the Towertown district, close to Clarice and Letty. The roads were congested with horse drawn vehicles and other drivers generally behind the wheel of Model T or Model A cars. The brick roads made the tires whine as they spun. So long as the streets were dry, the car would not skid, and if the horses didn't balk at pedestrians, birds, or street hawkers, selling wares, then there would not be an accident. The brownstone buildings got taller and taller as Gregory drove closer to Irene's apartment building. Gone were any sign of poverty or despair Gregory had seen the last time he had gone to Irene's. The economy remained strong and Chicagoans seemed a contented lot. Parking was problematic, so many cars were lined up on the curb near the apartment. Recalling the back street where he had parked near Clarice's; the one near that little park, Gregory drove there and left the Ford where he hoped it would be safe. Briskly, he walked the several blocks to Irene's, his dark brown three-piece suit getting a little dusty. When he finally reached the doors to the entryway, Gregory straightened his brown fedora, and rechecked the knot of his tie in the window glass.

"Miss Irene O'Brien, please," he told the concierge standing behind the counter.

The short, heavy-set man, who was dressed in a navy-blue uniform with red stripes down the sides of the sleeves and pant legs, paused to examine a ledger in front of him. He had a small round cap, too, with a red stripe around the edge. "Name?"

Gregory thought a moment then said, "Davenport."

The man drew his forefinger down the page then tapped a spot. "There you are." He smiled, his bottle brush moustache twitching. "I'll ring you up." He reached under the counter for a telephone headset. "The elevators are to your right down that short hallway."

Gregory followed where the man pointed. He slipped his overcoat off and over one arm before heading for the elevators. They had elaborate grill work over the doors. When the elevator operator slid the door open, the operator had to push the grill work to one side.

"Sixth floor, please," Gregory said, stepping onto the marble floor tiles. Behind him the wall was completely mirrored with thick stripes etched into the edges. Other passengers entered, giving the operator their floors. Gregory ended up stopping on each floor, waiting for the operator to open the doors, the one or two people to exit, and the doors to close again before the elevator continued its upward movement. Finally, they reached the last floor and Gregory left the elevator, looking down the hallway for the apartment number on the dark wooden doors.

He knocked on the door of number 18. He heard rather than

saw the peep hole opening and closing before he heard the locks being released. Irene thrust her head out between the door and the jamb.

"Why hello there," she said with a smile. "Don't you look spiffy." Irene gestured for him to enter the marble tiled foyer. Just beyond was a tiny living room with two sofas facing one another and a small, wooden rolltop desk in the corner.

"These glad rags?" Gregory ran his right thumb and forefinger up and down the lapel of his suit jacket. "They're all right." He grinned down at her.

To him, she looked adorable in her periwinkle drop-waisted dress, with its scoop neck and short, short sleeves. A small charm dangling from her gold chain, hung in the pulse point of her throat. On her reddish blonde hair, Irene wore a feathered headband. Her eyelids were dusted lightly with a light purple shadow, and she had drawn her lips into a cupid bow with her rose-colored lipstick. When she giggled, her silver triangle earrings flashed in the light.

"Welcome, welcome." Two other young ladies came into the living room similarly dressed to Irene, but one in a yellow dress with tiny daisies, the other in a deep burgundy. "We're Irene's roomies. I'm Daphne and that's Zelda," the one in yellow said.

Zelda laughed and covered her mouth. "Irene has told us about you."

Gregory exchanged a look with Irene, who shook her head slightly. Apparently, their secrets were safe from these two, but maybe not for very long. "Shall we go?" he asked her.

"Just let me get my bag," Irene said, racing off to one of the rooms down the shared hallway beyond the living room. She returned with a clutch purse with a design in tiny colored beads. As she walked toward Gregory, Irene grabbed her fox collared coat from a coat stand.

"It's nice to meet you gals," Gregory said to the roomies, before clapping his fedora back on his head. He guided Irene to the door with a gentle hand on the small of her back.

"Are you ready to face your father?" He asked Irene as he pressed the buzzer to call the elevator.

"That's not an easy question to answer." Irene's tight grin softened her words. "Father has different expectations for my brothers than he has for me because I'm a gal. He might accept Geoff or even Neill questioning him, but me..."

Gregory squeezed her arm. "You are a very strong and independent person," he explained. "Don't you work for the progressive stockbroker Mrs. Eleanor Hall at S.W. Stearns?"

"You know about that?" Irene asked, chewing her lip. She giggled shyly. "Oh of course, Teddy must have said something."

Damn! She hadn't told him that yet. He needed to keep his wits about him. Gregory merely nodded. "That's not important. What matters is that you are a pioneer. Your father needs to recognize that."

"That very well may be true. Is true, but Father—,"

The opening of the elevator cut Irene off. "Floor please?" said the uniformed operator, his hand on the brass grate.

"One," Irene and Gregory said together and laughed as they entered the tiny mirrored box with marble flooring. The gears grinded and the elevator dropped six or seven inches in a rush before the entire mechanism lowered them and the three other passengers to the lobby floor. A mother with her young daughter and a businessman exited, allowing Gregory to walk out with Irene.

"The Ford is parked around the corner and some," he admitted.

"I'm glad I hire a cab or take the train," Irene remarked. "Parking is always difficult."

After they reached the car, Gregory helped Irene into the passenger seat, before he set the clutch and cranked the engine. When the car sputtered to life, he jumped into the driver's seat and took the steering wheel. He switched gears, eased the car into traffic and headed off towards the more expensive neighborhood where Douglas O'Brien lived.

Watching the road, Gregory took the opportunity of a four way stop to glance over at Irene. She seemed to be enjoying the ride. "What were you going to tell me about your father?"

"Oh," She resettled herself in her seat. "He might be difficult because I want to know the truth about Geoff. How could he think it better to believe my brother took his own life?"

Putting out his hand to signal a left turn, Gregory said, "I bet you dollars to doughnuts that he was protecting the rest of your family. There are too many hatchet men ready to take care of business, as my cousin Deanie was fond of saying."

Gregory finally turned up the elm tree lined Belmont Avenue and the driveway leading to Douglas O'Brien's sprawling two story, dark brick home with its mansard roof. The home would have looked perfectly fine at the center of rolling lawns with a formal garden at one side, but instead it sat between two equally luxurious town homes. He parked the car along the curb before leaping down to hand Irene out of the passenger side door. They walked up the brick sidewalk leading to the house with its large front porch. Gregory placed his hand gently on Irene's back as they approached the three wide, bricks steps set off by a flanged short brick wall. A flash of motion at the curtains covering the narrow side windows near the front door, almost caused Irene to miss-step.

"Saunders, Father's butler, has been peeking at the window," Irene explained.

Gregory barely had a chance to knock on the door, when it was opened by a tall, skinny man dressed in black and a white apron.

The man blinked in the sunlight, then his mousey face brightened. "Miss Irene? Is that you?"

"Yes, Saunders," Irene answered softly. "Is my father at home?"

Saunders bustled around them, ushering them in. "Yes, yes. Of course, he is for you."

Irene turned troubled eyes toward Gregory as she unbuttoned her coat and handed it to Saunders. Gregory smiled at her, trying to bolster her confidence, while giving his own overcoat and fedora to the butler. Once the wraps were stored in the entryway closet,

Saunders beckoned them to follow him through a dark hallway papered in a burgundy and green stripe, past an elegant dining room with a table set for eight, and two comfortable parlors. The butler knocked on a partially opened mahogany door, leading into an office packed with papers and books.

"Enter," Irene's father Douglas O'Brien said.

Gregory was about to move into the room when Irene grabbed his arm and stopped him.

"Your daughter is here to see you, sir," Saunders said seriously.

Gregory heard a heavy chair scraping back against thick carpet and smelled the fumes of cigar smoke as it came closer to the doorway.

"Irene, dearest," O'Brien said, bursting out into the hall and clasping Irene up into a bear hug. A fat cigar remained clamped between his teeth. "I'm so happy you've come. What brings you to see me?"

"First," Irene said, muffled by her father's hug. "Allow me to introduce Gregory Davenport, a cousin to Deanie O'Banion."

O'Brien released Irene, who coughed due to the cigar smoke, and turned toward Gregory, putting out a thick hand.

Gregory took O'Brien's hand and shook, briskly. "You've met my brother Harrison, sir."

"Oh, yes, yes. I recall. Sandy brown hair, built like a full-back," O'Brien chuckled.

The man was one to talk. O'Brien was broad shouldered as well as tall, and his arms and legs filled out his suit like tree trunks. Even his well-rounded face seemed larger than life. No wonder he could command confidence as a politician. Irene had to take after her mother because she was dainty and had fine features.

"Come into my office and we'll talk," O'Brien said, moving into the office and returning to his chair behind his desk. Irene followed after and began moving newspapers and books from the sofa near a tall grandfather clock with a moon face. She placed the mountain of paper onto a leather club chair nearer to the desk, clearing space for Gregory and her to sit.

Once he was comfortable, O'Brien stared across the desk at them. "Well, well, what's this about, my dear. I want to go to the exchange."

"It's about Geoff, Father," Irene began, wringing her hands in her lap. The pulse point at her throat fluttered.

"Your brother was a troubled young man." O'Brien flicked the ash from the end of his cigar into a large marble ash tray at the corner of his desk. "The mustard gas addled his brain. That and the horrors of that terrible war. He never should have gone to Europe. I blame myself for that."

"No, Father," Irene started.

At the same time, Gregory said, "He wasn't as troubled as you thought. He never jumped into that train. He was pushed."

"The doctors said it was a result of post war syndrome." O'Brien took a large handkerchief out of his coat pocket and began to mop sweat from his wide forehead.

"They were wrong, Father," Irene said, reaching a hand toward him.

"The South Side mob deliberately chose Geoff in order to frighten you into supporting Capone and his agenda." Gregory added.

Irene's father jumped up, the chair almost tipping over backward from the force. "Neither of you knows what you are talking about!" O'Brien's face reddened in anger.

"I know you have his West Point graduation ring hidden in a velvet jewelry box in that desk," Gregory said firmly, pointing at the desk in front of them. He wasn't going to cloud matters by mentioning the séance and Geoff's presence. O'Brien was a practical and realistic man who would never believe him anyway.

O'Brien towered over his desk, smoke coming in puffs from the cigar in the corner of his mouth. "How dare you," he said in a quiet, cold voice.

"You have the ring," Gregory held firm.

O'Brien sank back into his chair, deflated. His face fell into his hands, the cigar stuck out between them like an extra fat finger. "I could never part with it. How could I? It represents all the evils they perpetrated against my beloved boy." He looked up over his hands at Irene. "Your brother never deserved what they did. They should have come after me, instead."

Gregory and Irene exchanged a glance.

O'Brien seemed to come to a decision. He leaned down to the left, and they could hear a drawer being opened. O'Brien fished around for a short time before he emerged again and placed a long, black velvet covered box on the far edge of the desk. "You really don't want to look, Irene, dear."

Gregory got up and scooped up the box, preventing Irene from doing so. A sour smell emanated from the box, created a sense of dread in Gregory. *Did he even want to see? Couldn't he just take Geoff's word?* On a bed of yellowed cotton wool was a grotesque, blackened partial fourth finger, complete with a yellowed fingernail. Gregory gaged. Holding his breath, he saw a large silver ring banded the finger. The emerald at the center of the ring blinked in the light of the room and *West Point 1918* was engraved in the silver setting around the stone. Gregory covered the box again. "It's Geoff's ring," he told Irene, holding the covered box out to her.

She shook her head. Her right hand went to her throat.

Gregory nodded and handed the box back across the desk to her father.

No wonder Harrison was so angry when he came back from this meeting before. Gregory understood why his brother had told O'Brien that Geoff would be avenged. That was not a viable option for them right now, though, Gregory thought. "I'm so sorry, sir," he told O'Brien. "Geoff never deserved that."

"Bugs Moran would go after more South Siders if he knew," O'Brien admitted. "I haven't said anything because there has already been enough killing."

"Have you thought about going to the Prohibition Investigation Bureau?" Gregory asked.

O'Brien slammed an open palm down against his desk. "They have *no* power against Capone. That would only put a target on my own back."

"We must bide our time." Gregory suggested. "In time, the Treasury Department may have evidence and yours would help them finally trap Capone and others in the South Side mob."

O'Brien nodded. He returned the box with its gruesome content back into his desk drawer. "When you know they have enough proof to make an arrest, come back," O'Brien told Gregory. His voice softened, and to Irene he said, "You, on the other hand, might come visit your old Father more often. I miss you, gal."

"Of course, Father," Irene replied. She began to stand, cluing Gregory that he too should get up. "Thank you, Father."

"Maybe you'll come to dinner with Neill and I next week?" O'Brien sounded hopeful.

Irene nodded. She clasped the sleeve of Gregory's suit coat and urged him out into the hallway.

"Good meeting you, sir," Gregory couldn't help adding.

"Hurrumph." O'Brien returned his focus to the papers on his desk.

Saunders appeared at Irene's arm so quickly Gregory wondered if the butler had been listening in to their conversation. The man was holding their overcoats. Gregory took Irene's and helped her into the sleeves before he slid his own overcoat on, right arm then left, hiking the coat onto his shoulders.

"Thank you, Saunders," Irene said.

"Please come see your father again," the butler said, concern in his hazel eyes. "He really misses you."

Irene nodded curtly before she and Gregory slipped out the front door and raced down the walkway to the parked Ford. Gregory handed her into the passenger seat, went and set the clutch, before going to the front of the car and cranking over the engine. It seemed to take more effort than usual, but perhaps he was emotionally tired from the visit with O'Brien and that *ring*.

Both Gregory and Irene were subdued on the ride back toward Towertown. "Would you like something to eat?"

Irene shook her head, her silver earrings swaying near her earlobes.

Gregory snapped his fingers. He smiled. "I know. I'll take you home and you can rest up. Tonight, I'll come back at 7:30 and we'll go dancing. There's this club..." Gregory rolled his eyes and shivered with delight.

Irene giggled next to him. "That sounds just swell," she said.

Across town to the South, past the Loop, Carlo had just met with and then parted from Teddy O'Hannilon. As he sauntered along the crowded sidewalk, Carlo whistled softly between his front teeth. Happiness seemed to bubble inside him in time to the clacking of his shoes against the bricks as he headed for home. He would not mind one little bit helping Teddy find out about Geoff O'Brien. Carlo chuckled to himself. He could not bring to mind anything he would not do for that cat's meow with those penetrating dark eyes. Carlo stopped in front of a tailor shop window, eyes roving over the readymade trousers and suit coat. He also saw his own reflection – his large brown eyes, well defined brows, square chin, chiseled cheeks, and straight nose. He buffed his nails of his left hand against his lapel. *I'm not such a bad catch either,* he thought.

Being with Teddy was the most exciting prospect of his life. They would have to be extremely careful, of course, not to alert either outfit. Al Capone and his men already distrusted the Sicilians and had taken out many of Carlo's own extended family. Carlo smirked. His cousin Antonio Anselmo deserved to be shot. Still, Carlo had siblings and other cousins who were darbs – well loved, well liked, excellent people. Those were the ones he wanted to protect from the hatchet men belonging to Capone and to Moran.

There had to be an easy way to find out what happened to Geoff O'Brien, and why, without creating trouble for himself and his family.

Carlo turned away from the shop window and hurried on towards his family's flat. Maybe his family might know something, and his work would be done. Carlo' thoughts returned to Teddy O'Hannilon, and he sighed. His pace increased and he began to whistle once more.

After Gregory returned to the farm, he wanted to search for Clarice and Letty, but because of their hours at the club, he thought they would still be sleeping. He was itching to share what happened at O'Brien's with them. Even more, he wanted to tell them about Margaretta Anselmo; so, they could begin planning a rescue of the little girl that involved fewer people, especially fewer of those who could be traced back to the North Side mob. *We have to rescue her differently,* he thought, *in a way Capone won't be alerted.*

Gregory spent the day cleaning and preparing the séance parlor for the next evening. His brother, making good on his promise, had left the farm in search of potential gold and silver investments. Clarice and Letty remained holed up in their rooms on the third floor of the farm house. Finally, Gregory was able to change into his black silk three-piece suit with the pale, yellow shirt and black, silver striped bowtie. He thought he looked very snorky when he combed back his pomaded hair while looking into the large octagonal mirror standing on his dresser. His reflection stared back at him with green eyes sparkling and a large grin turning up the ends of his generous mouth.

The drive to Irene's flat was uneventful, and he was able to salute the doorman in order to be rung up. Even the elevator ride seemed smoother than earlier that day, probably because the prospect of dancing with Irene sent thrills of excitement throughout Gregory's body instead of chills of dread.

At Gregory's jaunty knock, Zelda – the roomie with the orange-red hair – opened the door wide. "She's almost ready," she told him with a stifled giggle. Louder, she shouted, "Irene, your beau is here," before giggling again behind her pale white hand.

"Oh, oh, I'll be right there," Came Irene's response from behind the right-hand door beyond the small parlor with its sofas and desk.

Irene sounded as excited as he felt, Gregory thought. When she emerged from her room, Irene appeared vibrant. Her evening dress with its dropped waist had a jagged hemline of rose and black beaded fringe that swayed as she walked. The sleeveless dress was basically rose colored with small black ticking that made the colors change in the light. Blush colored kid gloves encased her arms almost up to her elbows, but her throat and some of her back were bare. She wore a gold neckband with small clear, round stones set in it. Covering most of her red-blond curls was a blush-colored cloche hat with an emerald pin, stuck in the left side ribbon, that looked like a rose. Irene had shaped her brows into fine arches, dusted her eyelids with a light blue shadow, rouged her cheeks, and drawn a cupid bow onto her lips with her deep rose lipstick.

Gregory held out his hands to her as she approached him, taking her outstretched hands into his own, twirling her around. "Don't you look the cat's meow," he complimented her in a thickened voice. His heart raced in his chest. She was more beautiful each time he saw her and twice as smart.

"This glad rag?" She asked with a raised eyebrow, echoing his own words from earlier. "They're all right. You look pretty spiffy, yourself." A smile broke out on her face, twinkling in her blue eyes. *She was teasing him.*

"He's a real *sheik*," Zelda commented from the small parlor where she was fiddling with a large radio set Gregory had missed in his perusal of the room.

"I'll say," agreed Daphne, coming out of the left-hand door beyond the parlor.

Irene looped an arm through Gregory's and turned toward her roomies. "Well gals, he's taken so, let up." Irene's nose crinkled up when she laughed.

Gregory's heart skipped a beat. She was adorable. He wanted to tell her so, but instead he asked, "Where's your wrap? It may get cold or be cool in the club."

Irene indicated her fox collar coat on its hook at the middle of the coat rack. Gregory collected it, holding out the sleeves for her to slide her arms into them. She reached for a small black clutch and said, "I'm as ready as I'll get," and smiled up into his down turned face. Her familiar fragrance of Jasmine and Heliotrope surrounded him, wrapping him in memories.

"Swell," he sighed.

Irene practically pushed him out the door. "Is the Ford over by the park?"

Gregory centered himself. "Yes. Yes, by the park." He placed his hand over hers where she had caught his coat sleeve. "You are gonna love this club."

"Swanky?" Her eyes widened.

He nodded. They rode down in the elevator, her hand still resting under his, her grip on his arm firm.

After starting the Ford, Gregory joined Irene, who sat in the passenger seat. "The club is on North Wabash," he told her as he pulled away from the curb. "Coon and Sanders have a jazz orchestra, and they play almost every night."

"That's the Kansas City Nighthawks, isn't it?" Irene simmered with excitement. "I've heard them on WGN. They're the bee's knees," she giggled.

"So—" Gregory turned to glance over at her. "Not a surprise?"

"Oh—" Irene shook her head. "Better than."

"Oh—" He returned, copying her, and they both laughed.

The atmosphere in the Ford was cheerful as they drove past the crowded, business streets of Chicago. Towertown was close enough to the hotels in the Loop and 139 North Wabash. With Irene chatting softly about her work as an assistant to a broker on the stock exchange, Gregory's joy kept building. Even though her hands were in her lap and she seemed to toy with the fingers of her gloves, Irene was growing more comfortable with him, relaxing. She was becoming the woman he had loved so well in what he called his alternate timeline.

Traffic on North Wabash Avenue slowed as they approached

stone columned building with the six-foot tall arched windows, consisting of 20 square panes apiece. Announcing *The Blackhawk Club—Indian Room* was a heavy sign with lights over the vestibule leading to the doors. Nearby streets were crowded as couples in fancy cars and even nattier clothing collected to enter the large glass doors at the portico. There were flappers in short skirts and feathered headbands, and their male counterparts, the flaming youths, ragged out in racoon coats. The men tossed their car keys to the valets, who would do the parking, and the couples headed down the block to the entrance. Between the cars and the crowd, there wasn't much room to maneuver either on or off the street. Gregory thought about parking elsewhere, but at night everything was hopping. He almost coasted the Ford up to the valet stand, stopped the car and tossed his key as he saw the other men do, then went to help Irene out of the car.

"Gee," She said, "This place is hopping."

Irene tilted her head back to take in the sights. The tall buildings towered over them, blocking out the night sky. Because there were so many people, the area felt almost claustrophobic to Gregory who was used to the isolation of the farm and Norwood Park. He hastened to move her off the street, grabbing an elbow and escorting her towards the glass doors with their metal decorations.

Chatter from the patrons grew louder as he opened the door and was met by a host who carried menus about like a shield. "Table for two?" He tried louder, "For two, I take it?"

Gregory and Irene nodded.

The host gave them a "Follow me," gesture and led them to a small, round table covered in a white table cloth. He removed the extraneous two place settings and placed menus by the remaining two. Gregory stepped around him and held the brown wooden chair out for Irene, the curved back, solid in his hands. After Irene made herself comfortable, Gregory sat in the chair opposite, scooting his chair and place setting toward her right in order to be closer to her and better see the slightly raised stage where the nine men in black suits played a drum set, trombone, tuba, trumpets, saxophones, clarinets, a baby grand piano, and one had a variety of banjos, guitars, and a mandolin. The stage was set off from the highly polished wooden dance floor at the heart of the room by a low set of three railings, one above the other, made of shiny brass. The dance floor, itself, was separated from the tables by a huge Persian carpet, muting the noise of conversation while patrons ate.

As Irene picked up her menu, Gregory noted that the musicians were about to start a new set. Sure enough, they began playing *Sluefoot,* a fast foxtrot, with stride piano bass chords, and wailing brass muted by the musicians' hand.

Irene's head began to bob and her foot tapped in time with the music.

"Like this one?"

"Um, humm," She said, her eyes flicking over the fare.

"What do you think of this prime rib?"

"That sounds lovely," Irene replied.

"And of course, we can't miss the spinning salad bowl," Gregory pointed out.

Irene giggled. "No, of course not," she drawled.

Gregory rapidly gave their orders to a waiter, adding, "Two glasses of your giggle juice, while you're at it."

The waiter nodded gravely, reaching over to grab two champagne flutes from another waiter's tray as the man passed by. He set the two glasses down, one by Irene's knife, and the other by Gregory's. "There we are."

"Excellent," Gregory said. He held up his glass in a toast. "To more meals and time together."

Irene raised her glass and they clinked softly. She lowered hers to her lips, glancing shyly at Gregory through her long eyelashes as she sipped.

He desperately wanted to say "Baby, you are the cat's pajamas," but it might be too soon. Instead, he took a sip from his own glass, returned it to the table and asked, "Might I have this dance?"

Giggling, Irene then wiped her mouth with the thick cloth

napkin at her place setting. She placed her hand in his, allowing Gregory to help her to her feet and lead her through the small, round tables to the wooden floor where couples were already doing a rapid foxtrot. Gregory wrapped his arm around her waist, pressing firmly against the small of her back, swaying with the music, sensing the beat. He could feel the weight of Irene's left hand on his shoulder, while he held her right one up at shoulder height. Catching the rhythm, Gregory began striding forward, two steps, then taking two short, quick steps, rotating them 180 degrees, then starting over with the two long strides forward.

She settled against his body, following his every cue as they whirled around the floor. He tried taking his longer strides to the left first and spinning, then to the right in the Baltimore. Irene danced like a dream, her jasmine and heliotrope perfume wrapping them in a cloud of scent. Ultimately, he was able to spin her out away from him on the fast steps, and then back into his arms. During one very frenetic number, the couple next to them had separated, shimmying their shoulders forward then leaning back, then shimmying their hips to one side than the other in the Black Bottom.

Gregory caught Irene's eye. He shot a look at the couple and then checked back with her. She glanced over and they laughed at the same time.

"You have to admire their dexterity," Irene said quietly.

"And theirs," Gregory inclined his head toward three couples at the edge of the floor, tapping their feet, stepping to each side, then kicking forward then backwards in the Charleston.

Irene crinkled her nose before smiling broadly, showing her small, white teeth. "Yes very, um, athletic."

"We could try some of those dances, if you'd like," Gregory remarked.

"Maybe some other time," she giggled, looking directly into his eyes.

"Too strenuous?" Gregory raised an eyebrow.

"So close to a prime rib supper? Absolutely," Irene's eyes twinkled.

They flew through several songs, striding and spinning around the large dance floor so smooth under their feet. Irene looked flushed and very happy. Out of the corner of his eye, Gregory saw their food had finally arrived. He steered them back towards the table and when the song ended, he told her, "I believe dinner is served."

She bit at her lower lip, pulling it through her teeth in a way that made Gregory ache.

"We will definitely dance more later," he said, touching her forehead with his own. Her breath, warm from her exertion, puffing onto his face. "Come on."

She followed him to the table, letting him adjust her chair, which scraped against the Persian carpet. After Gregory sat, Irene picked up her napkin, draped it over her dress, then took her fork and knife to her food with gusto. "This looks good enough to eat," she said, giggling.

"I rather agree," Gregory laughed, taking in the rich, meaty odor of the ribs and the salty smell of the gravy. He too placed the napkin over his silk trousers then picked up the heavy silver knife and fork. The prime rib cut like butter and melted in his mouth. The peas and carrots had a savory sauce that went well with the gravy and mashed potato. Owner Otto Roth came over with a large rolling cart to prepare salad for four tables, including Gregory and Irene's. The famous, huge, spinning metal bowl had a slightly smaller one inside it filled with chopped Romain and leaf lettuce. Roth spun the inner bowl, pouring the Blackhawk's signature dressing into the salad. Once the bowl stopped spinning, Roth plated salad, topping each serving with anchovies and two small shrimp. The waiters passed the plates on to the patrons. Irene took hers and dug in.

"I like a gal with appetite," Gregory chuckled, accepting his own plate of salad with a nod of thanks to the waiter.

Around them, the noise of conversation and good music grew louder. They ate in silence, concentrating on the food. Occasionally,

Irene would study Gregory while she chewed a bite of prime rib. He watched her covertly as he nibbled a roll, or combined a bite of peas, carrots, and mashed potatoes. *What a Sheba,* he thought. He couldn't help noticing other men looking at her–his gal. He felt justifiably possessive in a manly sort of way. *Was that how Harrison felt about Lysette?* Gregory shook his head slightly to clear those thoughts away. He wanted to live in the moment, this moment, and enjoy it.

14

Gregory slept later the next morning than he had planned. He had not returned home from Irene's until close to three in the morning. After eating the delicious prime rib, they danced until after midnight. Then they sat in the Ford talking quietly until close to one thirty. Gregory had wanted to kiss Irene good night so very badly, but he knew rushing her would destroy her growing admiration. When she was ready, their budding romance would reach the level it had been in that other – what? Time? Reality? *Gregory didn't know.* Did it really matter? He asked himself while shaving. Finally, he decided he needed to move forward in his life and make the things he wanted to happen come about while preventing the horrors he had seen from taking place.

Harrison had left his newspaper behind on the corner of the kitchen table. Gregory was disappointed in missing his brother, but Clarice and Letty were the people he needed to see. Walking to the sideboard against the wall, Gregory took bread out of the large wooden box and used a sharp knife from the drawer to cut himself several slices. He plugged in the heavy bakelite based, silver colored automatic toaster, then fed a slice of bread sideways into the slot. The machine heated up with a hum, a faint red glow emanating from the top and the slot on the side. After a minute, the edge of the bread popped into view between the two edges of the slotted end. Gregory collected butter and jam from the ice box, placing them next to the toaster on the sideboard. He got a small plate from the cupboard and a butter knife from the drawer. Once he had toasted three slices of bread, buttered them and added jam, Gregory took his plate over to the kitchen table, where he sat down to eat. He reached over to pick up the *Chicago Daily News* Harrison had left behind.

The paper was folded, revealing an article about economist Roger Babson. Apparently, Babson warned the conference, *Sooner or later, a crash is coming.* He also discussed the way more people were borrowing and speculating than ever before, making the security market less and less stable. Gregory read more of the article and hoped that Harrison had read it. Babson merely stated what Gregory had been trying to convince his brother of since April. Internationally, the lack of enforcement of the Kellogg-Briand Pact and the forgiveness of war debts also had a negative effect on the world economy. Harrison had to see the danger his investments were in. Gregory wondered if he should make certain his brother read Babson's remarks, or if he should let it go.

While he sat eating his last piece of toast, Clarice and Letty came down the stairs, laughing about something. They had pulled silk lounge coats tightly over their pajamas.

"Gregory. Good morning," Clarice said when she noticed him sitting at the table.

"Morning," echoed Letty. She headed over to the stove to make a pot of coffee for herself and Clarice.

Gregory saluted them. "Gals."

"What's the rumble about O'Brien?" Clarice asked, sitting opposite Gregory, a cup of steaming coffee in her hands. She took a careful sip.

"He might be willing to work with the authorities at some point. Right now, Irene's father is still carrying a grudge against the South

Siders." Gregory looked pointedly at Clarice and Letty, who sat beside her girlfriend.

"Well," Letty said, "Who can blame him?"

"I certainly can't," Gregory agreed, "But we can't allow anger to endanger people we care about."

Clarice raised an eyebrow.

"Harrison for one." Gregory tapped a finger against the oak table. "Teddy O'Hannilon and Carlo Anselmo – you don't know them or not very well right now, but –"

"We're going to be good friends?" Clarice finished for him.

Gregory nodded. "That West Point ring set off a spiral of terrible events. We have to stop it before Capone and his men go off the track."

Clarice and Letty shared a look. Everyone knew about the mob murders taking place all over Chicago, as well as the bad-tempered natures of Capone and Moran. Either leader was capable of committing horrible violence seconds after sitting and smiling. The women both placed their coffee cups on the table. "We're in," Clarice said.

Gregory released the breath he didn't realize he had been holding. "Another thing that will create trouble is Margaretta Anselmo." He held up two hands, palms facing Clarice and Letty. "She is a cousin of Carlo's. I think she's about eleven now, and she's been caught up in Capone's human trafficking operation since she was five."

"We've got to get her out," Clarice straightened, anger flushing her features.

Gregory laughed lightly. *That's exactly what she said last time.*

"We can't leave her in a *can house*," Letty said forcefully. "She's a baby!"

At the same time, Clarice hissed, "That's disgusting. An eleven-year old!"

"Oh, I completely agree," Gregory said, holding his hands up again. "We need a plan."

"Let's get a van and make it look like a delivery truck," suggested Clarice.

Gregory pulled on his chin.

"Oh," Letty said, her lips forming an "O." "Already done it."

Gregory pointed a finger at her and nodded. "Yes. We have to be quieter and involve fewer people in order to have a clean sneak."

Clarice tapped her fingers on the table. "Ideas?"

"I think we need to grab the girl by coming in from the roof. She's on the top floor of the apartment building next to 2222 Wabash."

"The *Four Deuces*?" Clarice asked, the color draining slightly from her face.

"Unfortunately." Gregory said, collecting his plate and taking it to the sink. He rinsed it off using the water pump and set it on the drain board. *They needed a plan that didn't involve any of the North Side mob.*

"Are you sure she's there?" Letty asked.

"Teddy can have Carlo go in and check, but I don't want either of them involved in the actual rescue." Gregory turned around and leaned against the sink, crossing his arms over his chest. "It puts them into too much danger."

"The three of us can do it," Clarice and Letty said at once. "Duck soup!"

"We need to see what sort of fire ladders or drain pipes, or whatever the buildings have on the sides and if the roofs are connected in any way. If we have Margaretta climb out the window and we pull her up onto the roof, we can get to street level through some building down the street that is not connected to those owned by the South Side mob."

"Brilliant, Gregory," Clarice said, snapping her fingers.

"Carlo can check out the building, and we will develop the rest later." Gregory tapped his chin again. "I could see what ladders are available. Carlo needn't do that. I need to speak with Teddy. Carlo would do almost anything for him, but when he learns his cousin is involved, well – we will have difficulty stopping him wanting to charge in to save her himself."

The two women got up, rinsed out their coffee cups, and walked towards the door to the kitchen. Clarice turned and looked over her shoulder. "We'll wait for Carlo to report back, meanwhile, Letty and I have work to do." She gave Gregory a quick smile, and they left.

Although cook could have cleaned up the breakfast dishes, Gregory did it because the mindless task gave his brain an opportunity to relax. He knew Teddy would convince Carlo to find information about rescuing Margaretta, but he was less certain about keeping Carlo out of the actual rescue. He remembered how last time Carlo adamantly insisted on being there for his young cousin even though they did not know one another.

While Gregory toiled in the kitchen, Harrison strode the streets of downtown Chicago. The tall skyscrapers altered the skyline and the widened streets permitted more traffic while allowing pedestrians a safe space to walk along the store fronts. Harrison stopped to peek into the Marshall Fields' shop windows, where the designers had set up two realistic female mannequins, holding tennis racquets. The left one stood tall, with her racquet resting against her leg, while the right one held the racquet up as if she were about to serve the ball. Both were dressed in fashionable tennis attire. Harrison marveled at the ingenuity of the window dresser who lured shoppers into the store through imaginative scenes passersby saw through the huge pane glass. Other buildings down the street had the decorative fronds of Egyptian palms at the tops of traditional columns, or huge animal heads, staring out at the street. The City of Broad Shoulders had altered so much since he was a newsy as a young boy. Back then the narrower streets remained dusty or muddy and the horse drawn vehicles outnumbered automobiles. Today, the opposite was true. Harrison often found himself turning in a circle with his head back in order to see the artistic changes.

Finally, Harrison reached the Chicago Stock Exchange building at 13 North LaSalle Street. The thirteen-story building was one of those decorated with Art Deco designs, making it look modern and classical at the same time. Harrison entered the thick doors and went out in search of his broker, who he hoped was in his office and not on the floor of the exchange. Walking up to the semi-circular desk opposite the elevators, Harrison tipped his fedora even further at the brunette powdering her face using a multicolored, enameled compact, hanging from her neck on a very long silver colored chain. The gal–Tikki Southern, served as a receptionist to the brokers, announcing their clients' arrival and answering the telephone. She finished patting her nose with the pad and snapped the compact closed before looking up and blinking her overly large brown eyes at Harrison.

"Can I help you?" She asked in a nasal twang.

Harrison leaned toward her slightly and smiled. "I want to see Stick MacBride."

"Oh," Tikki sat up straighter. "Mr. MacBride has a client right now, but I could squeeze you in when they wrap up."

"Swell," Harrison said. He nodded then went to sit in the narrow semi-circular arm chairs surrounding a coffee table covered in old issues of *The Chicagoan.* Once seated comfortably with the back of his coat hanging through the slit in the back of the chair, Harrison tented his fingers. On the one hand, Harrison wanted to continue to invest in the Bull market that had brought the brothers so much return. On the other hand, he was moved by Gregory's new conviction that the market was unstable. Gregory had changed so much since April. His opinions were stronger, and he was more forceful about implementing his ideas. The Art Deco renovations, for example, and hiring Clarice and Letty. *He had nothing against the two gals; in fact, they were the cat's pajamas, but he would not have thought to give those two the jobs they now did so well.* Most critical was his brother's insistence about the stocks. Harrison had seen some evidence of weakness in the market during recent weeks. Then, too, he had read the article in the *Daily News* this morning. Babson's remarks merely backed what Gregory had been saying since the raid. *That's why I'm here,* Harrison thought.

A thin, very tall, gray-haired man dressed in a dark gray pin-striped suit strode across the light green, stone tile floor, hand reaching forward to shake Harrison's own. "Harrison, my boy," Stick MacBride said, his eyes twinkling behind thick, gold-wire framed eye glasses. "Let's go into my office."

Releasing Harrison's hand, MacBride led the way to his narrow office. His small wooden desk stacked with documents faced away from a six-foot tall stained-glass window with an animal design. Light filtering through the window cast a unique glow around the silver papered walls. He indicated Harrison take one of the two leather-covered, skyscraper shaped chairs in front of the desk. Harrison flicked back his suit jacket and pulled up his pants at the thighs as he dropped onto the chair.

"What deal might I help with today?" MacBride had taken his own large desk chair and leaned forward over the desk toward Harrison.

Harrison swallowed–his throat suddenly dry. "I want to sell all my holdings except Standard Oil, Coca-Cola, and Electric Power and Light."

MacBride sat back hard. His mouth formed an "O." He raised his right hand and stroked his pointed chin. "Of all my clients, my boy, I didn't think you would be one to leave the market."

"I'm not totally," Harrison put in quickly. "I want you to take the earnings and buy gold bars and silver, you follow?"

"Diversifying, I see," MacBride said thoughtfully. "Yes, yes. I can help with that."

Harrison clamped his hands on his knees. "I'm glad, sir." He sighed quietly. *Maybe this was going to be easier than he thought.* "Whatever monies come out of those other investments need to go into either gold or silver, whichever you are able to buy at good prices."

"Currently, gold is $22.60 an ounce. Not a bad time to buy in."

MacBride continued to stroke his chin. "Let me see if I can't get you the highest prices for your stock sales from a precious metals broker, and I will notify you."

"Berries!" Harrison rose to his feet, reaching his hand across the desk.

MacBride stood and shook hands. "Good day."

Harrison saluted touching the brim of his fedora before he turned on his heel, leaving the office. As he headed towards the elevator with its fancy brass grill, sporting stylized deer, Harrison noticed the tall, broad figure of Douglas O'Brien, cigar clamped between his teeth, exiting. Increasing his speed, Harrison raised an arm, waving at the older man. "Councilman O'Brien," Harrison called.

Looking right and left, trying to find the source of his name, O'Brien stopped in his tracks.

Harrison raced up, holding out a hand to shake. O'Brien automatically clasped the outstretched hand, pumping it up and down. "Don't know if you remember me, Deanie O'Banion's cousin—Harrison Davenport? I met you several times with my cousin."

A smile broke out on O'Brien's face. The cigar remained at the corner of his mouth, smoke curling upwards towards his black felt Homberg. "Yes, yes. Harrison. I remember. Saw your brother the other day with my daughter, Irene. Ah–"

"Gregory. He told me he had spoken with you." Harrison nodded.

"Are you here to corner the market?" O'Brien asked.

Harrison, not wanting everyone exiting the elevator to overhear, gently clasped O'Brien's sleeve and steered Irene's father further into the large reception room as well as closer to the columned walls. "Actually," he began in a lowered voice, "I'm trading many shares for gold bullion and silver bricks."

O'Brien leaned closer. He took the cigar out of his mouth, between forefinger and second finger, tapping the ash into a nearby tall, free-standing spittoon. "Get a tip, did you?"

Harrison nodded. "Liquidating anything that seemed unstable in the past weeks."

"Hummm." O'Brien puffed on the cigar, sending a cloud over their heads. "Gold and silver," he muttered to himself. "Can't go wrong with that."

That's what Gregory has been saying, Harrison thought. "Exactly, sir."

O'Brien shook Harrison's hand. "I'll take it under advisement."

Harrison touched his fedora in a salute. "Good seeing you again."

O'Brien nodded and walked away with a wave of his large hand.

Harrison headed back towards the elevator, hoping that he had done the right thing.

Gregory knew he was doing the right thing, seeking out Teddy O'Hannilon. He had to get help casing out the building where Margaretta Anselmo was being held captive because he would be recognized by the South Siders and could not go himself. Teddy should be at his flat at this time of day. Gregory was counting on that. He strode down the elm shaded sidewalk from the El stop, searching down the broad expanse of West Brompton Avenue for 528. A few cars drove by, but generally there wasn't much traffic. He knew he was looking for Tudor-styled lions and shields, decorating the columns of the brick building, and a knight in armor poised above the entry. Eventually, he discovered the four story walk up. Stepping over the two entryway steps, Gregory opened the thick oak door into the foyer. He found the stairs at once, heading for the third floor where Teddy had his flat.

Gregory knocked on the heavy paneled door. "O'Hannilon!!" he called. Banging again.

From inside, Gregory heard rustling and light footsteps. Finally, locks scraped and the door opened a crack.

Hair mussed, bleary eyed, Teddy peeked through the door and the jamb. "Davenport?"

"Teddy, let me in," Gregory said. "Let's not do this in the hallway."

The door swung open as Teddy stepped back. He was clothed in a black silk smoking robe with velvet cuffs and trim. He held out an arm in a "come-in" gesture. After closing the door behind Gregory, Teddy rubbed the back of his neck and stumbled into the living area of his two-room flat. The door to his bedroom remained closed. The small living room had a single low sofa in the modern style. Beside it was a granite topped brass table with legs that looked like Egyptian fronds. A fireplace with small plaster shields holding up the mantel occupied most of the wall to Gregory's left. Opposite the sofa were two squat arm chairs covered in the same lemon yellow velvetlike material as the sofa. A tall Philco radio set made of oak with pecan inlay dominated the corner between the sofa and the fireplace wall. Three large windows, one on the fireplace wall, and two on the wall to the right of the entryway permitted a lot of light into the room. Enough light that Teddy was blinking. *He must have had a lot of giggle juice last night.*

Showing Gregory to a chair, Teddy lounged back on the sofa, one arm along the low back. "I'd offer you some joe, but this joint doesn't have its own kitchen."

Gregory shook his head and waved his hand. "You're fine."

"What's the rumble?" Teddy asked, looking Gregory in the eyes. He took a cigarette out of the mother of pearl and silver box on the side table next to him, lit it and blew a puff of smoke into the room.

"I'll be square with you," Gregory said. "I need your help." He held up a hand, forestalling questions. "Carlo has a cousin he doesn't know about. She's in Capone's *can house* and we – Clarice, Letty, and I want to get her out. She's only eleven."

Teddy sat up. The cigarette in his right hand sent smoke curling into the air. "Eleven! That's a baby. Of course, you have to get her out." Putting the cigarette to his mouth, he took a puff.

"I don't want either you or Carlo to be involved in the actual rescue – you follow? It's too dangerous seeing you are Moran's cousin and he's *Sicilian.*" Gregory stretched his legs out in front of the chair, crossing the right ankle over the left. "I just need Carlo to make certain the girl is on the fourth floor and which flat. We are thinking 4E, but we need to be certain."

"He would do that. They would never suspect him, seeing he's from the right mob," Teddy responded, crushing his cigarette into a nearby ashtray. "I'll ask him." Teddy rose from the sofa and headed to the closed door nearby. He knocked softly, twice. "Carlo?"

Not giggle juice necessarily, thought Gregory, *love.*

"Dangle," a groggy voice came from behind the door. "Fade."

Teddy knocked again. "Carlo, please. I'm not going away."

The door opened, revealing Carlo disheveled and half dressed, shirtless beneath a cotton dressing robe. "Can't it wait?"

"No, baby." Teddy reached up a gentle hand to cup Carlo's stubbled cheek. "It's important. Gregory, here, needs your help."

Carlo glanced around, saw Gregory and quickly jerked his robe closed then ran a hand through his hair as if to smooth it out. Teddy wrapped an arm around Carlo's waist, guiding the younger man into the living area and the sofa. The two men sat next to one another, Teddy's arm remaining around Carlo.

"I better start over," Gregory suggested. He told Carlo what he had shared with Teddy, finishing with his urgent plea for the two men to remain participants in the collection of information only and not the rescue. "And, that's the crop."

Carlo's eyes grew larger and rounder when he heard about Margaretta. His head seemed to clear. "I'll go tomorrow morning when the *Four Deuces* will be closed and check the flats. I can dress differently, too, so no one will recognize me. It'll be duck soup." Carlo ran his hand through his hair again. He yawned, quickly raising a well-manicured hand to cover his generous mouth.

Teddy looked longingly at Carlo. "Go back to sleep. There will be time later to get ready."

Carlo nodded at Gregory and, so quietly Gregory almost didn't hear him, Carlo muttered to Teddy, "Baby you are the cat's pajamas." He rose and returned to the bedroom, closing the door behind him.

Teddy stood, causing Gregory to jump to his feet. "We'll give you the rumble."

"Thanks, pal." Gregory grabbed Teddy's arm just below the shoulder and shook his other hand. He moved toward the door, wanting to leave, now that his efforts had born fruit. Teddy walked with him, letting Gregory out into the hallway. He shut the door almost silently, leaving Gregory alone. *That went well.* Gregory hastened down the steps and out onto the sidewalk. Traffic had increased, with more cars on the street. He strode down to the stop where the Elevated would collect him, sunlight poking out behind a cloud.

15

Getting up before the sun, Carlo left Teddy's flat and used the elevated to return home to his parents's crowded flat. His family would be at their various places of work – his father and brothers at the ironworks, his mother and sisters at various downtown hotels, cleaning. He would have the flat, and even more significant, the wash area to himself. Carlo dressed carefully in drab short pants, light brown shirt and double-breasted tweed jacket which he had borrowed from his older brother Vincento – a good egg if ever there was one, who wouldn't mind. He knew any of his own rags would be too hotsy-totsy by South Side standards to go unnoticed at the *Four Deuces*.

Carefully, he pomaded his light brown hair with a left-sided part, then decided that a center part made him look even less like his normal self as his reflection peered back at him in the tiny dresser mirror. Without asking, he appropriated an old black fedora from his father, one he discovered on the floor of the armoire containing his parents' clothing. Placing the hat on his head so the brim came down almost over his nose, he concealed his wide set brown eyes and most of his facial features. Rather than donning his usual two-toned shoes,

Carlo looked for a lace-up boot, one that would come up over his ankle – something *he* would never normally wear.

Finally, when he felt ready, he went and checked himself in the tall, oval, free-standing mirror in the corner of his parents' bedroom. Carlo turned one way and then the other, slightly bending the leg closest to the mirror and holding one arm on his hip. "Jake!"

Satisfied no one would recognize him, he walked to the kitchen cupboard, taking the sugar bowl off the shelf. Buried deep within was a small white envelope where his mother hid a few bills. Carlo took out a dollar before concealing the lot and returning the sugar bowl to the cupboard. *That will get me there and back.*

He turned on his heel and left the flat. Once on the street, he began to walk with purpose, whistling softly to himself. Over all, Carlo was happy. Never had he dreamed some handsome man, some sheik, like Teddy O'Hannilon might be in his future. Just the thought of Teddy made Carlo's heart speed up. They were good together, and that's really what counted most. When he reached the train station, Carlo had the ticket seller make change. He pocketed the ticket on the right and put his coins in the left front pocket of his pants where they would be more difficult to steal. The train was not very crowded because most people were at work. *A good thing because very few would see where he came from and where he went.*

Wabash came up quickly enough, and Carlo exited the car. He made his way up the sidewalk, tall buildings towering over both sides of the road. Carlo walked with purpose, as if he were walking home after a late-night shift. Finally, he approached 2224 South Wabash where Capone had his refurbished furniture store – part of the larger building at 2222 that housed the *Four Deuces* – Capone's leading speak easy, can house, and gambling joint. Beyond that was the four-story, reddish brown, brick apartment building with the flat where his young cousin was being held prisoner.

Carlo surreptitiously glanced about him beneath his fedora. While cars moved along the street, very few pedestrians were about. He quickly climbed the stairs and went through the archway and the doors leading inside the apartment building. Taking the stairs, he reached the landing on the fourth floor, where he stopped, listening. A baby wailed in flat 4"G" and music from an old-style gramophone played a scratchy tenor singing in Italian behind the door of 4"H." Gregory had mentioned Margaretta would be in Flat 4"E" and that's where he needed to check.

Approaching the wall where 4 "E" and 4 "F" had doors on opposite ends, Carlo tried to catch any signs of the inhabitants.

Suddenly, a young girl shouted, "No! That's baloney!"

"It's an art, sweetie," drawled a woman's voice, heavily accented in Italian. "The palookas will adore you."

"I... *don't* ... care!" the girl retorted. "I'm *not* learning to do *that!*"

A throaty laugh. "Oh, I say you *will* and what's more, you're going to *love* it."

"Or what?" The girl was sulking, Carlo could tell because she sounded just like his youngest sister Maria.

"He will come deal with you," the woman said nonchalantly.

"Noooo," moaned the girl.

Carlo had heard enough. He knew where his cousin was, and they needed to rescue her, immediately or her very innocence would be lost forever. He spun on his heel and almost flew down the steps to the street, running for the street car.

Carlo pounded on the door to Teddy's flat. "Teddy! Teddy!" He slammed the heal of his fist against the heavy wood again.

"Coming, coming," Carlo heard as if from a great distance. "Don't knock the door down." Chains rattled and the lock unlatched before Teddy started to open the door.

Carlo pushed in, noting that his boyfriend was already dressed in a navy blue, three-piece suit. *They wouldn't have to waste time waiting for Teddy to get ready.* "We need 23 skiddo! My little cousin," Carlo gasped. "Oh, Teddy. She's in such trouble." He pressed his forehead against Teddy's strong shoulder, holding back a sob.

Teddy griped his shoulders firmly with a hand on each side. "Tell me what happened and we'll go see Gregory."

"No." Carlo said, "I'll tell you on the way. Let's blow."

Teddy nodded. He hugged Carlo then set him back on his feet. "I'll get the key to the heap." Teddy strode over to a small drawered table and tugged at the brass knob. Collecting a ring of keys, he also grabbed an overcoat and his fedora. "Come on."

Teddy drove them to the farm and the *Hair of the Dog* as fast as his old Rambler Model C would go. As the tall buildings gave way to smaller shops and then to dwellings and the number of trees increased, Carlo shared the events of his morning. "It is flat 4"E" and they are forcing her to do things no eleven-year-old should know about, let alone do."

"Scandalous doesn't even cover it," Teddy finally said, around the cigarette between his lips. "My cousin, and O'Banion before him, never dealt in *can houses*. It's just *not* acceptable." The gears of the car grinded, then screamed, as Teddy switched them in preparation for the gravel drive into the farm.

"I just hope Gregory, Clarice, and Letty are prepared to go tonight," Carlo muttered. "I can't bear thinking of that poor child enduring one more day in that horrid place."

Teddy reached over and patted Carlo's knee. The smile he gave was sorrowful, but sympathetic.

Parking the car on the widened strip of gravel that served club patrons, Carlo and Teddy hopped out of the Rambler and ran up the brick steps to the white door of the farm house. This time it was Teddy who pounded on the door, after tossing the burnout remainder of his cigarette to the ground.

Klein came almost immediately to let them inside.

"We need to see Gregory," Teddy said.

"I'll announce you at once. He is having lunch in the kitchen." Klein waved for them to follow, and he took them down the hallway to the steps at the very back of the house which led to the kitchen basement. "Teddy and Carlo, is it?"

Carlo nodded, a front curl shaking loose.

"Teddy and Carlo are here to see you, Gregory," Klein said,

blocking the way into the bright, white walled kitchen. Carlo could almost see Gregory seated at the table with a plate of half-eaten something in front of him.

Gregory pushed his plate with cold ham, snap peas from the garden, and applesauce away from him as he rose from his chair. He raised his right hand, offering it to Teddy and then to Carlo for a strong shake, maneuvering around Klein, who nodded and seemed to disappear back into the farmhouse. "Teddy, Carlo." Gregory said, smiling. "What brings you?"

"I'll let Carlo tell it," Teddy said, "It's his rumble."

Gregory waved them into empty places at the table. "Ham? Coffee?"

Carlo and Teddy shook a hand and their heads. "It's too upsetting to eat," Carlo added.

Gregory knew then that Carlo had been to the flat on South Wabash. *That is the only thing that makes sense and would upset them like this.*

For the second time, Carlo detailed the events of the morning. His face growing more and more pale as he talked. Teddy slipped a comforting arm around his boy-friend's shoulders, encouraging him to tell Gregory everything.

When Carlo finished, Gregory jumped to his feet. "I'll get Clarice and Letty. We have to go tonight. I think we will be able to make a clean sneak if we get Margaretta out over the roof tops."

"What do we do?" Carlo asked.

"Oh no," Gregory shook his head. He raised an open palm. "Don't get sore, but you two are staying here or at Teddy's flat. You can't be anywhere nearby."

Carlo started to protest and Teddy's features hardened.

"If Capone suspects North Side involvement, you'll be iced," Gregory said, firmly. "If he realizes Carlo has been involved, you'll be iced. It's lose-lose for you pals. Noooo, no! Stay away."

"Clarice and Letty can take care of themselves, Gregory," Teddy said. "I worry about you."

"I'll be fine. Clarice and Letty will do the so-called heavy lifting. Everything will be Jake." Gregory threaded his fingers through his hair. "You can stay here if you'd like. There's an open room on the second floor."

Carlo looked at Teddy, who looked back and nodded. "Ok," they said together.

"Actually," Gregory said, tapping his chin with a forefinger. "There is something you could do."

Teddy and Carlo jumped up. "What's that?" they asked in unison.

"Margaretta is going to need some boy's clothes and a wrap. There is a trunk in the attic with Harrison's and my old rags. She's about so tall," Gregory held his hand, palm facing down towards the floor, about four feet in the air. "Find something suitable for us to take to her. I want to leave everything from that place behind us."

Carlo poked Teddy. "We're on it." The two men rushed out of the kitchen and Gregory could hear them thumping up the steps.

Now he just needed to get Clarice and Letty.

Harrison had no idea Gregory was busy looking for his accomplices to report Carlo's findings, when he leaped out of the street car and walked down Michigan Avenue to find MacBride. Together they would meet with Pickle Dooley, a precious metals broker. MacBride peeled away from a street lamp, where he had been leaning, speeding to catch Harrison.

"Dooley has invited us to dine at a smorgasbord on Herring Alley. Pickle swears they serve the city's best Swedish meatballs in town," Stick said, falling in step with Harrison.

"How do we find him?" Harrison asked.

"Rather, he'll find us," Stick replied. "There's his car!" Stick pointed down the street at a silver Rolls Royce coming towards them. He waved at the driver and the large car pulled over to the curb. "Come on," Stick urged, hastening over to where the uniformed driver had opened a car door.

Harrison slid into the back seat next to Stick. He could smell rich leather upholstery and wood trim. Beside him, the car door closed with a deep thunk. Flynn, Dooley's driver took his place behind the wheel, then worked the starter. Harrison never knew a Rolls could purr catlike, but it did as Flynn edged back into traffic. Sitting closest to the far door was a short, rotund man with an oversized black derby. His hair might once have been blond, but now it was pure white. His round face, with its double chins and bulbous nose, seemed jolly enough due to his genuine smile. "You must be Harrison," he said in a bass voice, thick with an Irish brogue.

"That I am," Harrison could not resist saying, his eyes twinkling.

"Stick here says yer wanting to buy a bit of gold and silver."

"Yes, sir. I do."

"Well between us, Stick and I, I think we got you covered." Dooley faced front again. "Flynn, Herring Lane if you please."

The Swedish part of town reflected its population. Tiny grocery stores advertised goods Harrison had never heard of – exotic fruits, venison, and seafood; especially seafood. Street peddlers shouted in Swedish, selling wares of all sorts. Finally, Flynn pulled up to a large six story building with a huge electric sign. *Smorgasbord,* Harrison read. Patrons joined a line heading for the double glass doors. Harrison could see patrons continuing into a side entry within the building. Dooley collected them and the three men followed through the outer doors, past an inner archway in a huge, open room with wood paneled walls where lines of patrons passed by heated trays of various foods.

A waiter handed Dooley, MacBride, and Harrison large plates. "Choose what you like," he explained. "Pay by the plate. I recommend Swedish meatballs and herring balls in current sauce."

Dooley chuckled. "No one makes Swedish meatballs like their cook."

"Have you had their herring balls?" Stick MacBride wanted to know.

"If they recommend it, gotta be tasty," Dooley said, smacking his lips.

Harrison craned his neck, trying to see past those ahead of them in the line. He could see steam curling up from some trays, but not others. A mixture of smells tantalized him. Onions, thyme, cardamom, and dill, dominated the seasonings. When he reached food, he pointed to this and that. Lutefisk, and smelts looked too fishy for his taste, so he passed them, selecting instead some of the rich seafood stew and thick sliced brown bread. From behind the food laden tables, servers dished out portions onto plates held out by patrons. Harrison made certain he got Swedish meatballs and just a taste of the herring balls. He counted eight different varieties of smoked herrings. Another server ladled out creamed ham with chucks of potato and cheese. Passing by trays of sausages, ring bologna, and some sort of wild game, Harrison's eye was drawn to the sweets table laden with coffee cakes, marzipan, petit fours, candied orange peel, and something smelling strongly of anise and saffron.

Dooley, MacBride, and Harrison selected a booth table with red leather covering the bench and backing. Placing their plates onto the thick oak planked table, the three men were seated. Around them tables were packed with people of all ages. Parents helped young children, or seated toddlers on their mother's lap, laughing and eating. In another corner businessmen congregated, talking quietly. At long tables, peddlers and factory workers finished with their shifts sat ignoring those beside them, but for the most part, groups – small or large – seemed to chatter joyfully over their plates brimming with foodstuff.

Dooley dug in, forking up a meatball, shoveling it into his mouth, and closing his eyes as he chewed. "Magnificent," he judged. "Try, try," he urged, gesturing with a meaty hand.

Harrison tasted his meatballs and had to agree. Cook presented a blend of flavors –fennel, onion, and something Harrison could not name – that seemed to sparkle on his tongue. In addition to the meatballs was a creamed potato dish – a cross between a soup and a stew, seasoned with fresh parsley and dill. While the fare was excellent, he hoped Dooley was not planning on discussing their monetary exchanges here. *How could he hear above the din?*

Dooley returned for food two more times, gathering up a clean plate each time. "When it comes time to pay, they count the number of plates. It's two-bits a plate." He laughed expansively, tucking his cloth napkin up under his double chins.

Stick and Harrison each only had their one plate. A person could pile on enough food for several meals, and the choices were endless – or seemed that way. Dooley insisted they try baked goods for dessert. Harrison's almond pastry melted in his mouth. He had a good excuse now to patronize that Swedish Bakery on North Clark Street famous for their cakes, cookies, and sweet rolls.

Once Dooley had eaten his fill, he paid their bill and directed them outside. Once again, the silver Rolls stood at the curb waiting for them. "Come into my office," Dooley chuckled, his belly jiggling.

Flynn opened the passenger door for Stick and Harrison, who took seats inside. Stick sat in a folding chair facing Dooley, while Harrison sat beside the heavy-set man. "Harrison, here, wants to buy gold bricks and silver bars," Stick explained to Dooley.

"I will arrange that for him." Dooley offered them a box of cigars, flipping it open. Stick took one and bit off the end. Harrison followed suit. "Just telegraph me the details this afternoon and I will have the precious metals delivered within two weeks." Dooley stared directly at Harrison. "I take it you have a safe place for them? Bars and bricks take up lots of room."

Harrison thought of the cellar concealed beneath his office at *Hair of the Dog*. He was really doing this—trading one type of securities for another. Hooch filled quite a bit of the space, but there was plenty of room in the further corner for hiding gold and silver. *Who would suspect gold and silver that far beneath a farm house? There were plenty of more obvious places to look.*

Gregory searched the Farm for Clarice and Letty, finally tracking them down past the old barn where they had set a target on a hay bale to practice shooting. He heard the pop, pop from the tiny weapons they carried just before he actually saw them. "Well here you gals are," he said, waving a greeting. He did *not* want to surprise them and risk getting shot.

Clarice and Letty lowered their weapons. Smoke curled into the air from the silver muzzles. Clarice walked towards him first, snatching up her suit jacket which she had folded carefully at the base of a tall tree. Letty came up behind her, looking somewhat plain without her long, double strand of pearls. A two-inch long pair of earrings shaped like elongated triangles dangled from her ears, and she had completed a full make-up, rouge, light brown eye shadow, and red lipstick. So, not completely as nature intended her.

"Did you get all the crop from Carlo?" Clarice asked softly, even though no one else could overhear them. An orchard of trees stood between them and the house. Clouds drifted over the blue sky, overhead.

"I did," Gregory nodded. He shared Carlo's story and need for urgency. "We'll go early tomorrow morning before the sun rises."

"I agree," Clarice said. She rested a hand on her hip. "Peddlers won't be out yet hawking."

Letty nodded. "Patrons of *Four Deuces* will have left, while occupants of flats will still be asleep."

"I think we will take the Ford truck, a six-foot ladder, a six-foot plank, and some rope. Everything should be in the old barn. That way we can use an external fire escape on the building beside 2220, and cross over the roof." Gregory had to suppress a smile as he remembered a Harold Lloyd film using a ladder similarly. *But wasn't that the one where he ended up hanging from the huge clock minute hand?* Gregory shook his head to clear it.

"Drop down onto the ledge and open Margaretta's window, and go back the same way," Letty smacked her fist into her open palm. A bird sang and wind rustled leaves around them. "Gregory – you're the bee's knees!"

"Carlo and Teddy are rummaging through my brother's and my old clothes. They will find something for Margaretta's disguise," explained Gregory. He slapped at a bug trying to bite his neck. "If we can't all fit in the truck on our return trip, you, Letty and Margaretta can always take the street car. Who would notice a couple and their son riding together?"

"Son?" Clarice's eyes widened.

"Don't get sore, but you and Letty are old enough to have a son about nine or ten years-old." Gregory knew the two women were in their early thirties, even though they could look younger if they wished.

Instead of anger, Letty and Clarice roared. They slapped each other's shoulders, and their own knees as they bent forward, gasping. "We never talked about children," Clarice admitted.

"What baloney!" Letty finally got out.

Clarice suddenly looked serious. "We could take her in. We certainly can't attempt returning her to the Anselmos. Even if they want to keep her, Capone or his mob would certainly track her down and take her back."

Letty's face brightened with understanding. "Yes. We'll take her, rear her, teach her to shoot."

Clarice started laughing again. She looped an arm over Letty's shoulders, tugging her close, and kissed her where her black hair parted. "It's decided."

"Come on. Let's go back to our house. We all need rest before tonight, or should I say, tomorrow morning?"

On the way past the old red barn, Gregory slipped inside and found several lengths of sturdy rope, a ladder and plank needed for Margaretta's rescue. When he came back outside, he found the two women discussing Margaretta's adoption. When they saw Gregory, they turned back towards the house. Gregory let the women go ahead of him while he secured the ladder and other things in the back of the truck. *Teddy and Carlo must have found some usable clothing by now.*

When he reached the house, Teddy and Carlo greeted him at the door, where Clarice and Letty held an armful of clothing.

"Success," Teddy said.

"Duck Soup," Carlo added.

After a light supper in the kitchen together, Clarice, Letty and Gregory agreed to meet at three a.m. in order to reach 2220 South Wabash while it was still dark. Gregory said "Good Night," to Clarice and Letty as well as Carlo and Teddy, who still looked a little sorry that they were not included in the early morning adventure. Gregory headed to his rooms, knowing they all went to theirs.

As he climbed the stairs to the third floor, Gregory thought about how he had wanted to speak with Harrison, but his brother was not anywhere to be found. Although he wondered where Harrison had gone that afternoon, Gregory could not dwell on his brother. Too many other worries occupied his thoughts. His sleep was fretful with lots of thrashing about in his bed as he dreamt of that other timeline where Margaretta's rescue resembled nothing like a clean sneak. In his dream, Two-Gun – actually a cartoonish version of him – causes a rumpus at *Four Deuces*, drawing a gun, so, shooting begins.

Gregory's wind-up alarm clock jangled, jarring him awake. His mind was muzzy. He blinked in the total darkness, feeling around his bedside table to jab at the off button. Silence wrapped the room like a thick blanket. When he remembered Margaretta and his purpose, Gregory threw off his covers and jumped out of bed. Washing quickly and running a comb through his curly hair, he dressed in his darkest and oldest suit, wanting to be unremarkable if he were noticed at all. Then, Gregory tip-toed down to the second floor where Clarice shared rooms with Letty.

Rapping softly on their door with a knuckle, he hissed, "Clarice, Letty."

He heard rustling and footsteps from inside the rooms. "Clarice, Letty," a little louder this time.

Rustling footsteps came closer, the floor creaked, and the door cracked open. Letty's brown eye pressed against the open jamb. "Oh, it's you," Letty whispered. "We'll be out soon."

"Are you going to leave me in the hallway?" Gregory hissed. He slapped a hand to his forehead.

He heard rather than saw Letty release the lock they had added to their outer door. *Security against wayward patrons they had said.* When she actually swung the door open, Gregory saw she had decided to wear her most drab outfit. A yellow and brown plaid pleated skirt with a dropped waisted brown jacket on top made her look like a school marm. She wore no earrings nor a hat of any sort. *So unusual for Letty who seemed so flamboyant.* Clarice strode out of the connected bedroom. She too dressed for action in a black cloth suit, her hair pomaded back to look black and as manly as possible. Like Letty, she wore no makeup. Rather than sporting a fedora, she wore a black newsboy cap similar to the ones Carlo liked. Clarice also carried another newsboy cap, only this one was brown.

"If we put Margaretta's hair up under this," Clarice held up the brown cap, "we won't be made."

"Berries!" Letty said. "Do you think we should grab some apples, or bread from the kitchen?"

"Fine," Gregory agreed, his stomach already rumbling.

Clarice pushed Letty out the door, waited for Gregory to walk out, then closed the rooms up behind him. "We've got to breeze. If the sun comes up..." She allowed her words to trail off. They all knew they had to be gone with Margaretta before sunrise.

"I'll start up the truck, you get food and meet me out back. Just hurry," Gregory told them, rushing down the stairs and out the front door. He set the clutch, cranked the engine over, and sat in the driver's seat, tapping his thumbs against the steering wheel. Clarice and Letty were out almost as soon as Gregory settled into the driver's seat. They squeezed in; Letty then Clarice, who closed the passenger door beside her.

Gregory's head lights drifted over the gravel driveway, bushes, and trees. Overhead an owl hooted. By the time they left the area near Norwood Park and entered the city, lights from Chicago brightened the sky even though it was still night. Road noises seemed louder in the dark. Gregory headed down Michigan Avenue with its sky scrapers and its many trees, turning left on 14th Street and left again on Indiana because it was less traveled than the main drag. While lights gleamed from the windows, they knew most everyone was asleep. They neared 21st and Indiana where Gregory started looking for a place to park the truck. Traffic was so light, they would not be seen; or, so they hoped.

Pulling up to the curb closer to 21st Street gave them less of a walk down Wabash. Clarice leaped onto the sidewalk and held her hand out to Letty, who clasped it tightly and hauled herself out of the truck. Gregory grabbed the ladder and the plank, pressing the wooden board against the ladder to make it easier to carry. The wood felt rough against his fingers and barn odors lingered on it. Letty took the newsboy cap from Clarice, stuffing it into a satchel where the women had concealed the clothing Carlo and Teddy had found. Clarice grabbed the pieces of rope. Letty strapped the satchel to her back, keeping her hands free.

"Ok?" Gregory asked.

"Let's go," Clarice said softly.

The three of them walked purposefully down 21st street, past Michigan Avenue, stopping just before they reached where Wabash and 21st crossed. Two cars, one going uptown, the other headed further south passed them, then Wabash was quiet. Gregory inclined his head. They crossed the street then walked swiftly towards the building two doors closer to them than the *Four Deuces.* By not passing Capone's club, they had less risk of being noticed. The alleyway where the external, steel fire stairs were attached was extremely dark. A rat scurried by them causing Letty to jump. *Thank God she hadn't shrieked,* Gregory thought and they carefully climbed up towards the roof, four floors above them.

"I'll get a slant on things from here, but it should be duck soup," Clarice said. As she moved closer to the edge nearest Margaretta's building, Clarice startled a flock of pigeons, who warbled before flying off.

Overhead, stars competed with street lamps. Tar paper covered the roof which had several chimneys and other protrusions. A cornice of stone outlined the edge of the building just as it did for the apartments at 2220. Large pipes protruded near the center of the roof edge closest to their target. After looking around, Clarice gave the others a thumb's up.

Gregory used one length of rope to secure one end of the ladder to the roof while straining to drop the other end of the ladder on the cornice of Margaretta's building. The first attempt failed, Clarice rushing over to catch the ladder so it wouldn't crash loudly against the stone wall of the building below them. Gregory was successful his second attempt. Clarice – the rest of the rope tied around her waist – climbed onto the ladder, testing its stability, then nimbly walked across to Margaretta's roof.

Gregory slid the plank across to her, creating a makeshift bridge for the girl to cross. *Neither Clarice nor Letty with their background in Vaudeville needed more than the ladder*, Gregory knew. He handed Letty up onto the plank. She crossed to Clarice. Gregory remained where he was to maintain the stability of the ladder bridge. He watched as Clarice tied a length of rope around Letty's waist then fashioned a safety type harness with it. Then Letty took the satchel of clothing, strapping it to her own back.

Gregory's heart beat in his throat. Everything seemed to take so long. Clarice helped Letty lower herself down one floor to the window they decided was Margaretta's bedroom. At one point, Gregory heard the rope straining under Letty's weight and his heart skipped. He held his breath.

Clarice paused her hand over hand release of the rope, hissing "Are you secure?"

"Keep going," Letty whispered back, her feet dangling.

Clarice began lowering the rope again. Letty's feet tapped softly against the steel ledge that fed into the fire escape system. Once she was confident in her balance, Letty worked at the window. When it resisted her efforts, she pulled a small file from a pocket in her skirt, wiggling her file between the sill and window. Finally, it gave and Letty eased the window upward, sliding it open. She pulled aside dark fabric window covering; so, light from street lamps below might enter the room and Gregory could watch, coming to their aid if needed.

Gregory watched as Letty gently shook the sleeping child awake. The girl seemed confused and frightened, flailing at Letty with her arms and fists. She talked and shook her head. But Letty told her something, and the child smiled. Margaretta climbed out of bed, disappearing out of sight. When she returned, Margaretta had exchanged her white shift for Harrison's old, faded blue shirt, and tweed jacket, and Gregory's last pair of short pants, which hung loosely around her ankles. He hoped she could wear that old pair of shoes Clarice brought. Margaretta couldn't go barefoot. Their clean sneak depended on not taking anything away with them, nor leaving anything behind. As he watched, Letty gathered up Margaretta's long, thick curls, twisting them up and self-tying them into a top knot. Letty covered it completely with the brown newsboy cap, transforming Margaretta into what appeared to be a nine-year-old boy.

Gregory had to smile to himself. *No one would recognize her now.* The window raised even further, and Letty handed Margaretta out onto the open metal mesh. Her borrowed shoes must have been too large because the little girl's feet scrabbled against the stone wall of the building. She mistakenly glanced down and turned bone white. However, Letty nimbly scrambled out beside her, using one arm across Margaretta's back as a stabilizer. With her other hand, Letty quietly closed the window.

"Clarice," Letty hissed.

Clarice leaned forward over the cornice of the roof. "I'm here." She lowered another length of rope which she had fashioned into another makeshift harness. Letty caught it, fitted it onto Margaretta, then tugged it gently once. Letty helped hold Margaretta steady, while Clarice pulled hand over hand, hauling the precious load upward toward the roof. Gregory pitied her since Margaretta seemed to fear heights. Clarice, being cautious, hoisted more slowly than she had lowered Letty, which caused the little girl to spin in the air. When Letty's hands could no longer touch Margaretta's shoe covered toes, Letty stealthily headed down the open, metal, fire stairs leading to the darkness of the alley below them. As Letty disappeared from sight, Clarice got an arm around Margaretta, lifting the small girl over the cornice and onto the roof with a quiet huff.

Gregory returned to the bridge, holding the plank steady against the sandstone. Clarice brought Margaretta over to the roof's edge across from where Gregory stood. He could hear Margaretta whispering, "I have to cross that?"

"Have they offered you better?" Clarice asked with an arched brow.

Margaretta shook her head violently.

"Careful," Clarice chided softly, "don't displace the hat."

"Oh," Margaretta covered her mouth with a hand.

"You go ahead," Clarice said. "I'll be right behind you. Now, everything will be Jake. Go hands and knees, if that's easier."

That's what Margaretta did. Clarice helped her to the plank, and Margaretta crossed on hands and knees. When she reached the center of the board, a gust of wind must have hit her because Margaretta shifted her weight to the left and Gregory gasped as he felt the board tilt. He pressed with more body weight on his right side, attempting to stabilize the plank. Clarice, also, worked at steadying the board on her side. She shot Gregory a terrified, wide eyed look. Gregory placed his right knee up on the board as a counterweight, reaching out toward Margaretta's shoulders.

"You've got this," he whispered to Margaretta. "Just a little further now."

Staring into Gregory's face, Margaretta lifted one hand, then another before sliding her right knee forward. With a sigh, Gregory's fingers brushed Margaretta's shoulders. Feeling him connect, she launched herself into his arms, crying silently. Gregory lowered her to the roof, her small frame even lighter than he imagined. He reached for the rope harness, and nimbly untied Clarice's knots.

After the rope slipped free of Margaretta, Gregory collected it, looping its length over one shoulder.

"Swell," Clarise said praising Margaretta, as she started across their makeshift bridge. Unlike Margaretta, Clarice moved as if she were on a garden path, rather than four stories above South Wabash Avenue. Once at his side, Clarice freed the ladder from the pipes where Gregory had secured it. Gregory collected the plank and ladder, hoisting them over the shoulder protected by the coiled rope. Clarice reached over and took Margaretta's hand, giving it a slight squeeze.

She nodded at Gregory, who nodded back before the three of them carefully descended the metal fire stairs into the darkness of the alley. Clarice stopped suddenly as they approached the bottom.

"The steps don't reach all the way to the street," she told them.

Gregory slowly edged past Clarice, and lowered their ladder from the bottom step to the brick surface below. "I'll hold it steady. You go first, Clarice and catch Margaretta. I'll follow after."

Gripping wood smoothed from long use, Clarice quickly descended rung to rung, almost gliding to the ground. She held up her arms, beckoning to Margaretta, who cautiously lowered herself to Clarice. The woman clasped the little girl to her side as Gregory joined them. He pressed the plank back against the ladder and shouldered both. The sun was just beginning to brighten the far horizon as they peeked out into Wabash Avenue. The hum of car tires running over brick had gotten louder and more frequent.

"We haven't much time," Gregory told Clarice. "Letty will be at the truck by now."

"Let's skiddo," Clarise said, making Margaretta giggle.

As before, they walked briskly across the street and over to 21st where they headed past Michigan Avenue. Traffic had begun to increase, and on to Indiana where Letty stood by the truck, peddlers were beginning to hawk wares. Gregory secured the ladder and plank in the back, using some of the rope while the rest he simply tossed into the truck bed.

"Do you think we four will fit inside?" Gregory asked.

"Long enough for you to drive us to a street car stop some miles from here," Clarice offered.

"Pile in," Gregory said, setting the clutch through the window before cranking the engine. The two women squeezed into the passenger seat, Letty folding Margaretta onto her lap like an oversized pretzel. The girl's head, bent at an odd angle looked very uncomfortable. He got behind the wheel, sitting slightly displaced himself to give the women more space.

"Here," Clarice said, when they had gotten to a street car stop in The Loop, five or six miles away from the *Four Deuces* along Michigan Avenue at Adams Street. "This will work."

Gregory pulled over to the curb, letting Clarice, Margaretta, and Letty spill out into the press of morning pedestrians. They waved before each gripping Margaretta by a hand, directing her to the streetcar stop where early morning workers were already bustling. In the distance, Gregory could hear the car approaching. Already, those wanting to ride began lining up. *They would not have to wait long. It was safest if no one saw them together.* He drove off. Gregory knew they would all breathe easier once they had Margaretta at the farm. He sighed. Then, they all could get some sleep.

16

Clarice and Letty bustled their child onto the streetcar, cramming in with thirty or more others rushing to work. Margaretta's eyes grew wider and wider as she encountered a broader variety of people than she ever had before in her short life. Clarice could tell the gal wanted to ask millions of questions and respected her restraint. *There would be time to share and explore the world – later*.

Three stops further along the route, just in the northern part of The Loop, a tall, coarse man in a dark three-piece silk suit leapt up onto the back of the street car. His large nose, rounded cheeks, and thatch of dark brown hair sent shivers up Clarice's spine. She leaned around the car's support pole, where they stood amid passengers, to whisper in Letty's ear.

"Keep your peepers on my face, darling," she hissed, a warning in her deep voice.

Letty turned her head slightly, in order to better see Clarice. A moue formed on her lips.

"At the back of the car, near the doors," Clarice continued. "That hood is Jack McGurn."

Letty's blood drained from her cheeks. Her gray eyes widened. "What'll we do?" she whispered back. Letty glanced down at Margaretta, who sensing their fear, ducked down, making herself seem even smaller. Letty's hand tightened over the girl's. "We can't just breeze. It'll call attention to us – trying to cut through this bunch. He'll make us."

Above them, the streetcar bell dinged and the car pulled to a stop. Passengers around Clarice, Letty, and Margaretta pushed and shoved their way through the press to reach the exit. Others, who had been waiting, joined the crush inside the car.

On the street nearby, a peddler, hawking scrap paper and rags, shouted "Buy ya paper, buy ya paper." The older man, dressed in worn dark wool of an indistinct color, turned his attention to McGurn, who had been standing near the back rail of the car. "What flimflam you running now? I'll drop the dime on you, just wait and see."

McGurn jumped down, out of the car, rushing the man. Before anyone could say a word, he had his gun out.

Letty gasped.

Clarice pressed Margaretta's face deep into her middle, preventing her from seeing.

"That palooka gives me the heebie-jeebies. Is he gonna croak him?" Letty hissed.

"Naw!" Clarice barked, but nodded, wishing she could free the hand gripping the pole and hug Margaretta even tighter.

But instead of shooting, McGurn raised his pistol, bringing its butt down hard on the peddler's forehead. Blood trickled out of a large gash in his skin, sticking to his face. McGurn struck again, the blow sounding like an exploding melon. This time the old man crumpled to his knees, with an agonized cry.

"We can't help him," Clarice said, quickly. "Come on, let's go." Her heart raced, and she had never been so glad she hadn't eaten much that morning. *They had to get the child out of there.*

While other passengers stared at McGurn, who now was berating the peddler, Clarice and Letty dragged Margaretta forward through the crush of passengers toward the front exit. They no longer cared if they made a stir because their efforts detracted very little from the drama taking place in the street. Their mutterings of "Excuse me," often won them ugly looks and nasty words. One man who smelled like bad whiskey and cigarettes made a crude remark, but neither Clarice nor Letty cared. They forced their way through. Once they got out of the streetcar, Clarice pulled them off down the street.

"The cops are sure to come, and we don't want to be anywhere nearby," Clarice told Letty. *They had enough on their plate.* "Let's find a hack to drive us back home."

"I'm with you," Letty agreed, breathlessly. "We can't get there soon enough for me."

Gregory paced back and forth in the front parlor, waiting for Clarice, Letty and Margaretta to get home. Several hours after he, himself, had made it back, they burst through the door. He caught each one by the arms, squeezing them with joy. Relief flooding through him. "I was so worried about you three."

"Rightly so," Clarice said. She summarized their adventure, ending with the nice driver of the cab, who promised to get them home as fast as he could. "It was pure luck stumbling on that hack, or we might still be out there in the City."

"We are exhausted." Letty added, rooting around the boxes in the front parlor, looking for a cigarette.

"And hungry," Margaretta pipped up.

"You poor child," Gregory said, by way of apology, waving the three toward the kitchen downstairs. Clarice led the way, followed by Margaretta. Gregory glanced back at Letty, who had grabbed several cigarettes from a box near the hearth and a lighter from her handbag. She hustled after the others, tilting her head at Gregory's raised eyebrow.

"It helps me relax," she said with a slow smile before catching up with Clarice.

While Clarice, Letty, and Margaretta made themselves comfortable around the rectangular oak table, Gregory gathered up some smoked ham, thick slices of bread, and butter from the cook's larder. He placed the small platters on the table and gave each woman a plate. "Do you want to fix Margaretta something?" Gregory asked Clarice, looking rather innocent with his large hazel eyes.

I can see what Irene finds pleasing, Clarice thought to herself.

"I am very well able to make up my own plate," Margaretta piped up with spirit.

"Down gal," Clarice laughed. "Here," she said, putting her own empty china in front of the girl. Holding out a hand, she snapped her fingers for Gregory to give her the third plate, which he did. *Was he a little jumpy?* Letty and Margaretta began taking bites of ham and the brown, molasses bread, between sips of tea cook already had on hand. Letty also found an ash tray, adding puffs from her gasper to her rotation of bites and sips. Clarice lifted her own cup, allowing the comforting scent to sooth her jangled nerves.

"I'm glad you are all here," Gregory began, his hands clasped over the table top.

"We are too," Letty chimed in, before taking a drag. She had cupped her right cheek in her right hand, all the better to smoke with the least movement. Most of her food had disappeared from her plate, and Clarice could tell how exhausted Letty was from the way her eyelids were beginning to droop.

"I was wondering if the three of you would come to tonight's séance?" Gregory spoke softly.

Almost as if he were suddenly shy – uncharacteristic of the man she knew, thought Clarice. She set aside her fork, sitting straighter against the wooden chair. "Ok. Give us all the crop."

Gregory held up his palms in surrender. "It's another special séance. At least, I am hoping it will be, especially for Margaretta."

"You're not planning on giving her the heebie jeebies, are you?" Letty asked, a warning in her voice.

Gregory shook his head. "Absolutely not."

"Then, of course, we'll come." Clarice relaxed. "The usual time?"

He nodded. "Back parlor. Eight p.m. sharp." Gregory rose to leave. "I'll leave you gals to your own devices. I'm sure you are quite done in."

"Later alligator," Letty began, her gray eyes glittering with humor.

Gregory waved over his shoulder, saying softly under his laughter, "After while crocodile." His shoulders twitched until he turned the corner and disappeared into the house.

Clarice turned back to Letty and Margaretta. "We need to find suitable clothing."

"I like these," Margaretta said. "Very liberating."

"I suppose they are fine for the moment, but if you are going to be our daughter, you are going to be the cat's meow, not what the cat dragged in." She laughed, softening her pronouncement. *How could she deny Margaretta the comfort of male clothes if she herself wore them?* Clarice gave a little shake of her head to clear it. *Something to be decided in future – not today.*

"Let's get these things cleaned up and go into the attic," Letty said, raising from her chair. "There's more clothing up there to choose from." On her way to the huge metal sink, Letty rubbed a hand along Margaretta's back. The girl scrambled up after her, grabbing up her plate, cup, and silverware.

Carlo watched his mother collect the tableware and head for their small cluttered sink. He headed for the portion of the flat he shared with his brothers, reaching for the armoire and grabbing his suits. He placed them carefully on the closest bed, then retrieved his under clothing, socks, and ties from his drawer in the chest against the far wall. When he had his things collected, he pulled down the attic storage stairs. Amid the dust and debris, he saw it – his father's old traveling valise. Carefully, he dragged the leather case out of the crowded cramped space, plunking it down the ladder into the bedroom. A cloud of dust plumed into the room.

"Damn!" Carlo cursed. He took a towel from the wash basin and rubbed the brown leather until it gleamed. Looking at the towel, Carlo frowned. It had turned black and grimy. He shrugged. *What could I do?* He carefully folded his suits into the valise, covered them with the divider, then packed his underclothing, socks, shirts, ties, and cuff links. Toiletries went into the zipper compartments in the divider and the underside of the leather lid. Carlo glanced around the crowded bedroom with its cot like beds covering the floor and the dressers against the walls.

"I'll be glad to be away," he said to himself. He thought about life with Teddy at his flat and warmth suffused his body, energizing him. Leaving the locked, packed trunk on his cot, Carlo walked out of the room. Teddy and he would come for the trunk later with the Rambler. *Getting that trunk onto a street car – horse feathers. It'd be easier to find a flying pig.* He laughed.

"I'm happy to see that million-dollar smile," his mother said, glancing over at him from the sink.

Carlo swept his heavy-set mother into a hug, before pecking a kiss to her round cheek. "Later, Mama," He saluted her with two fingers, gathered up his best overcoat and newsboy cap, before heading out the door.

He strode down the sidewalk packed with pedestrians, peddlers, and other traffic. Stalls of fresh meats, fish, flowers, fruit, and other wares created competing smells with the exhaust from the motor cars, horse drawn vehicles, and nearby industry. Carlo hopped up on a streetcar heading for the Loop. He planned on eating at the Green Mill before meeting up with Teddy, who had been summoned by his cousin Bugs Moran. Even though the car was packed, and Carlo was pressed between two businessmen, his thoughts carried him far away.

Various futures with Teddy spiraled outward before his eyes, each happier and more outrageous than the last. His attention so rapt, Carlo almost missed his stop.

He exited the street car in a hurry, walking the few blocks to the white stone building that housed the now famous Green Mill. Opening the doors, noise from talk and laughter within blasted Carlo with an almost physical blow. He allowed his eyes to adjust to the low light inside the deep brownish-red wood paneled interior. An empty spot at the bar beckoned him. He wasn't interested in sitting in one of the booths anyway and certainly had no desire to run into Capone, who frequently sat in a booth near the back. Carlo pushed his way through the patrons seated at tables between himself and the bar, then flicked back his suit jacket before taking the bar stool.

"Roast sandwich," he told the tall, balding barman, "and a seltzer."

The man tossed his cleaning cloth over his right shoulder and nodded. He disappeared for a moment, returning to draw the seltzer, handing the tall glass of fizzy water to Carlo, who had settled and waited for his food. Carlo took his drink, sipping carefully. Bubbles tickled his nose.

Men at the next table guffawed loudly. "I'm telling ya," the smaller of the two said, "those Irish mooks better watch their backs."

The larger of the men, rubbed his bulbous nose, and replied, "Capone wants to rub-em all out. Every hatchet man I know is gunning for them."

"Here ya go." The bar man placed a hot sandwich in front of Carlo, steam curling from under the thick bread and delicious smells of onions, roasted beef, and mustard hit Carlo full in the face. Carlo nodded his thanks, grabbing up the food with both hands, glad his napkin already covered his lap. While the sandwich tasted divine, Carlo couldn't help thinking about what the men had said. *Teddy was an Irish mook—not to* him *of course, but to* them. He had scarcely finished and wiped his greasy hands off on the white cloth napkin, when Carlo heard a stir beyond the bar.

Jack McGurn, Carlo recognized the voice, owner of the Green Mill and underboss to Capone, gave a shout of laughter. Another man – not Capone, more likely John Scalise, made a retort. McGurn came around the end of the bar, looked around the room. His eyes landed on Carlo, who unconsciously hunkered down further over his empty plate. Normally, he would not have been afraid, but after those comments, his thoughts felt guilty.

"You," McGurn shouted.

Carlo tapped his chest with a forefinger, not risking a word that might offend him.

McGurn towered over Carlo, who could smell the onions he had for lunch. "Yes, you, Sicilian." His cheeks were flushed. "You'd better watch where you step, see? Put one toe over the line, and we'll cut it off, you savvy?"

Carlo gulped and nodded. *His family was in danger, too!*

Warning delivered, McGurn turned and headed off into the back.

Hastily, Carlo pushed his three bits across the bar to the barman and practically ran for the street.

Across the City with Broad Shoulders, not that far from the florist shop once owned by Deanie O'Banion, Teddy O'Hannilon hastened to a meeting with his cousin George Bugs Moran. Since Carlo could not accompany him, the Sicilian returned to his family flat to pack some of his clothes. Teddy smiled as he recalled the huge valise Carlo wanted to bring with him, the one almost the same size as a steamer trunk.

"One has to make sacrifices," Carlo had said, "to be snorky."

What could Moran want now? Teddy worried. He brought the butt of his cigarette to his mouth, taking a drag with each step as he entered the ritzy area near the Parkway Hotel where his cousin had his flat. *Lincoln Park West was a swanky address.* The

Parkway offered his cousin many amenities, while being close to the heart of the city. Teddy looked skyward, up the twelve brick stories to the penthouse. While the first two floors shared what looked like huge arched windows, from the outside, the rest of the stories all had single windows, until one looked at the corniced top floor. *Moran, naturally, would want to live on the best, fanciest, floor*.

Teddy pushed his way through the large brass and glass doors into the cool marble floored lobby and strode around the half-circular, cream colored couches dotting the open flooring. At this time of day, early afternoon, clusters of guests waited to check in or out. Teddy didn't need to speak with a desk clerk. He knew his way up to the elevators and his cousin's flat. The elevator operator cranked the folding metal doors shut before sending them up to the top floor.

Bing! The operator snapped the doors open. As Teddy walked out into the wide hallway, he left behind the odor of stale cigarette and cigar smoke. The carpet under his expensive Italian leather shoes felt soft and thick; the red, yellow, and black strands forming exotic patterns. Knocking on Moran's door, Teddy wondered which goon would answer. He took out a new cigarette, lighting it with the last remaining ashes of the last one.

Finally, Lefty Stiles responded to Teddy's summons. As hatchet men went, Lefty was a decent sort. He greeted Teddy like a prodigal son, leading him deep into the rooms of the flat. Teddy glanced around at the art work on the white walls and the sparse furniture. He couldn't be certain if his cousin had added anything or not when Morgan grabbed him up into a bear hug.

"Teddy. Good to see ya." Moran's round cheeks pulled upwards into a broad smile over his small, dimpled chin. Since Teddy had last seen him, his cousin's hairline had slightly receded, especially on the right side where he wore his part. Moran's fleshy nose had the beginnings of tiny veins showing, probably from drinking, but his wide set eyes still glittered with good humor – for Teddy, more likely with craziness for anyone else.

Teddy gasped a greeting, glad when his cousin released his bear hug. He took a drag on his cigarette to calm his nerves.

"I wanted to chin with you," Moran began, his large hand spanning Teddy's back just below the shoulder. He directed Teddy into a sitting room, furnished in a modern style. Short, rounded arm chairs faced each other while an RCA radio set sat in an alcove built into the wall near the door. After Teddy folded himself into a chair, cigarette trailing smoke in a lazy curl, Moran began pacing. "What did that palooka say about Capone and Belmont-Sheffield Bank?"

Palooka, Capone? Belmont... Oh. "They were depositing gold bars every week," Teddy replied, blinking. So much had happened since that day at Woolworth's, he had forgotten.

His cousin rounded on him, pointing. "Exactly. And, what are *we* gonna do?"

Teddy crossed his legs and tapped his long fingers against his knee – waiting.

"We're going take it – take it all," Moran said almost calmly. "What fantastic revenge. Get him and his riches."

"I see," Teddy said so softly, he could scarcely hear himself. He raised the cigarette to his mouth and puffed.

"I want you to have dibs," Moran continued. "Maybe your pal Harrison Davenport, too. You both could use extra kale, you savvy?"

Teddy uncrossed his legs. Things were going so well with Carlo. He really didn't want to fall into his cousin's schemes – not now. "Can I talk it over with Harrison?"

"You do that. But cousin, don't take too long. We're talking millions here." Moran's eyes sparkled. "My guys won't hold off for long. They like it that we are launching a full war against those dirty palookas. None of 'em are safe."

Teddy gulped then nodded. He levered himself up out of the narrow arm chair with both hands, pinching the cigarette out with his fingers. "I'll let you know."

"You do that," Moran said, more gruffly, holding out his meaty hand for Teddy to shake.

Teddy gave his cousin's hand one good pump before, calmly as he could, he turned and walked to the front door. "Thanks, cousin George," he said a little louder, before letting himself out.

Carlo wouldn't want him to participate in any robbery against Capone. Not that Carlo felt any love for the mob boss, but such a robbery definitely would set Capone against us. I need to talk this over with Harrison and Gregory – that's what I need to do, he thought as he raced toward the street car.

17

Gregory knew the back parlor was as ready as possible for the séance tonight, but he headed back just to check the armoire one more time. Just as he turned the corner around the stairwell from the second-floor landing, he saw his brother Harrison coming in from the foyer.

"Gregory! Just the one I wanted to see," Harrison hailed him. His brother's voice sounded excited matching the energy causing him to bounce on his feet. Harrison stuck one arm through the crook of Gregory's own practically dragging him down the hallway into the tiny dark office which had served their father. It was now a tradesman's parlor. The place they hung their extra overcoats and hid their rubber shoe covers. Leaving Gregory's side, Harrison darted around the tiny space, checking lamps to switch on those that worked. The two which did cast a dull, yellow light over the small, dusty desk with its upright wooden chair and the bookcase with filing cabinet still containing old farm documents. Harrison turned to face him, resting his behind on the edge of their father's desk. He crossed his arms in front of his chest.

"You'll never guess where I was." Harrison's blue eyes glittered and his cheek dimpled.

"You got me," Gregory chuckled. Subconsciously, he mimicked his brother's stance, crossing his own arms.

"A really strange guy named Pickle Dooley," Harrison laughed, showing his straight, white teeth. He held up a palm, staving off any remarks. "He's a precious metals dealer. My stockbroker Stick MacBride set it all up." Harrison stared at Gregory. He tsked. "Don't you savvy? I sold the stocks—all but three – so almost everything we have sunk our kale into. I bought gold bars with as much as I could and the rest is in silver. Just like you asked me to."

Gregory stood tall, dropping his defensive posture. "Harrison, that's wonderful news!" He rushed to his brother's side, gripping Harrison's biceps in brotherly affection. "Come December, we'll celebrate again, but for now – everything's copacetic." Joy rushed through Gregory. He renewed his clasp on his brother and began dancing them around the room.

"Don't go off the track or I might regret my decision." Harrison allowed Gregory his antics for about 30 more seconds before pushing him away. "Stick was worried but since I kept Electric Power and Light, Cocoa-cola, and Standard Oil, our very best and most stable stocks, he went along."

Gregory relaxed, idly fingering a porcelain figure on the shelf of his father's bookcase. "With this investment, we will be protected," he said, softly. "You needn't accept anyone's offer to do a bank job."

Harrison stared at him as if Gregory were crazy, but the look vanished as Harrison shrugged. "Guess that slug grazing your noggin did more damage than I thought," he mumbled. "Just what are you talking about?"

Gregory fixed his brother with a glare, then glanced away. "I'm saying if Teddy or Moran come to you with a tempting box job involving Capone's bank, don't do it."

"Job? What job?" Harrison sounded incredulous. "I'm not risking anything right now even if Deanie's ghost came back and asked me to take one. When those bricks and bars come, I'm gonna put them deep with our best hooch. You follow? Everything we own will be tied up with this farm. I am not willing to lose any of it. What about you?"

"I am copacetic, brother." Gregory felt as if his grin were splitting his face. He held up a palm in surrender. *He wouldn't bother Harrison again unless his brother decided to do something stupid. Would that be enough to save him?* Gregory hoped so.

"Let's go. The rats and mice crowd come in early today," Harrison said, holding his arm out in invitation to leave the office.

"Clarice and Letty are coming to the séance tonight. They won't be there as help with the dice table during that time," Gregory told him.

"Fine. I'll see to it myself." Harrison turned off the lamps and urged Gregory forward.

Gregory lifted an eyebrow.

Harrison mimicked Gregory's earlier gesture of surrender. "Won't join in either. On our parents' graves."

Gregory's smile earned one from Harrison as he walked down the steps to *The Hair of the Dog Club*. Gregory returned to his third-floor rooms, taking out his purple smoking jacket and gray trousers for the séance. He shot the cuffs on his crème silk shirt before hefting the smoking jacket over his shoulders. His gray trousers rode loosely over his hips, leaving plenty of room for tools needed in the past to replicate ghosts' knocking, or making other noises. *Please Lord,* he prayed, *let Melody Anselmo appear tonight.* Finally, he adjusted his silk tie at his collar, smoothing the shirt over it and making certain the knot looked presentable. When he was satisfied with his reflection, Gregory headed on downstairs to the back parlor.

Klein, dressed in his black, three-piece suit and white shirt, was already in the parlor, moving the chairs, and adjusting the crystal ball on the table. "Darryl and Mrs. Kempt, Nancy and Ned Thompson, Councilman and Irene O'Brien are among your participants tonight."

"Clarice, Letty, a young girl, Teddy, and Carlo will also be attending," Gregory told him.

"I will bring in another chair," Klein said, rushing off and appearing moments later with the heavy chair. He placed it far from Gregory's place near the armoire. "Hopefully no one will inquire into politics," Klein commented, indicating a list of attendees.

Gregory nodded. The names on the page he scanned reflected a high number of people connected with politicians or political agendas. The Thompson's were relatives of Mayor Thompson. Kempt, and his similarly overweight spouse, belonged to the poultry union. O'Brien was a councilman, but he most likely wanted to contact Geoff. He hadn't realized Irene was to be included tonight. *Maybe she must be in order for Melody to appear.*

Klein filed the attendees into the parlor, showing them to the places Gregory wanted them to sit. He would bring refreshments if required as well. However, his main duties were to watch the lights, collect wraps, and lend assistance if a guest needed to leave suddenly. While people took their seats amid quiet chatter, Gregory went around the room, lighting candles.

"Ladies and gentlemen, please finish taking your seats so we may begin," Gregory announced, standing at his place in the circle. *Where were Teddy and Carlo?* he wondered, glancing around the parlor.

Klein hustled Clarice, Letty, and Margaretta into the vacant three chairs at Gregory's left, putting the little girl in the seat between those of the women. Somehow Clarice and Letty had found more suitable attire for her. She was dressed in a simple pale-yellow frock belted at the waist. Gregory couldn't tell if she was excited to be out among adults, or if the prospect of the séance frightened her.

Councilman and Irene O'Brien approached Gregory's right. He smiled at them and noted Irene wore an outfit he hadn't seen before. Her frock – a red chiffon drop-waisted dress, consisting of three flounces decorated with increasingly smaller scalloped hemlines, had narrow shoulder straps held together by large beetle shaped buttons. Around her long, white throat a wide matching scarf was wound twice, covering her soft, alabaster bosom exposed by the deep, boat neckline.

Behind her, long tails of the scarf fluttered along her back with every movement. In place of pearls, Irene wore a necklace of fine, golden rope, the tassel at the end serving as focal point. He watched her closely as her father assisted her with her chair, handing her fox collared coat to Klein. Heart thrumming in his chest, Gregory reminded himself, *tonight was about Margaretta, not Irene; although Geoff might reappear. She was so very lovely.* He almost sighed out loud.

Once they all had been seated, Gregory took a clearing breath. "Please clasp the hands of the individuals seated on either side of you, and remain as quiet as you can. We will attempt to communicate with the spirits tonight, as we do at all seances here." Gregory scanned the faces of the participants, noting Nan Thompson and Margaretta's paleness. "Klein, lights if you please."

Klein dimmed the lights, casting the room into deep shadows thrown by the flickering candles. Mrs. Kempt coughed behind her handkerchief. Ned Thompson, the mayor's cousin, sneezed. Margaretta shuffled her feet beneath the table. Gregory held up his hand, palm out. Everyone settled. A slight movement by Klein momentarily stopped Gregory from beginning. Over by the door, Teddy and Carlo had silently crept in.

"Spirits, we seek you. We need your counsel. Please come to us," Gregory intoned in his deepest voice. He waited several heart beats, then began reaching for a button connected to the knockers under the table, but before he could push any button, the room's temperature dropped, and there was no need. Irene, on his right, shivered in her thin, sleeveless dress.

"Geoff O'Brien? Have you returned to speak to your sister and father?" Gregory's throat started closing up, tightening. He felt as if he were shrinking in stature, even though physically that was not possible. "Melody Anselmo, sweet –" Gregory wanted to say child, but his voice and body were no longer merely his own.

"How do you know me?" a childlike, soprano voice came out of his throat.

"I have brought---" Gregory rasped, but was a passenger in his own body unable to tell Melody what he had planned.

"I am Melody – Marietta Anselmo, cousin to the Genna brothers," her tears joined her sobs.

"Sister," Margaretta called out. She tried to jump up from her chair, but Clarice and Letty held her in place. "That's my sister. I must help her."

"Margaretta?" Melody asked, shock in her voice. "Are you here with me?"

"Yes, yes! I am. I am." Margaretta strained toward Gregory.

"Oh, my dearest, dearest girl. Are you..." Melody hesitated, her voice hoarse, "free?"

"They helped me. I've gotten away, far away, as you could not," Margaretta told her sister. Tears filled her brown eyes, finally spilling over and running down her cheeks.

"I might have come seeking revenge," Melody told them, "but I did not. I had come to beg for my sister's liberation, that she might avoid my horrible fate."

"We'll punish them," Margaretta growled.

"No. No, dearest, sister. My fondest wish for you is granted." Melody's happiness seemed to make the candle light brighter. "Be free to make your own choices. Be safe."

"I will," Margaretta swore.

"Promise me," Melody demanded.

"We will protect her," Clarice and Letty said in unison. They squeezed Margaretta's hands.

"I love you, Margaretta." Melody's voice was beginning to wane. "Never forget."

Margaretta sniffled. "I love you too! I'll remember always!"

Gregory's head fell forward onto the table as Melody Anselmo, finding peace at last, departed. Beside him Clarice soothed the crying little girl. Further around the table, Gregory could hear the sibilant noise of whispered conversations.

"That poor child," from Mrs. Kempt, frown lines deepening on her forehead.

"Wonder what happened to her?" questioned Mr. Thompson, who leaned toward Margaretta.

"I hadn't heard her voice for six years. We had been kidnapped together. She always protected me." Margaretta hiccupped. "I always wished I could have saved her."

"Wasn't anything you could have done, child," Letty said. "You weren't much more than a baby."

"She doesn't blame me. She just wanted me to be out of that horrible place." Margaretta pulled her hand and Letty's closer to her eyes to rub away the tears.

"She'll move on now to a better place," Clarice said softly, looking over at Gregory with admiration and kindness in her expression.

Gregory cleared his throat, finding it slightly rough. He coughed. "If we can settle the room, we can try and communicate with another spirit." The whispering stopped.

"Spirits," Gregory intoned again. He felt the invasion, violent takeover of his body. A familiar laugh rang out into the room from his throat. His cousin Deanie's laugh.

"So, me boyo," Deanie chuckled. "You been wanting to have a chin?"

"Deanie O'Banion?" It was Douglas O'Brien. "Did you know my boy Geoff was murdered by those bastard South Siders?"

Gregory shifted his head to face O'Brien. "Was he now? Then he's another we'll be needing vengeance for, but *you're* not to do it. Nor my cousins Harrison and Gregory. Not those innocent lives. NO!" Deanie shouted and banged Gregory's fist on the table. "I want Bugsy to do it. George Bugs Moran. He's the one tasked with vengeance."

"But, Deanie," O'Brien tried to protest, his face beginning to redden with anger. "Geoff—"

"I said none but Moran." Deanie laughed but this time his normal voice sounded mangled, a horrible twisted version of his once sweet tenor. "That crazy son-of-a bitch, Moran is just slippery enough to get my revenge and not be touched by those bastards. He can do it and live to tell the tale. God love him!" Deanie shouted, and he was gone.

Gregory felt completely drained of energy. His cousin's spirit had been a force of nature, sapping him dry. Releasing Clarice's and Irene's hands, Gregory rubbed his temples. "Lights, Klein. That's all tonight. Please return in a few days, and we'll see if we can't find other beloved departed."

After the lights came up, chatter in the room became intolerable for Gregory. The Thompsons demanded that their grandfather be amongst the spirits summoned at the next séance. Kempt and his wife raised questions about Melody–who had taken her and where. He wanted to go to his own rooms and rest. Even his desire to visit with Irene was not enough to hold him.

"Irene," Gregory began, taking up her left hand.

"Gregory," she said almost at the same time.

"You first," he said.

She looked down at her beige pumps. "I should go with Father. He needs comforting after what Deanie O'Banion said tonight."

"Yes. He needs you," Gregory whispered, turning her hand over in his. *He hoped she could not sense his relief.* "We can go dancing again tomorrow – I'll call you at your flat?"

"Swell. That would be Jake," Irene said, smiling up into Gregory's eyes.

He raised her hand to his lips, then released it. She slipped her arm through her father's, as Klein gave O'Brien their overcoats, and her father bundled them both out the door.

Clarice and Letty, whose arm hung loosely over Margaretta's shoulder, said good night. Clarice gave him her now familiar, "we'll talk later," look before the three followed the O'Briens out into the hallway. They understood and, besides, had Margaretta to comfort. Near the door to the hallway, Teddy and Carlo stood, a shared haunted expression on their faces. Gregory shook hands mindlessly as Klein made certain each wrap went to its owner. He made his way over to the door. Grasping Teddy's upper arm, Gregory tugged gently. Both Teddy and Carlo sidled further from the threshold, allowing other patrons space to leave. Gregory drew closer to them, blocking them from prying eyes with his body.

"I can tell from your faces we need to talk," Gregory began.

Both Carlo and Teddy nodded.

"Since you were here at tonight's séance, I know you'll understand why postponing until tomorrow will work best?" Gregory's expression took on an earnestness he wanted them to see.

"That's just copacetic," Teddy replied, a hint of sarcasm in his tone. He slid a protective arm around Carlo's waist.

Gregory noticed the brief flicker of disappointment that passed over Teddy's chiseled features. "Look – don't go back to your flat. Stay here – that same set of rooms on the second floor. You can stay as long as you'd like. Please. I'm all fagged out, couldn't really hear what you want to tell me tonight. I promise I'll be all yours first thing in the morning."

A broad grin spread first across Carlo's face and then Teddy's as if the sun were rising. "Sure," Teddy said, mollified.

"Berries," Carlo added. He looked lovingly at Teddy.

Capturing Carlo's gaze with his own, Teddy said softly, "We know the way."

Gregory's entire body relaxed as the two men turned and headed up the hall leading to the staircase. "Klein –"

"Don't fret, I've got this," Klein cut in. "Go rest."

Gregory nodded and gave a quick wave of thanks before he headed for his own rooms on the third floor.

18

Teddy and Carlo dressed quickly after jumping out of bed around nine the next morning. Teddy shrugged into his black silk suit, while Carlo grabbed his houndstooth vest and trousers, stepping into his pantlegs as he walked around the room. Neither spent their normal amount of time facing their small dressing mirror, before mounting the steps to the third floor. Teddy rapped on Gregory's bedroom door, knocking out the rhythm "pa, papa, pa, pa" so Gregory would know who wanted to see him. It was an old but popular code Teddy and Harrison shared as newsies. Teddy knew that Gregory would recognize it. He knocked again and waited.

"Thump, thump," the answering rhythm came from within. "Give me a minute, or five," Gregory sounded hoarse and sleepy. Teddy and Carlo could hear the whisper of silk against chair upholstery when Gregory grabbed his clothing, as well as the klunk, klunk of slippers against the wooden floor. Water splashed in a basin, then silence.

Carlo turned his large brown eyes to Teddy's. "He doesn't seem very awake. Maybe we should go back to our room?" Running a finger down Teddy's sleeve, Carlo smiled in that slow burning way he had, and Teddy's stomach filled with butterfly wings.

About to grab Carlo and drag him back to the second floor, Teddy remembered his cousin Moran's ardor about getting revenge on the Italians and his plan to rob Belmont-Sheffield bank. "We can't" Teddy shook his head. He pressed his forehead against Carlo's. A stray brown curl fell into Teddy's eyes. He used a forefinger to tuck the lose lock back behind Carlo's ear. "Remember why we're here?" he whispered.

"Yes," Carlo sighed. "I'm trying to forget."

Teddy kissed him quickly, stepping away. "We need to get past the mob bunk and decide on a plan. If we don't, we are easy marks from all sides."

Carlo's eyes widened as his fear from yesterday returned.

Gregory has to help us, Teddy thought. *This new, solid Gregory is the go-to man. He seems to have answers before everyone else, even Harrison.* That surprised Teddy because the Davenport boys, men, were younger than he, and previously seemed less experienced. That raid on the club had changed Gregory for certain. *That's no baloney.* Teddy knocked again.

Feeling rejuvenated, Gregory opened the door. "Morning, gents," he said with good humor. *Teddy and Carlo looked frazzled, unkempt, for them. Carlo, especially, had dark circles under his large brown eyes.* He looked the men up and down. Usually impeccably dressed, today, Carlo's houndstooth trousers, white shirt, and houndstooth vest looked wrinkled as if he'd slept in them. Teddy's black silk suit seemed fine, but his hair looked tousled. Instead of meeting Gregory's eyes with a defiant stare, Teddy's gaze roamed the hallway, lingering on Carlo with worry.

"Aren't you inviting us in?" Carlo finally asked.

Gregory shook himself out of his reverie, combing his right hand up over his forehead and through his hair. "Sorry. Of course, you are welcome to come in, but let's go down to the kitchen for some coffee.

I know cook has prepared cinnamon rolls," he smiled gently. "I'm starved."

"Sounds copacetic," Carlo said.

"The bee's knees," Teddy added, placing his left hand on Carlo's broad back, guiding the younger man toward the back stairs.

Sunlight filtered through the curtains hanging in the windows high on the wall of the kitchen opposite the metal sink. A pot of coffee steamed on the sideboard, while a plate of soft, sticky buns sat nearby. Gregory went and took three plates from the cupboard along with forks, setting them down on the table. Teddy and Carlo sat at two of the places, while Gregory grabbed newly washed coffee cups from the drainboard next to the sink.

"Joe?" he asked.

Teddy and Carlo nodded, subdued. When Gregory pointed to the cinnamon buns, the two men shook their heads.

After pouring out two cups, putting them in from of his friends, Gregory poured a cup of coffee for himself, breathing in the steamy, dark aroma. He turned towards Teddy and Carlo, who sipped cautiously. "All right," Gregory said. "Out with it."

"I overheard—" Carlo began.

"Cousin George—" Teddy started.

"First," Gregory pointed at Teddy, flicking his coat back behind him as he carefully slid into his chair. "Then, you," indicating Carlo.

Teddy straightened. He pulled a pack of cigarettes from his vest pocket, tapped one out, rolled it on the table top, before sticking the smoke between his lips. Replacing the box of *Lucky Strikes* into his pocket, he fumbled out his lighter and lit the cigarette. He took three deep drags, allowing smoke to filter out through his nostrils. "I saw Cousin George yesterday. He all but summoned me." Teddy took the cigarette out of his mouth, between two fingers and examined it. "He is planning a bank job. The Belmont-Sheffield bank, to be exact. He wants the North Side mob to steal gold bars from the vault." He returned the cigarette to the corner of his mouth, talking around it.

Gregory's stomach plummeted towards his feet. He almost dropped his porcelain cup.

Carlo set his coffee down, leaning forward across the table towards Gregory, "Tell him the worst part."

More smoke filtered from Teddy's nose. "His real plan is revenge on Capone, since the gold mostly belongs to him. It's all part of a new war against the Italians, targeting the South Side mob. He's got hatchet men already on payroll, ready to take out as many as possible." Teddy glanced furtively at Carlo.

"Capone won't take this laying down," Carlo picked up the story. "He started eliminating competition back in 1926. He croaked all Sicilians in power – first the Genna brothers, then the Anselmos, now the North Side leaders. You know all that," Carlo turned wide eyes to Gregory's face. "Yesterday, I heard from Jack McGurn that the boss is gunning for all North Side hoods—or anyone who might cross his path wrong. The Saint Valentine Day massacre this past February was only the beginning." Carlo shuddered, curling his hands around the coffee cup for warmth.

"Last night, Deanie O'Banion's ghost merely confirmed that a mob war is starting," Gregory concluded. "He practically said he has given his blessing to Moran."

"And we—" Teddy drew his cigarette away from his face, tracing a heart in the air with the glowing butt end.

"Are like star-crossed lovers with feuding parents," Gregory offered.

"I wouldn't go that far," Teddy said, his dark brown eyes narrowing. "But definitely threatened by both Italians and Irish alike." He tamped out his cigarette in an ashtray near his right elbow, then reached across to Carlo, taking the younger man's darker skinned hand into his own. "Any of them – all of them, seem to be gunning for the likes of us."

Gregory nodded. "I've been thinking about your jam."

Teddy and Carlo looked at him intently. Hope flared on their faces.

"I was thinking a long vacation in Germany, but then the economy there is terrible. So, Paris—Paris would be delightful, and Parisians are so accepting of different lifestyles. And-- you'd have no mob affiliations either for or against you," Gregory leaned back against the wooden slats of his chair. "Harrison, well Harrison and I, would be willing to lend assistance when or if you should need it, but were you both to travel to Paris, neither Capone nor Moran would remember you exist. You would be safe to –" Gregory waved his two hands in the air in front of them, "well, to be together and enjoy what life has to offer."

"Paris?" Teddy's eyes widened with surprise.

"Paris," Carlo whispered, delight sweeping over his features. He squeezed Teddy's hand.

"Then, you'll discuss it?" Gregory asked.

"Certainly," Teddy said, standing and pulling Carlo to his feet.

"That might solve everything," Carlo hissed into Teddy's ear, making Teddy and Gregory smile albeit each for his own reasons.

"By the way," Gregory stopped them at the door, "If Moran wants to rob the bank, you let him," he pointed at Teddy, "but *you* stay away."

"I never wanted to take him up on his offer," Teddy admitted. His shoulders seemed to relax as if relieved of a burden. He stubbed out his cigarette.

"That's swell," Gregory said. "That job is simply fraught with dangers and has very little pay off."

"I don't want any dibs. I don't want any part of it." Teddy told them. "I'm afraid to tell Cousin George, though, he ... he has a lot invested in this job."

"Paris?" Gregory raised an eyebrow. "With an ocean between you, he won't be able to reach you."

Teddy nodded, a smile beginning to twitch at the corners of his mouth.

"Paris," Carlo echoed dreamily.

Teddy all but dragged Carlo out of the kitchen toward the back steps and their room several floors above. Gregory could hear Teddy and Carlo offer a greeting before their footsteps faded away. In their place, Gregory heard the click-clacking of high heeled shoes and lighter weighted tread of men's leather soles. Clarice, dressed in a midi-blouse over brown worsted trousers, and Letty garbed in a large pocketed, blue and white, gingham dress, came around the corner of the hallway.

"Morning, gals," Gregory said with a grin, saluting them with his coffee cup. "May I offer you some cinnamon bun with your Joe?"

"We'll help ourselves," Letty replied, still giggling over something Clarice had told her. She collected two plates, used silver tongs to place a sticky bun on each one then passed a plate to Clarice, who had poured two cups of coffee.

Once they had settled into the chairs previously occupied by Teddy and Carlo, Clarice said, "What a wonderful thing to do for our little gal. She is still over the moon." Clarice sipped at her coffee.

Letty blew over her cup, cooling the steaming brew. "She truly believed she'd never speak to her sister again. They were apart for six years, after never being separated."

"You can be square with us," Clarice leaned closer toward Gregory, who busied himself eating a bun. "Melody told you, didn't she? That's how you knew to rescue Margie."

"Of course, she did," Letty said. "He's told us."

Clarice slapped Letty playfully on the arm. "I just like hearing. Serves as a small reminder that he's actually the bee's knees." She smiled broadly, first at Gregory then at Letty.

"We have important things to do," Letty said, wrinkling her nose.

"Thanking Gregory is certainly on that list," Clarice insisted.

"I think getting Margie some clothes, books, and –" Letty began.

Clarice cut her off, waving the remark away. "We agreed on all that. Isn't that how we're spending the afternoon?"

Letty sent Clarice a pointed look. Clarice shook her head so briefly Gregory almost missed it. *What were they cooking up?*

"Secrets? –"

"Good," Harrison said as he rounded the door jam, "Good. Gregory, I need to talk to you." His brother, dressed in brown trousers, vest and white shirt, had dashed up from his office in such a hurry he had forgotten his coat and his fedora.

Clarice and Letty excused themselves, whispered between them, covering smiles behind their hands. They bustled out the door and down the hallway. *They were definitely up to something,* Gregory thought. He turned to his brother about to rise from his chair when they heard the door knocker.

Gregory and Harrison, gripping the door frame, glanced at each other. From upstairs in the foyer, they heard the tinkling of laughter. *Irene?*

Clarice's voice drifted down to them from overhead, "Irene, baby, you are prompt. Come in and join us while we get dressed."

"We are so glad to have your help," Letty said. "Just look at that darling frock. Herringbone is the cat's meow."

Irene laughed. "An invitation to shop on my day off – who could resist."

So that's what they were up to. Maybe he could see Irene later today. She looked so forlorn when she left with her father after the séance.

"Gregory," Harrison said, interrupting his thoughts.

Gregory coughed and looked at his brother. "Harrison give me the crop." He wiped his sticky hands on a cloth napkin from the table.

"You know that investment you wanted me to make?" Harrison began, coyly.

"You mean, selling the stocks, buying gold?" Gregory found himself whispering.

Harrison nodded. "It's coming today. I had a wire from Dooley. I need your help with the cellar. We need to move some of the hooch around to make room from my – ah—investment."

Gregory stroked his chin, considering. "The cellar under your office is completely secure. We could move the bottles and barrels from the very back corner – it's so dark there, even if someone were to go down there, they won't see it."

Harrison nodded again. "Exactly my own thought on the matter."

"They won't be driving up in a bank truck?"

"No. Dooley mentioned a Quick Rise Dough van from his son-in-law's bakery making the delivery," Harrison chuckled. "It's ten bars weighing in at almost thirty pounds apiece and the strong box with the silver. Had to be a big truck to carry all of it and the two men, protecting the lot."

Gregory got up, pushed his chair back under the table and followed Gregory down the hallway. Upstairs, the door knocker sounded, clanging through the house.

"That can't be them," Harrison said. "It's way too early,"

Walking up the steps and down the hall towards the foyer, they heard George Moran's booming voice.

"They'll see me, my good sir, we're practically family," Moran told Klein.

"Oh, no," Gregory whispered, wondering what Moran wanted.

"There you are, Harrison." Moran held a hand out. Harrison rushed forward to take the offered hand and shake it. A warm smile lit up his brother's features. Moran clapped a large hand on Harrison's bicep. "Good to see you, and Gregory there." Moran glanced over at Gregory.

"Teddy was supposed to mention an upcoming job. I would like to recruit the two of you, especially you Harrison." Moran moved them into the front parlor, waving the Davenport brothers into chairs while he settled himself on the small sofa, his size making it look like giant armchair. He looped his arms out over the wooden rail topping the damask covered back and stretched his legs out in front of him, crossing his ankles. Moran took a moment to admire his shiny black and tan leather, two toned shoes. "Have you spoken with my wayward cousin recently?"

"No, sir," Harrison said. "But tell us what you've planned." He took a fat cigar out of his vest pocket and lit up, drawing in a calming breath.

Gregory sighed in relief, silently thanking his brother for diverting Moran's attention. The head of the North Side mob didn't come to the Farm or *The Hair of the Dog* often – a good thing for the Davenport brothers. *What did he want today?*

Moran focused his intensity on Harrison. "I'm planning a job, and I need talented pals to pull a clean sneak."

Harrison remained silent and Gregory waited for the ax to fall. *At least Harrison wasn't bouncing with excitement over the prospect.*

Stroking his clean shaven, square chin, Moran continued, "It's a complicated job. I need a box man and several thugs. And drivers of course."

Harrison smoked his cigar. Gregory held his breath.

Raising an eyebrow, Moran smiled. "Not gonna ask what the job is?"

Tapping the ashes of the cigar into the metal ashtray on a small side table next to his chair, Harrison said, "You'll tell when the time is right."

Moran slapped his knee, laughing heartily, sending his jowls to quivering. His finger jabbed the air in Harrison's direction. "I like you, son. Hahahaha. I do like you. Remind me of Deanie." He took a few deep breaths, regaining seriousness. "There's gold in Belmont-Sheffield bank. Lots of it, and most of it belongs to Al Capone. I plan on stealing it all. We're going to need a few trucks and enough mooks to haul those heavy bars out of the vault." Moran rubbed his chin again. "I'm hoping you and Teddy might want dibs."

Gregory's heart skipped a beat. *Here it was—his nightmare!*

Harrison leaned back slightly against the thin cushions of his chair. "I can't speak for Teddy, Sir, but we've been caught up here in our repairs after the damage from that raid."

"You don't need the kale?"

"I have to focus my attention at home," Harrison said softly. He sounded responsible rather than dismissive.

Moran's poleaxed expression fleetingly crossed his round face before he composed himself. Harrison hadn't been disrespectful and while turning down the offer, did so allowing Moran to save face.

Gregory piped up, "I was shot in several places, sir, and Harrison has been attending to me as well as the club." Reminding Moran might not be a good thing, or it might swing the balance in their favor. But Harrison nodded.

"I've had quite an increase in responsibility," Harrison said. "I'm honored you have brought the job to our attention, but..." he spread his hands out, indicating the entire room, the whole farm, their operation, "my best efforts are needed here."

Moran pursed his lips, tapping them with a forefinger as he thought about Harrison's words. Suddenly, he sat up with a start, clapping his large hands over his knees before getting to his feet. "I'll leave you to it then." He wasn't angry, nor was he pleased, but he did not seem inclined to press them. Heading toward the foyer, Moran tossed over his shoulder, "You know how to reach me if you want dibs."

Gregory and Harrison reached the doorway just as Klein handed Moran his bowler and overcoat. They glanced at each other, faces relieved when Klein closed the door and they were alone again.

Gregory sagged against the door jam.

Harrison stood with his back against the wall. "Was that the bank job?"

"Yes," Gregory hissed.

"Even if you hadn't warned me, I wouldn't have wanted to do it," Harrison said. "He's going directly against Capone."

"Last night cousin Deanie joined us," Gregory began.

"Wait," Harrison held up a hand. "His ghost?"

"In a manner of speaking. He seemed maniacal, almost ranting that Moran be the only one to wreck his vengeance on Capone," Gregory finished. "A gang war is gearing up, it seems."

"Best to stay as far from that as we can," Harrison said.

"After being shot in the last wave—" Gregory nodded, "you won't get me to fight you on that one."

Harrison clapped him on the shoulder. He smiled, then shot a hand into his vest pocket for his watch. Glancing down at it, Harrison blanched. "The bakery truck should be here soon. We have to get ready."

"Wowzer! Moran almost saw your investments." Gregory's stomach lurched.

"That would have been a fine kettle of fish as mother used to say," Harrison replied. He grabbed Gregory's arm. "Come on. I need your help in the cellar." When Harrison turned and rushed down the hallway to the stairs leading down to *The Hair of the Dog*, Gregory raced after him. *How long would it take them to clear a space for all those gold bars?*

19

Apparently, it took four hours to move barrels and bottles of hooch from one spot in the second cellar beneath the hidden door in the floor of Harrison's office. Cousin Deanie had been behind the design, wanting to be certain any rival gang members would *not* be able to find the club's stash of alky. Concealed beneath the Persian carpet in Harrison's office, Deanie had a pull up trap door installed that opened onto narrow stairs circling downward yet another story into blackness. The walls of this cellar were hard packed dirt with some wide planks of wood used to restrain the clods from escaping. Because the cellar contained a fortune in hooch, Deanie spent some money on installing a stone floor of two-foot square slabs of sandstone. Lighting was dim at best because Deanie feared gaslight was dangerous in such enclosed space; therefore, anyone going into the alky cellar had to carry a lantern.

Back in 1921, Harrison and Deanie with Teddy and Gregory's help built the shelving on site so that the bottles and barrels could be organized by place of origin, quality, and price. At least the back corner, perhaps because it was so dark, held only barrels of hooch rather than shelving that would have been more complicated to move. Today, the brothers were thankful for Deanie's foresight.

After Harrison closed the trapdoor, Gregory helped his brother replace the carpet over the wooden floor. Harrison wiped the grime off his hands, brushing the palms against one another.

"Who would look under that carpet? We're three stories underground already," Harrison said, dusting the back of his pants.

Gregory used his fingers to swipe away dirt from his own trousers and vest. His brown pants and vest were his oldest fashionable clothes. Fortunately, he hadn't put on his navy-blue pinstripe, or he'd had to have words with Harrison. He found a small hole near the buttons on the vest where the worsted rested against his waistband. *Perhaps the tailor could patch that*? He thought poking his finger into it. "How about something to eat?" Gregory asked, thinking that he spent a lot of time in their kitchen lately. His stomach rumbled.

Harrison nodded as his stomach gurgled. "Moving those kegs was hard work" he said, laughing.

They made their way back to the kitchen, finding sliced ham in the ice box and fresh bread in the white enameled breadbox. Harrison left for a minute, while Gregory put their sandwiches together and returned with two icy glasses of beer.

"Nothing goes with ham like a cold beer," Harrison said, putting a tall frothy glass near Gregory's place.

Gregory brought the plates with sandwiches piled with ham, tomatoes, lettuce, and pickles. He gave a plate to his brother before sitting down at his own spot. Gathering up the sandwich in both hands, Gregory took a mouthful and savored the salty, sour and sweet flavors. "When will that truck get here?" he asked, mumbling over the mouthful of food.

Harrison took out his watch, flipped it open and smiled. "we might have time to finish up these sandwiches before they pull up." He laughed then dove into his own lunch.

Just as Harrison predicted, they had cleaned their plates when

Klein came looking for them. "Delivery," Klein announced when he tracked them down.

Harrison tossed his napkin down on the table, getting up to follow Klein to the delivery entrance. Dropping his napkin on the table, Gregory gathered the plates, placing them in the metal sink and pumped some water over them, before leaving the kitchen to go after his brother. Through the windows by the back door, Gregory saw three burly men in light blue uniforms jump out of the Quick Rise Dough bakery van. One of them went to the rear, opening the narrow double doors. He reached in and took out a medium sized, black metal, strong box that strained his back and arms. Rather than setting the box on the ground, he staggered toward the porch and the door used for access to *The Hair of the Dog*. One of the other men ran over to help, but the first man yelled, "You two start bringing in the loaves."

"Loaves?" Gregory asked Harrison.

"Gold bars, I suspect." Harrison said, opening the door before the man needed to knock. "Over here," Harrison told him.

The man with the strong box made his way up the two board steps to the doorway. "Where do you want this?"

"Down in the club office," Harrison told him.

Gregory wondered how they were going to lower that strong box down into the hooch cellar, but Harrison might have already considered that problem. *They certainly weren't going to confide in these men.* The two men had collected several of the thirty-pound gold bricks apiece, shuffling carefully under the weight as they followed the first man into the small entryway within the farmhouse where Clarice and Letty or other cappers screened those wanting access to the club. Stacking the bars inside would prevent anyone arriving at the farm from seeing Harrison's investment. When Gregory saw the size of the gold bars, he was glad they had cleared such a large space in the hooch cellar. *But where would they store them while the men carried the gold to Harrison's office?*

The men had cleared everything out of the truck, but they were only halfway done with their task, fifteen bars remained just inside the hallway. Harrison showed them the way down the stairs that spiraled down two stories to the club. Gregory chanced to glance up, and he saw a cloud of dust in the distance. A white or cream soft-topped car with a sporty, steel gray body, a Duesenberg J model? --it was hard to tell for certain with the sun shining in his eyes for certain—raced toward the driveway and the Club entrance. Clarice and Letty were still in Norwood Park shopping with Irene and possibly Margaretta. That meant no one but Klein was manning the door.

"Harrison!" Gregory called out. "Someone is coming. I don't think Moran is returning. He owns a Bugatti Type 41, besides his car is black and this one is definitely dark gray."

Harrison ran up behind Gregory. When he saw the approaching car, he blanched.

"What?" Gregory asked, his sandwich doing flips in his stomach.

"That's Jack McGurn's car," Harrison whispered. "What the devil is *he* doing here?"

"What a jam!" Gregory smacked his forehead with the heal of his left hand. "You'd better hurry those men to clear out the rest of these -- `loaves' or McGurn will take them." Gregory shoved Harrison away from the window and toward the stairs to the club. He remembered the story Clarice and Letty told him about McGurn pistol whipping that street peddler. He did not want his brother or himself to be next.

Harrison struggled to pick up three of the bars, rushing off to his office in the club, leaving twelve bars behind. The car was still bumping along the driveway, having slowed down to negotiate the washed-out places. "Klein," Harrison called out, "a little help here."

Klein came into the hallway from the middle parlor, dropped his dust cloth, and went to pick up three more of the bars. He turned to follow Harrison down the stairwell. *Now there were nine remaining bars.* The car approached the carriage way at the side of the farmhouse where drivers would leave patrons for the club, or patrons might turn their keys over to the boy who parked the cars for a small price.

Two of the blue, uniformed men came towards Gregory returning from their trip down to the office.

"Hurry up," he hissed. "We need to get this put away."

They ran over to the remaining gold, each gathering up four bars, one more than they had carried on all the previous trips. Huffing, they worked their way to the stairs. Gregory could hear them straining as they descended. Now only one bar remained. From outside, car doors slammed.

Gregory grabbed for the gold bar. It was heavier than he imagined and cold to the touch. He curled his fingers beneath it, and hoisted the thing to his shoulder, supporting it with two hands as if it were a baby. His father's old office was around the corner and down the hallway close to the back steps leading to the kitchen. Gregory headed that way, thinking he could conceal that one gold bar under the cushions of his father's old desk chair. He felt along the office wall for light switch, twisting the dial for the gas. In the flickering shadows, he dashed over to the desk, knocking a knee on one of the small tables beside an armchair. Stifling a shout of pain, Gregory tossed the cushion from his father's chair to one side, plunked the gold down in the center of the seat, then grabbed up the cushion when the door knocker sounded. He tossed the cushion over the gold bar, and ran to the club entryway door.

McGurn stood on the stoop, in his fedora and overcoat. He had two gals wrapped in furs with him, one clinging to each arm. They both wore identical deep red headbands with two feathers bobbing over their faces. "I'm here for the show," he told Gregory. "But I'm also looking for that weasel Anselmo. I heard it from a reliable mook that he might be holed up here."

"The club hasn't had any guests of that name," Gregory said hastily, acting as if he were Klein. "You are welcome to come in, but our entertainment won't begin until half-past nine, tonight." His heartbeat thundered in his ears as he thought about Carlo and Teddy being upstairs on the second floor of the farmhouse. *They can't go to Paris soon enough,* Gregory thought.

McGurn stared at Gregory with a gimlet eye. His features hardened. His lips formed a thin line across his face.

Please don't let him go off the track, Gregory prayed. He opened the door further and extended his arm in welcome, even though that was the last thing he wanted to do. "Please," he said.

"If I find him here, of all places, he's going for a ride." McGurn chuckled as if he had made a joke. Pushing the women in ahead of him, McGurn came into the entryway. "I wouldn't be here myself, if I weren't tracking that palooka down."

"We heard da Jazz was really good here," the gal on McGurn's right piped up.

"The bee's knees," said the one on the left.

"If Anselmo ain't here, we're going back to the Green Mill. I *know* the music there is jumpin'." McGurn swept down the short hallway towards the circular stairs, spiraling down to the club floor. As he did, the three men in the light blue bakery uniforms nearly ran into him. "Watch where you're going, ya bums," McGurn yelled. "Get outta our way, ya savvy?"

The men said nothing, just rushed past Gregory and out the door. Outside the truck engine cranked over and the wheels rumbled on the crushed gravel, before the noise of the delivery van gradually grew further away.

"What kinda joint is this?" McGurn demanded, competing with the sounds of the truck off in the distance.

"Baby," the gal on the right whined, "I wanna dance."

The one on the left threaded a finger around the outer edge of McGurn's ear, teasing him. "Yea. I wanna dance, too."

He looked at one then the other, finally smiling down into their upturned faces—the one on the right oval with soft red curls and the one on the left heart-shaped with huge blue eyes. "Sure," he said, "anything for my two beauties." McGurn cuddled the women closer to his thick body.

The women giggled as they disappeared down the spiral stairs, heading for the club.

Gregory's heart slammed in his chest. *Surely, the bars are all hidden somewhere by now. It was early for dancing and music. Hopefully, a few glasses of giggle water will satisfy them. When he doesn't see Carlo, maybe they'll leave.*

After McGurn and the women were gone, Gregory raced up the front stairwell, taking the steps two at a time. He had no idea what Teddy and Carlo were doing right now, but he had to warn them. Reaching the oak door to the second-floor rooms he had given to Teddy and Carlo, Gregory stopped to catch his breath. He ran his right hand backward through his hair, smoothing it down. Once he felt composed, Gregory knocked on the door. Pa, papa, pa, pa. He waited for a response.

"Hold your britches, I'm coming," Teddy said, rather loudly, from within. He cracked the door rather than giving the knocks Gregory expected. "Yes?" Teddy asked, elongating the word into a long sibilant.

Through the door jam, Gregory could see Teddy wore a chocolate brown smoking robe, loose sand colored trousers, and slippers. "Looks like you are calling it a night early, but –" Gregory cut himself off. He rubbed the back of his neck. "Can't a fellow come in?"

Teddy nodded and backed away so that Gregory could push the door open. "Jack McGurn just came into the club with two gals, but that's not the worst of it. He's looking for Carlo, and he's not happy."

Carlo rushed in from the other room, hastily tying his houndstooth robe around his narrow waist. His eyes grew round in his face, and if he hadn't had stubble, he might have looked boyish. "Did you say McGurn?"

"Unfortunately." Gregory glanced at his hands. "Just what did he say to you at the Green Mill?"

"He told me that we Sicilians needed to watch our step," Carlo's eyes narrowed. "If we put one toe out of line, the hatch men would come after us." He went and stood by the unlit fireplace, leaning his head against the coolness of the mantel. "Capone and his mob have murdered the most powerful men in my family," he whispered. "Maybe they will only be happy when we're all dead."

Gregory began pacing. He stroked his chin.

Teddy sat down on the small green damask covered loveseat, took a cigarette from the ivory box on the occasional table, and lit one end with his lighter. After taking a few puffs, he rested his arms along the back of the loveseat, smoke from his cigarette drifted out from both nostrils, above his thin moustache. "Paris?"

"As soon as possible," Gregory agreed, stopping and staring down at his brother's closest friend.

"There's an early morning train to New York City." Teddy drew in more smoke, before making a smoke ring, pursing his lips. "They leave almost every day."

Carlo looked over his shoulder at the other men. "But what about tonight? What if McGurn decides to search the house?"

"Now that I've warned you, we'll all watch and try to prevent McGurn from heading your way," Gregory suggested.

"Meanwhile, everything I own is in a trunk at Teddy's. We could go to his flat. You," Carlo turned to Teddy, "could pack, and we would be able to leave at dawn."

"McGurn won't look for you at Teddy's," Gregory said, nodding.

"No," said Teddy, "But wasn't cousin George looking for me? If he goes to my flat and finds Carlo there, we'll both be dead."

Gregory smacked his forehead with his palm. "I forgot about that." *They really were safest at the farm until they could get the train to New York and the steamer to Paris. Where could he hide them?*

Loud voices came through the door from the ground floor.

"Unhand me," shouted a liquor roughened male voice that Gregory recognized as McGurn. There were scuffling noises.

Carlo visibly blanched. Teddy rushed over to him and slid an arm around the younger man's waist.

"But sweetie," whined a female voice – either gal right or left. "I wanna stay for the dancing."

"There'll be plenty of dancing' at the Green Mill, I tell you," McGurn yelled. "You gals stay here while I check upstairs for that little weasel. He wasn't at the club, but he may be here at this house."

"Only the family goes past the ground floor," Klein's calm tones did not convince McGurn. Gregory could tell from the scuffle and footsteps pounding on the stairs.

Carlo and Teddy froze near the fireplace, a study in fear.

Gregory put up his hand for silence. "Stay here," he mouthed. "I'll take care of him." Before the tramping feet could reach the second floor, Gregory slipped out the door to Teddy and Carlo's rooms. He moved into the rectangular hallway, heading for the stairs. McGurn came puffing up, with Klein several steps behind.

"I could not restrain him," Klein said, giving Gregory a speaking look.

They could not afford to offend McGurn too much or Capone would return and destroy the club and the farm. Gregory nodded.

"Mr. McGurn," Gregory said calmly. "May I assist you?"

Pulling himself up to his full height, McGurn stared directly into Gregory's eyes. "Told you, I'm looking for Anselmo." He took several steps forward, forcing Gregory back toward the guest rooms.

"We have no Sicilians here," Gregory lied.

McGurn stumbled slightly, putting a steadying hand against the wall closest to the door Gregory had just closed behind him.

"This is speakeasy is independent. Anyone can enjoy our giggle water and music," Gregory began. He hoped his dread remained hidden. "Moran will be here soon to enjoy the delights of *The Hair of the Dog*. While you might want him dead, I know you don't want trouble right *now*."

McGurn swayed close to Gregory, grabbing the lapels of Gregory's suit jacket, bunching the expensive silk in his massive hands. "If you see Anselmo, let the little bastard know I'm looking. If he knows what's good for him, he'll come see me at the Green Mill, ya follow?" McGurn's face took on an unholy glee, his eyes sparkling hotly, and his dimpled chin raised. Under his breath, he said, "I'm going to take him for a ride and when I'm done with him, no one will ever find him." He released Gregory's coat, rubbed the rumpled fabric twice as if to smooth it flat, and turned stumbling back down the stairs.

"Come on, you skirts," McGurn slurred. "Let's blow this joint."

His two women giggled and began chattering at him. They snarled fingers in his hair, and stroked his cheeks. McGurn leered at them, especially when the left one kissed him.

"This way," Klein said. After footsteps scuffled against the marble tiles in the foyer, the door banged shut. "They're leaving," he called quietly to Gregory, "And good riddance."

Gregory heard the Duesenberg's engine roar and tires skid on the drive. His heart thudded in his chest. "They're gone?"

"Yes," Klein answered.

Gregory practically flew upstairs. "Teddy. Carlo," he called, rapping on their door. "McGurn is gone—at least for now."

Teddy and Carlo peeked through their cracked open door. Their eyes seemed huge and their faces pale. "I don't know what we'd have done if he'd come in here."

Gregory shook his head. "Come on. Harrison needs your help. That should get your minds on other things." He led the two men down the back, spiral stairs to the club floor. "Go on into his office." Gregory then shouted, "Harrison, I've brought some extra hands."

He patted Teddy and Carlo on their shoulders. "I'll be right back," he told them, pushing them towards Harrison's door, before dashing off to his father's old office where he had concealed the remaining gold brick under his father's seat cushion. He hoisted the gold onto his shoulder and rushed back down to Harrison's office. He found Carlo and Teddy had already descended into their hooch cellar with Harrison. Below, lantern light flicked strangely and their voices drifted up to him.

"I'm coming down with our last loaf," Gregory called out,

warning them. Cautiously, he negotiated the narrow, steep steps to the stone floor. His shoes made odd scraping noises that echoed around him.

"Back here," Harrison called out. He had taken off his suit jacket, leaving it folded on top of a whiskey barrel. Beside it were Teddy's and Carlo's dressing robes. They had rolled up their shirt sleeves and sweat trickled down their faces in the lantern light. All but three of the gold bricks had been neatly stacked in the back corner. Beside the pyramid of gold stood the black steel strong box which held Harrison's silver. Harrison allowed Carlo and Teddy to move the last gold bars, so that he could inspect his silver investment. While his brother turned the two dials on the strong box, Gregory placed his gold bar on top of the rest.

"Take a look at this," Harrison said, opening the strong box. Inside where stacks of silver tiles and several small bags of coins. He fingered the tiles with wonder.

Gregory picked up one of the bags, opening it to examine the coins inside. Turning his back on the others, he palmed a handful of silver, slipping it into his pocket. *Carlo's family will need this,* Gregory thought and Harrison would never miss that small amount.

When Teddy knelt beside Harrison, talking quietly about leaving for Paris, Gregory approached Carlo. He slipped Carlo the handful of silver and indicated the Sicilian should put the money into his pocket. "For your family, I wish I could do more for them—but that's an endless proposition," whispered Gregory. "With you and Teddy gone, at least they will have a little set by."

Carlo stared up at him in amazement. He tried several times to speak.

Gregory placed his finger to his lips and shook his head. "Teddy is family – now so are you. We always look after our own. Cousin Deanie taught us that."

Carlo smiled, his entire face brightening. He nodded then as if he could not help himself, gave Gregory a quick hug.

Harrison and Teddy stood. After relocking the strong box,

Harrison said, "Come on. Let's get cleaned up and celebrate. The club won't be busy for hours."

Cook brought several plates of cold meats and sweets to the front parlor, setting them out on the narrow buffet standing against the wall furthest from the front door. Teddy and Harrison stood near the fireplace, smoking. Teddy made smoke rings with his cigarette while Harrison chewed the end of his cigar. Carlo sat close to Teddy in an overstuffed chair covered in cream velvet. They laughed and joked about their past exploits as newsies.

After his light supper, Gregory walked over to the gramophone, and opening the cabinet below the machine, he scanned the titles of their books of 78rpm records. He would not have another séance until tomorrow night. *Listening to the gramophone would be nice for a change.* He sighed. *If only Irene were here.*

Clarice, Letty, Irene, and Margaretta returned to the farmhouse just as darkness fell and the stars twinkled in the cloudless sky above. They chattered gaily about different shops they had visited, praising some of the newest styles, while criticizing others.

"That little mint green frock was darling on Margie," Letty said, knocking on the door.

"It was, but I liked the dark red one even better," Clarice replied.

"She seems to enjoy those knickers you picked out even more," Irene countered, ruffling the short-cropped curls on Margaretta's head.

Clarice studied the little girl as she stood beside Irene. Margie had traded her hand-me- down boy's clothing for a smart frock of pink with a green ribbon at the neckline and dropped waist. Her thick brown hair had been cropped into a curly bob. She had transformed from the white faced, frightened little girl, into a gamine creature with large brown eyes, which looked a lot like her cousin Carlo's. She had his Mediterranean complexion, too. *What a little charmer,* Clarice thought, smiling.

Klein rushed past the opened doors of the parlor. A blast of air surged through the room as their front door opened. Clarice, Letty,

Margaretta, and Irene came chattering into the hallway. Gregory rushed out to greet them, his heart racing with excitement.

Clarice stood sliding her plaid wool coat down her arms, revealing a mid-length rose colored sportscoat belted at her waist. Her white blouse showed behind the narrow lapels, and she had tied a black bowtie at her throat. Instead of a skirt most women would wear with their sports suit, Clarice wore black trousers. Letty's mink collared, cream coat hid a green gingham wrap dress with long sleeves that came to a point on her hands and a square cut neckline. Down the front hung her ubiquitous strand of pearls. She wore flesh-colored stockings and black pumps with a glittery buckle. Her matching cylindrical cloche hat remained over her dark hair.

Irene, though, in her light blue frock with its flanged, chiffon sleeves, tunic top, and uneven pointed hemline, stood out above the crowd for Gregory. The three-inch coiled circle pattern repeated from the rounded neckline to the scalloped hem below her hips, drawing his eyes up and down her figure. She wore her hair in loose curls, free of covering, and gold drop earrings swung from her ears. *That dress! Those large blue eyes.* Heat coiled inside him.

"Come," he invited, "all of you come join us. There is food and – we can provide dancing." Clarice and Letty nodded their willingness while Margaretta looked pleadingly at them, squealing joyously after they assented. When Irene turned and smiled at him, Gregory's gut warmed. He held out a hand to her.

"Give us a moment to get rid of these wraps," she said, her blue eyes dancing with good humor. "I believe we would love a bite and dancing." After passing her fox collar coat and gloves to Klein who already held Clarice, Letty, and Margaretta's, Irene reached for the hand Gregory had offered. With his other hand, he beckoned Clarice, Letty, and Margaretta to join them.

With her soft fingers fitted between his, Gregory led her into the parlor with the others following behind. "Look who I have found," he said to the men.

Harrison glanced up. "I should have telephoned Lysette. Maybe I can catch her, and she will join our party." He excused himself, leaving Teddy and Carlo. Teddy moved closer to his boyfriend, and sat on the overstuffed arm of Carlo's chair. He wrapped an arm over Carlo's shoulders possessively, their cigarettes sending tight curls of smoke into the room.

Gregory turned to Clarice and Letty. "You know Teddy O'Hannilon and Carlo Anselmo," he said, indicating the two men. "These lovely ladies are Clarice Daniel, her girlfriend Letty Carlyle, and their daughter Margie. Of course, you are already acquainted with Irene O'Brien."

Teddy and Carlo stood and bowed. "A pleasure, ladies," they said in unison.

Clarice bowed back, while Letty, Irene, and Margie quickly curtseyed. Gregory showed the women where Cook had left plates and silverware as well as the delicious ham, candied pears, cold chicken, cheeses, and pastries. While they ate, Gregory returned to the recordings, selecting several hefty volumes. He placed them on the octagonal table next to the Gramophone. Blowing dust off the top volume, Gregory took a recording out of its paper sleeve. Holding it with one hand, he lifted the lid to the gramophone case with the other. After placing the record on the turntable, he gently wound the crank powering the machine. Carefully, he lifted the arm with its steel needle, setting it down on the record. A crackling noise came from the speaker vents before Esther Walker's voice filled the room as she sang "I left my baby standing in the rain." He noticed that Harrison had returned and was talking with Carlo and Teddy.

Gregory found his favorite artists amid the recordings, stacking them into a tower. When one disc finished, he replaced it with another. Bessie Smith followed Esther Walker, then Louis Armstrong, and Fats Waller. After eight songs, the gals have eaten their fill and set their plates to one side. Lysette joined the party then, in time for the dancing, garbed in a red ruched dress that complimented her translucent skin and bee-stung lips. After giving Harrison a sultry kiss, Lysette rushed over to the women in a flurry of silk ruffles and sat opposite Letty's chair, near Irene. Gregory lined up a fast-moving fox trot on the gramophone. Once the music began, he strode across the parlor to where Irene sat near where Clarice and Letty shared an overstuffed armchair, and Margie perched on a footstool.

"May I have this dance," Gregory asked, his left arm behind his back, his right outstretched hand open beckoning towards Irene.

She looked up into his face and smiled, eyes twinkling and there she was, the girl of his dreams—the Irene who loved him – at least so much closer. She took his palm in hers, allowing him to pull her to her feet, her light blue strappy pumps shining. Going into his arms, he felt her check nuzzle against his chest. Her perfume surrounded them both as they swept up into the fox trot, dipping and turning. Gregory smiled and joy exploded inside his chest. *What a girl, what a night,* he hummed. *Wowzer!*

Behind them, Clarice stood, offering her hand to Letty, who laughed. "Why not?" Letty said. They, too, began dancing.

From the corner of his eye, Gregory saw Carlo poke Teddy. At first, Teddy shook his head, but Carlo's persistence won out. They joined in. Not to be outdone, Teddy twirled Carlo around an upheld arm, spinning his partner first away and then toward his chest. Their antics made everyone laugh, but no one missed a step. The three couples had finished two records and were beginning a third when Harrison and Lysette joined them in the center of the parlor.

Harrison held his arm out for his girlfriend, and there were four couples dancing. Margie clapped in time with the music, a huge grin on her face.

"Black bottom," shouted Carlo.

"A challenge?" Harrison asked, laughing. He and Lysette began shimmying, bumping their hips.

Gregory captured Irene's eye. She nodded. They also shimmied and touched hips, then rotated in a circle before clinging to one another.

Teddy and Carlo did flips and other fancy steps, making everyone stop to watch and clap.

Gregory's insides swelled with happiness he had not felt in years. Irene's sweet body pressed close, and she held him as if she never wanted to let him go. His brother and his girlfriend smiled up into each other's faces as did Clarice and Letty and Teddy and Carlo. *This was his family now. If only he could protect them from the hardships to come.*

20

Teddy and Carlo packed steamer trunks, put the rest of their meager things into storage, and found a tenant to sublet Teddy's flat in preparation for their long trip to Paris. They had purchased tickets for the New York train and the ocean liner for France, giving themselves a week to put their Chicago lives into dry dock, as Teddy's sailor father used to say. Fear of McGurn lingered, retreating into the background of their lives. Carlo still looked over his shoulder when they walked on the streets, but his eyes had lost that strained terror which had griped him after he had seen McGurn. Additionally, Teddy avoided any old haunts he knew his cousin might frequent. He did *not* want to answer any questions Bugsy Moran might have. Both men recognized this was not a lifestyle they wanted to continue living. They visited the Farm and Gregory once their travel plans had been solidified. Sitting in the front parlor where they had last danced, dreaming of a safe future.

"We have a flat already rented near the Sorbonne. I don't know how long we'll stay there," Teddy told Gregory, stretching his arms along the back of the loveseat and allowing his cigarette to dangle from his lips. "At least six months to a year. Long enough for my cousin to forget about me – us."

"Your cousin?" Carlo said, an edge to his baritone, "what about McGurn? Or Capone?" He glanced over his shoulder at Teddy from his perch on the ottoman he had moved next to Teddy's feet.

Carlo hadn't forgotten the manic look in McGurn's eyes Teddy could tell. He pressed a hand on Carlo's shoulder, pulling him closer so that Carlo's back rested against his knees.

"Hence Paris," Gregory mollified. "We are only a phone call away. Just let us know if you need anything. Anything at all."

Teddy nodded, crushing out his stub. Tapping a new cigarette against his pant leg, he flipped it into his mouth and used a match to light the end. *He was going to miss the Davenports and Chicago, but he had Carlo and Paris would have to be enough.*

Gregory's heart gladdened when Teddy and Carlo left for their train. He would miss their company, of course, but their safety was tantamount. Capone and his reign of violence continued and the Prohibition agents were unable to find enough evidence for a conviction. *When Elliot Ness takes over,* thought Gregory, *I'll try to convince O'Brien to help them and get justice for Geoff.*

October brought crisp, cool air to Chicago. Leaves began turning from green to orange, red, and brown. Patrons at *The Hair of the Dog* continued packing the club at night, dancing, drinking, gambling, and eating. They also fought over attending seances, new and old faces crowding around the table in the back parlor. Gregory spoke for daughters and sons, mothers and fathers, for lost souls and happier ones. None of them could warn of the crisis to come, lessening its impact. When he wasn't working, Gregory courted Irene. In his eyes, she grew more lovely each day. Today, her day off, they met at the small park near her flat. She was wearing her fox collared coat and a smart wool hat in a deep violet, sporting a jaunty feather on the left side. Gregory took her hand and they walked for a while before Gregory offered to push her in the wooden swing.

"There's talk in our office," Irene confided, "that the market is destabilizing. We have had several small dips in the past months, even I've noticed."

Gregory nodded, holding his tongue. *He knew what would occur near the end of October. Should he tell her?*

"My boss has taken a conservative approach much different from those of the male brokers." Irene tightened her gloved hand on the chains of the park swing. Gregory gently continued pushing her. Around them leaves swirled, and the scent of Autumn filled the air. "She has shifted her clients into more stable stocks, encouraging them to pay off margins, closing out puts or calls."

"Sound advice," Gregory said, knowingly. His tweed wool coat flapped in the growing breeze.

"I worry about Father," Irene confessed, biting her lower lip in a way Gregory thought adorable. "He stands to lose a fortune."

"He might have time to sell everything and get out of the market," Gregory said in a rush.

"Father?" Irene looked back over her shoulder straight into Gregory's eyes. "Horse feathers! He won't sell out. Not him."

"I thought that once about my brother."

"And?" Irene glanced sideways.

"Somehow – I convinced him," *with the help of economics professors and research by the Security Exchange Commission,* Gregory thought.

"Maybe he would listen to you," Irene hinted a plea—her faced turned up toward his.

"I could try – especially if Harrison were to approach him. That would be better," Gregory confessed.

"Would you?" The adoration in Irene's blue eyes came like a punch to his gut.

"Look at me that way, and I'll do anything," Gregory muttered, his world spinning.

Irene hopped off the swing, standing with it between them. Her short, blonde curls fluttered in the wind. She raised her hands to

Gregory's cheeks and pulled him closer to press a kiss to his lips. "Thank you," she sighed.

He didn't care that the swing banged his thighs. Gregory threaded his arms around her waist and kissed her as he had wanted for so long. Her lips softened under his and her breath sweet. He moaned, his fingers pressing deeper into the wool of her coat. Irene moved even closer, opening her mouth to his, insisting on more.

Somewhere a block over, a horn honked and they broke apart, breathing heavily. The chain of the swing chinked and clacked between them. While Irene hastily straightened her clothing, she seemed neither ashamed nor abashed by her forward behavior. Instead, Irene continued to gaze into Gregory's face as if memorizing his every feature. Her hands, although gloved, felt warm where they lingered on his forearms. He never wanted to let her go.

"Irene," he began, not certain what he wished to tell her.

"Tomorrow, then?" She asked.

He nodded.

"We'll go together with Harrison and talk to Father?"

Gregory gave himself a mental shake, refocusing his thoughts. "Yes," he said. "Yes, of course. I believe my brother will be available after lunch. Will that work?"

Irene giggled. She shook her curls and crinkled her eyes. Darting close to his ear, tickling him with her breath, she whispered, "I think I'm falling in love with you, Gregory Davenport."

"I certainly hope so," he whispered back. *Wowzers!* An electric current shot through him, excitement mixed with a little fear. He knew he loved her and now, finally, she loved him back. *Better work even harder to save O'Brien from Black Tuesday – might be my father-in-law.* "Come on. It's getting colder. Better get you back to your flat."

Irene slapped his arm lightly. "Trying to get rid of me, are you?"

"Baloney!" Gregory's eyes narrowed with his hoot of laughter. He came around the swing and wrapped his right arm around her waist, dragging her against his side. Dropping a light kiss on top of her head, Gregory breathed in the heliotrope and jasmine scent of her before guiding her down the street and up the steps of her apartment building.

After walking her to her own door, he gathered Irene into his arms for another passionate kiss. "See you tomorrow around two. Probably should check with your father – make certain he's able to see us then, wouldn't you say?"

"Duck soup, baby." Irene gently touched his cheek, then turned to use her key. "Gals! I'm home," she called into the flat to her roommates. Over her shoulder, Irene blew him another kiss.

He caught it, "Tomorrow," he said, and closed the door behind her.

Later that afternoon, Gregory sought out Harrison. He found his brother holed up in his office – the one their father had always used on the first floor of the farmhouse, not the larger one in the club.

Harrison shook out the newspaper he had been holding. "You have saved me a wad, brother. Look here," he pointed at a line of stock numbers. "These have begun falling in value. Two days ago, they were higher than ever. I don't want the headache of following the roller coaster pricing."

"It's only going to get worse," Gregory told him.

"And you know this how?" Harrison raised a light brown eyebrow and tipped his fedora further over his left eye.

"Crystal ball?" Gregory suggested.

"A ghost told you?" Harrison asked, suddenly serious. He took a cigar from a small wooden box on his desk.

"You might say that," Gregory said.

"Horse feathers!" Harrison sat up straight, suddenly. He cut off one end of the cigar and stuck the other into his mouth. From his vest pocket, Harrison extracted a small silver lighter which he flicked with thumb and forefinger. The flame touched the cut end of the cigar, curling the papers and tobacco as they began to burn. He jabbed the burning end toward Gregory. "When are you gonna tell me?"

Gregory stiffened. *He's my brother. If I could tell Teddy why not Harrison.* "The bullet wounds changed me, Harrison. I—"

Harrison waved his free hand in the air. He puffed on the cigar. "Maybe I don't need to know," he said softly. "You can talk to ghosts for Christ's sake. Why wouldn't you know the future?"

"Not everything, Harrison. Only through the beginning of next year. It's – I somehow lived through it all before," Gregory explained. Harrison continued puffing his cigar. "When you found me on the floor after being shot, I thought it was May 1930 not still 1929."

"So," Harrison took his cigar out of his mouth, studying it carefully. "You know the results for the horses? What about baseball?" Slowly, he tracked his eyes to where Gregory stood in the doorway of the office.

Gregory shook his head.

"Worthless," Harrison laughed, belying his words. He shoved the cigar back into the corner of his mouth. "You probably saved me hundreds of thousands of dollars."

"More," Gregory admitted quietly. "And I need your help to convince Irene's father to sell his holdings."

"And buy gold and silver?" Harrison pushed his fedora back over his light brown hair.

"Exactly," Gregory said, coming into the office and sitting in the chair facing Harrison. "Do you think your precious metal broker would work with O'Brien?"

"I can't think why not," Harrison leaned across the desk, closer to Gregory. "Don't get sore, but I believe we should ..."

They discussed plans for O'Brien almost until it was time for Gregory to drive over to Irene's.

"I'll speak with him first. We've meet at the stock exchange several times so he'll know me. Go get your gal," Harrison determined. "Later, alligator."

Gregory waved to his brother over one shoulder as he walked out of the room and headed for the barn where they parked the Ford. *She's falling in love with me,* he thought, driving through the Chicago streets, without paying attention to the automobiles or horse drawn vehicles beside him, using the cobbled and brick roads. Instead,

Gregory saw Irene's pout-painted lips in a wide smile, of a flash of humor expressed with her deep blue eyes. A flutter of a blonde curl warmed his belly. He began to hum to himself rather than concentrating on O'Brien and the upcoming visit. *Oh, what a night! Oh, what a girl!* went through his head. Before he realized, Gregory had turned the Ford up Irene's tree lined street. The oak trees were completely red, orange, and gold – giving them the appearance of flames, flickering in the cloudless blue sky.

After parking the Ford near the park, Gregory sauntered to Irene's apartment building. He slid a hand along the stair rail, almost skipping through the glass doors. Making a crisp salute to the doorman, Gregory made his way to the brass, caged doors of the elevator. He gently repositioned his fedora on his wavy, brown hair and wondered if he should take off his coat. The building was warmer than he expected, and he was beginning to perspire. By the time they reached Irene's floor, Gregory had folded his black woolen overcoat over his left arm. He strode out of the lift, making his way down the hallway, then rapped briskly on Irene's door.

Opening the door, Irene said, "I don't give a fig if it seems desperate or forward, but I'm letting you in myself." *Cat's meow,* Gregory thought, taking in her knee-length, orange, yellow, and cream striped, pleated frock, belted at her slender hips, exposing flesh toned stockings and her brown buckled pumps. Cap sleeves left her arms bare, except for the silver bracelet watch she wore on her left wrist. The collar of the dress, open at her throat, was tied loosely with a scarf of matching silk. Her gold bee earrings dangled against her slightly roughed cheeks. She had dusted her eyelids lightly with a blue powder, and outlined her lips in a cupid bow of the palest red. Gregory cleared his throat and entered the small entryway.

"Is it Gregory?" Daphne yelled from their small kitchen. She appeared in the doorway, dressed in a white blouse and blue pleated skirt which reminded Gregory of a sailor's uniform.

"Of course, it is," Zelda chided, popping out of her room to look Gregory up and down appraisingly. Her floral kimono and red hair tied up in a top knot caused Gregory to wonder if she still wore her pajamas.

He was glad he wore his pin-striped gray suit and two-toned shoes. The forest green tie gave him a splash of color, echoed by the handkerchief in his jacket breast pocket. Gregory was about to say something when to his left side, Daphne broke in, "See something you like, Zelda?"

"And then some," Zelda remarked with a slow grin. She placed a hand on her hip, shifting her weight. Her floral kimono dress rustled

Irene walked around Gregory, grabbed each roommate by the upper arm, and steered them away into the living room. Laughing she said, "Down gals. He's all mine, remember?"

They all giggled then, loosening Zelda's red hair in its topknot. Irene's eyes crinkled adorably, making Gregory's heart clench.

"Are you ready to go?" he asked Irene, but he really wanted to ask her something else, something more personal.

Their gazes met across the room. Irene flushed and nodded. "Let me get my coat."

When she came to his side after slipping into her fox collared coat, Gregory wound his right arm around her waist, giving her a one-armed hug. "Come baby, your father is waiting."

Once they were outside the flat, Irene gave Gregory a playful punch. "The gals are gonna think you are asking my father a certain question." Her eyes danced in her face and a grin spread over her mouth.

"Who's to say, I'm not," Gregory whispered into her pink shell of an ear. The bee earring bobbed against his jaw.

"Ohhh," Irene said, her eyes widening. "Be square with me."

Gregory mocked affrontery. He tapped his heart with his left hand, letting his overcoat slide back toward his elbow. "I'm over the moon," he whispered, unable to hold back any more. "You are the cat's pajamas, baby."

"That's easy for you to say," Irene said with a laugh, getting her composure back as they headed for the elevator.

Was she being dismissive? Had he been too forward, spoken too soon?

When they reached the Ford, he handed her in, went and turned the crank, before joining her on the bench seat. The side street by the park was strangely quiet. They were quite alone.

Irene reached a hand out and tentatively touched the sleeve of his overcoat.

"Did you mean it?" she asked quietly, stopping him from shifting gears and driving away.

He turned and looked down into her eyes. "Mean it?" he echoed.

She looked away, mumbling, "That you're over the moon?"

"Irene," Gregory groaned. "Darling gal, look at me. Please." He wrapped his right arm around her shoulders drawing her even closer within the confines of the Ford. He placed a gentle kiss against her cheek and under her ear, risking being struck by the hanging bee. When she continued to stare at her folded hands in her lap, Gregory murmured, "Do you want me to be?"

She nodded, her reddish blonde curls bobbing, tickling his nose.

Gregory took her small, almost pointed chin between his thumb and fingers, turning her face towards him and kissed her. She threaded her hands up around his neck, drawing him to her. Their breaths came in pants. Gregory felt alive, fed by her scent of heliotrope and jasmine as well as the softness of her body pressed against him. "Do you believe me?" Gregory asked between kisses, when he could speak.

Irene nodded. Joy radiated over her face. Gregory framed her cheeks with his hands, cupping her face gently. He kissed her again quickly. He wanted to stay there, kissing her, but he knew she would be sorry later when the opportunity to warn her father had passed. "Baby," Gregory whispered. "Kissing you, being with you – is hotsy-totsy."

Irene smiled into his lips. "Father?"

"Fire extinguisher," Gregory chuckled.

"As ever," Irene agreed. She gently pushed back against him, sitting once more at Gregory's side, rather than almost in his lap. Patting her curls back into order, she drew up against her door and looked down her pert nose. "Do I look respectable?" she asked, laughter in her voice.

"You look swell," Gregory said, smartly. "Come on." He worked the levers, shifting from park to drive and eased the Ford out onto the road. They drove down the streets in near silence, but it was the type of quiet that spoke of companionship and closeness. Joy filled the interior and Gregory did not wish to disturb it. All too soon, they reached Belmont Avenue and O'Brien's home. Harrison had taken their truck and it was parked in the turnaround behind and to the side of the house.

"I hope my brother has been successful," Gregory said, shifting the Ford into park and shutting of the engine.

"What and leave no challenge for us?" Irene giggled. She took Gregory's hand when he helped her from the passenger seat, and looped her arm through his elbow. They walked arm-in-arm up the brick steps towards the front door. Before they could knock, Saunders opened the oak door and waved them in.

"Your father has been waiting for you in his office," the butler told them, leading the way without even asking for their wraps.

As they followed Saunders down the dark hallway with its thick carpet and flickering sconce lighting, Gregory helped Irene out of her fox collared coat before shucking his own overcoat.

From down the hallway, Harrison's voice drifted to them along with the smoke from O'Brien's cigar. "Don't you remember the drastic drops in the March market," Harrison was saying, "where some stocks dropped more than 30 points, and again those falling prices a few weeks back in early September?"

"But the market rallied, just as Professor Irving Fisher predicted," O'Brien commented, his voice lowered with intensity. "The doomsayers have been proven wrong every time!"

When they reached the office door, Saunders took their outer garments while announcing, "Miss Irene and Mr. Davenport are here, sir."

"Come," boomed O'Brien, much as he had the first time, but instead of a cigar clenched between his teeth, the cheroot butt smoldered in an ashtray beside him. He perched on the front edge of his desk, legs clad in gray silk trousers outstretched and ankles crossed, staring down at Harrison, who sat in one of the chairs facing the large wooden desk. Harrison's face brightened upon seeing them, a wry grin curling his thin lips upwards, his fedora tilted rakishly over his left ear. The light brown hair on the right side of Harrison's head looked to Gregory as if his brother had been running his fingers through it in frustration.

Irene breezed past Gregory and into the office. She rushed to give her father a peck on the cheek. "Father," she said in a loving voice. While O'Brien did not shift position, he beamed down at his daughter.

"So good to see you, my dear," O'Brien told her, reaching out a hand to stroke her bare arm affectionately.

For Gregory, the office seemed smaller and more crowded than last time. Cigar smoke lingered in the air although O'Brien was not actively smoking. The tall grandfather clock with its moon face dominated a corner closest to the office door, it's ticking now sounding loudly in the silence. O'Brien's cluttered walnut desk took command diagonally across the room. Perhaps because Harrison was already seated and O'Brien leaned against the front of his desk, the office appeared to have shrunk. Gregory followed Irene in, a thick Persian rug muffling his footsteps. He stopped next to his brother's chair, placing a hand on its high back, and waited for O'Brien to acknowledge him.

Irene's father kissed her on the cheek, his face brightening at her appearance. "Irene, dear child," he said, holding her slightly away from where he had stood upright. "You are looking positively stunning."

Irene flushed at her father's praise, as if he were stingy with nice words, and she did not hear good things often. "Gregory has come with me, today." She indicated Gregory with an outstretched arm.

"Of course," O'Brien grumbled. He took a step forward, offering a hand to shake.

Gregory did so, stepping back afterwards, allowing Irene to take center stage.

"Harrison and I have been discussing the current stock market," O'Brien began.

"And?" Irene asked, one of her finely arched brows lifting.

"I am not entirely convinced that the market is unsafe for investments," concluded O'Brien. He rooted around on his desk, found a wooden box, and prized a cigar from it. Tapping one end against the desk, he took a clipper from his pocket to prepare the cheroot for smoking.

"Not for the lack of trying," Harrison said mostly in an aside for Gregory and Irene's ears. He leaned forward with his hands resting on his knees. Louder, he continued, "I mentioned Babson and his economic study already." Harrison glanced at Gregory and gave him a speaking look.

"Go tell it to Sweeny." O'Brien waved a hand. Afterwards, he turned the cigar to the right and then to the left, checking it, before tossing his clippers aside for a large lighter with a granite base. Puffing four times, the tip of the cigar reddened, and O'Brien blew out a ring of smoke. He returned to his comfortable position against the front edge of his desk, legs stretched out and crossed at the ankles, while he leaned his great weight against his arms where his hands rested on top of the desk between papers and ledgers. "I don't believe that baloney. Babson has been speaking of a bubble burst since the beginning of 1928 – it hasn't happened."

"That's because wealthy men like William Durant of General Motors have been pumping money into the market, a market – by the way, they cannot allow to fail," Gregory spoke up. "I've been tracking the market for a long time," he continued, taking his hat off and holding it at his waist like a shield. "Each time the market destabilizes, Durant, someone like him, or the head of the New York Federal Reserve steps in and helps speculators regain confidence. The market generally takes off afterwards, as if the fall in stock prices had never happened."

"I have noticed that too," agreed Harrison enthusiastically. "Ordinary investors just want to make as much profit as they can. They aren't looking at patterns in the market."

"Exactly!" O'Brien jabbed the air with the end of his cigar.

"But don't be deceived by that sort of thinking," Gregory said.

Harrison almost jumped to his feet. "My broker recently admitted that many of the smart speculators have begun to sell off their shares. The interest rate on loans has increased so much that its higher than the earnings from stocks. I've told you I've sold my shares in everything but three companies."

"Listen to them, Father," Irene pleaded, grabbing up one of his arms and clasping his large hand – the one without the cigar.

"Pick two or three of the companies you trust most—hold on to those stocks, if you will, but sell the rest," Harrison said earnestly. "I know my metals broker Dooley will help you buy gold or silver. He knows his onions, sir."

"Then why are important bankers saying the market is fine while the Federal Reserve hasn't said anything at all?" O'Brien asked quietly. He took his cigar from his mouth, staring at the burning embers at its tip.

"They are avoiding a panic, a run on the market," Gregory said and O'Brien looked over at him. His eyes had grown larger and rounder. "Just consider how speculators reacted after the *Times* Industrials dropped 12 points, and the bankers rushed in to back the brokers."

"If the bottom falls out of the Market – that would be disastrous for the whole country," Harrison jabbed the air with his forefinger. Harrison rearranged himself in his seat so he could lean toward O'Brien. "We're telling you, sir, selling out now is in your best interest."

Irene sent a pleading look at her father, pressing her hands together as if in prayer. "If not for you, Father, do it for Neil and the boys."

His cigar clenched between his teeth, O'Brien tugged on his chin, his jowls jiggling slightly. *Was he considering?*

"Look, sir, gold prices are at an all-time low," Gregory kicked his persuasion into high gear.

Harrison scooted yet closer, "What could it hurt to shift your resources into gold rather than the riskier stocks?"

"Getting out now while most of your earnings intact still keeps you ahead," Gregory put in, using his hat to emphasize "earnings" and "ahead."

"Hang on to the gold and silver," picked up Harrison. "Historically, gold prices tend to rise and bars have concrete worth..."

"Unlike the paper stock certificates are printed on," concluded Gregory.

"Gold and silver." O'Brien continued to stroke his clean-shaven chin. He looked down at Irene, who once again clasped her hands as if in prayer. "The market has taken several downturns in the past seven months as you pointed out." He cleared his throat, grasping his cigar so he could flick off the growing ashes. *He was thinking, maybe remembering the market falling.* "I could sell off the riskier holdings, as you say, and buy up some gold bars."

Harrison fished around in his pocket. He drew out his large leather wallet, and pulled a business card out, handing it across to O'Brien. "That's Dooley's card, sir. He's a good egg."

O'Brien took the card and scanned it. "I'm only thinking about this because you're Deanie O'Banion's kin, you savvy?"

"Oh, yes, sir," Harrison and Gregory said together. They both nodded their heads. "You won't regret this, sir." *Now if he'd only follow their advice.*

Irene risked a cautious smile. She gave her father a quick hug.

O'Brien eased the card into his vest pocket. "That's remains to be seen," he harrumphed, replacing his cigar between his teeth. "Now scram," he said, moving back around his desk to sit in his oversized desk chair. To Irene, he added, "Don't be such a stranger."

Harrison collected himself, standing up from the chair. He caught Gregory's arm, pulling him gently from the room. Gregory glanced at Irene, who nodded. She followed the brothers out of the office and down the hallway to the foyer. Saunders waited there with coats in hand, helping Irene into her fox-collared wool while letting Harrison and Gregory don their own overcoats.

"Thank you, Saunders," Irene said as they walked out the door.

When the solid front door closed behind them, Irene turned to Gregory and asked, "Well, what do you think?"

"He very possibly might sell some of his holdings," Harrison responded.

"Hopefully, he will decide before the 28th. He has a few days," Gregory told them.

"What happens on the 28th?" Irene inquired her blue eyes wide with curiosity.

Harrison also looked at Gregory, questioningly.

"Disaster," Gregory said, shaking his head. "Unmitigated disaster.

Gregory had taken Irene home, and he was sitting with Harrison in the parlor, listening to baseball over the radio set. Harrison took off his navy, pin-striped jacket, and loosened his tie, settling back into the plush cushions of the club chair with a cigar stuck between his teeth. The Chicago Cubs had been dominating the National League and were pitted against the Philadelphia Athletics in the World Series. While Gregory wanted the Cubs to win because they were his home team, Harrison – of course, had placed a wager on the Cubbies, which is why his brother yelled and screamed at the radio announcer and the players throughout the game.

"Aren't you going to check up on the club?" Gregory asked his brother, after Harrison almost knocked over a side table in his exuberance at a Cubs' homerun.

"Clarice and Letty have it in hand," Harrison retorted. "Now shush! Looks like we're ahead" he wagged a hand toward Gregory. "Come on Pat, toss a strike!" Harrison shouted at the radio, urging the Cubs' pitcher Pat Malone to make the current batter swing and miss.

Gregory settled back against his own chair cushions when the door knocker sounded. The announcer and the noise of the game receded from Gregory's attention. He could hear the rustling footsteps as Klein went to answer.

"Telegram," a reedy boy's voice announced, "sign here."

After a pause, Klein replied, "Here you go." The door closed and Klein came down the hall and headed straight for Gregory. "Telegram. I'm sure you heard."

Gregory took the folded paper, flicking it open. It read:

Arrived safely in Paris. Nightlife excellent. Lucky in our flat. Will write soon.

Teddy and Carlo

"Teddy and Carlo made it to Paris," Gregory told Harrison. *Everything would be Jake for them now that they were safe from Capone and Moran.*

"Hallelujah!" Harrison said, but Gregory wasn't certain it was because his friends were safe or because the Cubs got a man on base.

He had to chuckle. His brother was hale and whole – would never be shot escaping after a bank job. Their economic situation stabilized ever since Harrison bought gold and silver. They weren't going to suffer the bankruptcy that drove Harrison to desperate behavior. Furthermore, the club had grown in popularity, and their Norwood Park neighbors seemed to pack the place when it was open Tuesday through Sunday nights. Gregory limited his seances to Wednesday, Thursday, and Saturday to rest, even though he was in high demand as a medium and could have held several an evening. Word had gotten out that he actually connected with the departed, forcing Klein to turn potential patrons away, since only a maximum of 13 could squeeze around his table.

"Those bums!" Harrison slammed his fist on the side table, breaking Gregory's reverie. "They lost the Series."

Gregory shook his head. "How much did you wager?"

"It's the principle of the thing," Harrison said, when he normally would have retorted, "none of your beeswax!"

"How much?" Gregory insisted.

"After talking to O'Brien the other day – nothing," Harrison said quietly, puffing on his cheroot. "I know my onions. We can't afford to toss kale away on the Series."

"You are so right!" Gregory said. He walked over and clapped Harrison on the back. "Good move."

"I've put it all together, brother," Harrison admitted. "Bad times are coming, and you couldn't warn me enough."

Gregory made two imaginary pistols with his fingers and took aim at Harrison. "Come on. I think Clarice and Letty will appreciate us dropping by *Hair of the Dog*. Business has been the pig's wings."

"The tiger's spots!" Harrison chuckled, nodding in agreement, gathering up his suit jacket and slinging it over one shoulder. "The gnat's elbows!"

Laughing, Gregory steered his brother out of the parlor, through the hallway, and down the many steps to their club. Noise of clinking glasses and bottles, loud chatter and laughter, along with Clarice's deep voice singing "stairway to paradise," rose up to meet them.

21

Several days later, O'Brien pounded on the front door of the Farm, shouting, "Davenport, open up!" In the crook of his plaid wool covered elbow was a folded morning newspaper. His cigar, clenched between his teeth shook with his tension. Beyond the arched brick entry, fall wind picked up, causing fallen leaves to circle in small tornadoes, despite the recent heat wave.

Klein opened the door. "This way, sir," he said, backing away so O'Brien could make his way into the foyer without barging.

Harrison and Gregory, having heard the commotion rushed up from the kitchen just as O'Brien handed his overcoat to Klein. "O'Brien," Harrison said.

"There you are, sir!" O'Brien said. He slapped a copy of *Chicago Daily* he had carried in with him against his open hand.

Gregory couldn't tell if he were awed or furious. *Whichever, O'Brien felt strongly enough to seek them out before noon.*

O'Brien struggled with the flimsy paper, opening the folds, then held the newsprint up for the brothers to see.

Black Tuesday! Market Crashes! Is this the END of the Bull Market? The headlines practically screamed off the page. Gregory knew the *Chicago Daily* article went on talking about impending economic troubles for the country as well as for Chicago because he had read it before. Many men faced unemployment. *Bread lines like those in Europe weren't going to be uncommon.* He instantly thought of the tent city that had grown up in the park near Irene's flat and shuddered. Below the fold, Gregory noticed a smaller headline *Untouchables Fail to Find Enough Evidence for Capone Conviction.* He filed that information away for later.

"Prices are plummeting," O'Brien spluttered. "No stock seems safe."

Gregory and Harrison stood completely still. Klein disappeared after hanging O'Brien's overcoat in the hall closet, leaving them alone with Irene's father in the foyer. They shared a glance.

"It's bad," Gregory admitted, knowing even more than he would say.

"You warned me," O'Brien said, slightly awed. He stubbed his cigar out in the ashtray on the small wall table beside the entryway. "You *warned* me," then quieter, "how did you know?"

"Economist Roger Babson argued for a crash weeks ago, as we told you," Harrison put in, stepping up to place a hand on the older man's shoulder. O'Brien was visibly shaken. Harrison said, "That upward trend of stocks couldn't continue forever."

"Especially with people borrowing money to buy on margin, not having any real kale to back their loans," Gregory added, softly. "Talk about a straw house."

"If you boys hadn't come—if Irene hadn't come, I'd be as broke as most of my neighbors," O'Brien scrubbed his face with his large hand. "I'd be ruined."

Harrison clapped O'Brien on his broad back. "There, there. *You* are gonna be copacetic, ya savvy?" He directed O'Brien into the front parlor. "How about some coffee?"

Harrison led O'Brien to a large arm chair, easing the man's bulk down into the damask covered cushions. O'Brien stared up at

Harrison and then over to Gregory, who had followed behind them. Irene's father had a haunted, almost broken look.

"I went to the exchange early this morning, before I read this," he flapped the *Chicago Daily*. "Men clustered around the entrance, shouting. A few approached me, trying to sell their cars, for Christ's sake!" He shook his head. "I managed to get onto the trading floor. The din was painful, and the numbers scrolling across the ticker kept falling, and falling." O'Brien moaned. "It was the most horrific thing I've ever seen. Grown men sobbed, while others ranted. Pandemonium everywhere!"

I know. It was tragic. The clamor on the exchange floor had been deafening as brokers struggled to make deals, everyone wanting to sell. Gregory remembered Harrison's ashen expression when his brother had learned they lost almost everything. *It was heart wrenching, at least, I changed that much.*

"How are we to survive this?" O'Brien asked. "How is Chicago, the country to manage? The Federal Reserve isn't going to be able to buy us out of this one." O'Brien shook his head, then pressed his forehead into his large open palms.

Harrison spoke up first, "Fortunately, we sold our holdings, hedged our bets."

"How could our government allow the Market to break down so badly?" O'Brien wondered out loud.

Prior to the raid, he would have asked the same thing, Gregory thought ironically. *What no confidence in President Hoover? But who could have much certainty in these times?* "So many wanted the market to continue to rise. It reflects confidence in the economy and industry." Unfortunately, few looked across the Atlantic at Europe—Germany specifically where he knew conditions for people had become unbearable. He had seen the newspaper photographs of barrels of *Deutsche* marks being exchanged for two loaves of bread and the blocks long lines for buying fresh produce. *Hopefully, Paris was much better. The French had been on the winning side of the armistice, after all.*

O'Brien stared hard at Gregory, who remained by the white plastered wood of the fireplace and mantel. "You just listened to certain economists?"

Gregory nodded, not wanting to explain.

"How did you know which ones?" O'Brien pulled on his chin. He pulled a cigar from his vest pocket and a lighter from his jacket, igniting the end not caught between his teeth. Taking three puffs, Irene's father visibly relaxed. "I heard them all; read about 'em in the papers," he plucked his cigar out of his mouth and studied it. Smoke snaked into the room, bringing with it the scent of burning cherry wood, and the tang of good tobacco. "But without you, I wouldn't have pulled out. I truly believed the rise would continue."

"We know that, sir," Harrison said, taking a seat in the chair closest to O'Brien with a backward flick of his navy suit jacket.

"I'm not an economist," Gregory admitted, leaning against one arm, his hand on the fireplace mantel, "but the fairytale of getting rich quick had to end sometime. It's been ten years of almost steady upward sales." Gregory shook his head. "It just could *not* last."

O'Brien poked the air in Gregory's direction with his cigar. "I owe you," he said so softly Gregory almost couldn't hear the words. "In the end, it doesn't matter how or why you knew. You shared that knowledge with me. That means a lot."

Gregory looked across at O'Brien, catching the older man's eyes with his own. "I care a lot about Irene, sir, and her family."

O'Brien suddenly slapped his knee and gave a shout of laughter. "So, you've protected the old man because you're in love with the daughter." He threw his great, brownish red-haired head back and practically roared. "I should have guessed. Not the milquetoast Teddy O'Hannilan is, God bless his father's soul. Now you," he pointed his thick finger at Gregory, "are son-in-law material."

Harrison glanced over his shoulder at Gregory, with a raised eyebrow.

Gregory flushed. He felt as if his face had caught on fire. As much as he might have wanted to deny it, Gregory could not, because everything O'Brien had said was true. "All the same, sir—"

O'Brien wagged his hand from side-to-side, waving Gregory off. "No matter," he said, biting back down on the cigar. "You have my blessing son. Won't say a word to Irene. I'll let you do it in your own time."

"Hurrmph," Harrison grunted, trying to draw O'Brien's attention away from Gregory. "Have you bought gold yet?"

O'Brien sat back in his chair, letting his long legs stretch out in front of him. He took a deep drag on his cigar. Leaning his head back, he blew out a cloud of smoke before he said, "Yes. Just a few days ago. Just in time, ya savvy?"

"I do," Harrison said, nodding his head.

Gregory wanted to disappear, but knew diplomatically, he had to remain. Fortunately for him, he heard laughter and running feet coming down the stairs from the bedrooms above.

A shriek, then, "Try and catch me!" Laughter echoed through the hallway.

"You won't get away, Margie," Clarice said firmly. "Letty and I will find you," she added, but spoiled the sternness with chuckles.

Margie shrieked again, before she pelted into the front foyer. Her short, bobbed curls fluttered and her dark, round face was flushed with excitement. She darted behind the loveseat and the chairs. Her newsboy knickers, suspenders, and broadcloth shirt looked good on her in a boyish way, but also gave her the freedom of movement she needed. Clarice dressed in deep burgundy trousers, vest, and matching suit jacket strode swiftly into the room, her eyes darting here and there, looking for the girl.

"May we be of assistance?" Gregory asked, a grin curling his lips, and laughter threatening to escape his throat. He leaned even more casually against the decorative columns of the fireplace. "Lost something?"

Margie had completely transformed from the shadow of a girl into this highly animated gamine thing. Clarice and Letty had done wonders with her, helping her gain confidence and a sense of self-worth.

Harrison managed to keep O'Brien's attention, but the older man's eyes twinkled when he caught sight of the little girl concealed behind the large hickory case that held the gramophone and the Davenport's collection of 78s. *Was he remembering Irene as a child?* Gregory wondered.

"Have you seen Margie?" Clarice asked, placing a forefinger across her lips as she snuck across the carpeted floor on silent feet. "She seems to have vanished."

Gregory, Harrison, and O'Brien made a big show of scanning the room, not seeing Margie in her hiding place. She giggled, quickly covering her mouth to stifle the noise. Gregory shook his head.

"We haven't seen her," he said, keeping up the pretense, but unable to prevent a wide grin from spreading over his face. Margie placed a finger across her mouth. Gregory gave an almost imperceptible nod.

Clarice put her hands on her hips. "Hurumph. I wonder where she's gotten off to?" Her green eyes glittering, but her features impassive. As she turned to leave, Margie dashed out of her spot and flung her arms around Clarice's waist and the woman hugged her back.

Gregory marveled at the change in the girl. She seemed so happy now and well-adjusted after her horrible ordeal. *Old wounds must remain*, he thought, Margie had been a captive too long under Capone and his cappo's control. Nonetheless, Clarice and Letty were doing a wonderful job in healing the damage. Margie could eventually attend school, or learn a trade from Clarice or Letty. They had already begun teaching her to shoot and defend herself. When Margie went out into the world again, as she eventually must, she should not have to live in fear, constantly glancing over her shoulder for a hatchet man or a South Side bully.

In the weeks following O'Brien's visit, stock prices continued to fall, most bottoming out below a single cent. Chicagoans quickly feared for their savings, once secure in the banking system, and – like Americans around the country – stormed the banks in an attempt to get their money out. Radio programs, once filled with optimism, predicted continued economic disaster. President Hoover, on the other hand, gave speeches in those days of prosperity returning if only Americans were willing to practice tiny economies. Just the other day, Gregory remembered hearing the President repeating, "Prosperity is no idle expression. Every man will have a job," phrases from a campaign speech last year.

On the streets of Chicago, the city that shouldered burdens, Irene and Gregory walked by more apple sellers than there were street corners. Markets with long lines of men and women dressed in shabby coats, or no coats, struggled to provide patrons with even a single loaf of bread.

"I have heard," Irene began as she and Gregory walked toward the Ford past the tiny park, "that Capone has opened a soup kitchen downtown to feed the needy."

"I've seen it," Gregory admitted. "He even goes there to ladle the food, himself. It helps make people trust him. You know all the food comes from grocery store managers he has extorted. It's easy to be generous with other people's money."

"How horrible. That terrible man—" Irene stared down at where her hand curled comfortably in Gregory's.

"He looks like he's doing good deeds," said Gregory, "but they won't be enough to keep him from being convicted."

"Eventually." Irene added, "Not necessarily soon enough for us." She frowned, remembering her brother's treatment by Capone's men, by McErlane. The Prohibition agents and the Treasury Department remained unable to touch Capone, but justice for Geoff had taken a secondary place to survival.

More and more signs of the economic troubles grew, becoming readily apparent as they walked the Chicago streets. The tiny park near Irene's flat began supporting a few tent dwellers. When more weeks passed, the number of tents increased, and they collected into a small village. Today furniture and boxes of possessions lined the sidewalks and threatened to overflow into the street. A dark-haired woman clung to her bearded, but slightly balding husband, both them clad in threadbare tweed coats. She cried into his chest while their three-year old son kept tugging on his mother's skirt.

Irene pulled up short, tugging on Gregory's arm. "Wait—I know that family," she said, pointing at the people near their possessions. "They lived on my floor. Come on! I want to know what happened." Irene almost dragged Gregory across the street oblivious of honking horns blown by traffic. "Mrs. Feidleman?"

The woman raised a haggard looking face with red rimmed eyes to look at Irene. "Oh, Irene," the woman – Mrs. Feidleman, half sobbed.

Irene reached out a tentative hand towards Mrs. Fiedleman's arm. "What happened?"

"Mr. Amato evicted our family," Mrs. Feidleman whispered. Her face reddened with shame.

"We could not pay the rent," Mr. Feidleman explained. "He gave a few months grace, but with the banks failing, he had his men pack up our furnishings and put them all out on the street, as you see."

"I don't know where we'll go, Abe," Mrs. Feidleman shook her head. "I just don't know."

Irene patted her former neighbor's shoulder. She raised troubled eyes to Gregory. *There wasn't room at the farmhouse for the whole family. What could he do for them?*

"I'll talk to Harrison," Gregory whispered into Irene's ear, "but I don't see what we can do for them."

"I know," Irene said. "I just feel terrible for them." She told the Feidlemans, "I'm so sorry."

Mr. Feidleman remarked over his wife's shoulder, "I believe we will be able to move in with my parents. They have a farm in Minnesota. Because my two older brothers help work the land, they are all doing much better than we, who worked in the factory. At least, food is readily available." He patted his wife's back and cuddled his son against his leg.

Gregory and Irene nodded before walking back across the street and continued to Irene's flat. The Feidlemans were not the only family to lose their home. Men were either getting cuts in pay, or losing employment altogether. Businesses wanted to survive, but in doing so, threatened the survival of their workers. Just like the downward economic quicksand of the stock market, similar forces destroyed the workforce.

Irene used her key to open the door of her flat. They moved through the foyer towards the living room. "I'm not on the street like the Feidlemans, but Mrs. Hall let all us gals go today," she said in a quiet voice.

"I won't let you be out on the street, you know that," Gregory assured. As he took Irene into his arms, he felt her nodding against his chest. He held her a little away, "How about helping me with the seances? I could use an assistant."

"Really?" she asked, her blue eyes wide and bright with unshed tears.

Gregory nodded, encouragingly.

"That'd be swell," Irene said. She turned into his embrace, tightening her arms around his neck and kissing him passionately.

Gregory's hand glided over Irene's back, drawing her even closer. His blood sparked and he grew light headed. "You're the cat's pajamas," he whispered into Irene's ear before giving the lobe a gentle nip.

"Hello, kids!" Daphne called, coming into the living room from her bedroom. "Am I interrupting?" She laughed.

Irene and Gregory jumped apart. His nerves jangled, Gregory straightened his suit jacket and hair. Irene smoothed down her coat. "Where are you off to?" Irene asked. Gregory saw Daphne was wearing her waitress uniform with its yellow checked dress and full front white apron. She must have stuck her white cap into the large apron pocket because she wasn't wearing it yet.

Daphne moved to the closet to grab her wrap. "The boss had let several of the gals go. I'm grabbing extra shifts at the diner while I can." She threaded her arms through the sleeves of her wool coat, then turned to waggle her fingers at Gregory and Irene. "Toodles," she said, opening the front door. "Don't do anything I wouldn't do." Her laugh echoed down the hall towards the elevator along with the clap of her heels against the marble floor.

Gregory looked around the flat, searching for Zelda. Irene gave a smile.

"Zelda's already at work. She's been answering phones for the meat factory, but I don't know how long that will last. Her previous job was as a secretary, but the scrap business let everyone go who wasn't family," Irene explained.

"Seems like everyone is tightening their belts, even the well-to-do in Norwood Park," Gregory said, scratching the back of his neck. "Those bread lines are made up of the unemployed and seem to be growing every day."

"Same with those apple sellers." Irene returned to Gregory's side, wrapping her arms around his waist. "I don't like what's happening and can't help being a little afraid."

Gregory wanted to tell her he could keep her safe, that they would make it through, but he only knew what was coming for the next few months and no more. Then, he would be like everyone else, living one day at a time. He wanted to tell her he loved her and they would make their world what they wanted. Instead, he remained quiet and hugged Irene tightly.

22

Seances over the next few weeks revolved around money, bringing in new faces. As the patrons gathered around the large oak table in the back parlor, Mrs. Lipshultz, a short woman in her early thirties, and her second husband Nikoli begged Gregory to contact her paternal grandfather. Gregory had taken his seat closest to the armoire as was his habit, placing Irene on his right, when he looked down into Mrs. Lipshultz's plump, round face.

"I can't guarantee which spirits will appear this evening, dear lady," Gregory soothed, *cringing inside,* "but I shall try."

"Please," she pleaded, glancing between Irene and Gregory. "He always told us children stories about hiding some treasure." Mrs. Lipshultz patted her husband's hand, placed on the table beside her own. "Nikoli and I have questions for him."

Of course, you do, Gregory thought with a sigh. He had to laugh. *If the spirits wanted to speak – who was he to make judgements.* He took his three deep cleansing breaths and began, "Everyone take hold of the hand belonging to the people beside you." He gently squeezed Irene's hand and winked at her. She winked back, making his heart leap. Out of the corner of his eye, Gregory saw Klein beckon to

Clarice, whispering in her ear. He couldn't watch them, the guests around the table were growing restless. He released Irene and clapped his hands to disrupt the chatter in the room.

"Spirits we beseech you," Gregory said, when the room grew quiet and he had clasped Irene's hand again. He could hear the raspy breathing Mr. and Mrs. Lipshultz made, the sniffling made by Mr. Banbury near the far end, and Irene's soft sigh. "We beseech you to join us."

One of the participants at the other end of the table, Mr. Fine, or perhaps Miss Brannigan, coughed. Gregory was about to speak when he felt the now familiar tightness in his throat. A strident, female voice almost shrieked into the near silence like a ripping of fabric. "Ralph Fine, you little weasel. I knew I'd catch up with you. Are you casting your eye about again?"

Mr. Fine shrunk into his wooden chair so that the high-back seemed to rise up above him. "Nno, my ddear," he stuttered. "I loved only you." Fine, a small, skinny man with gaunt features, and an especially long nose, glared down it at Gregory.

"So, you've said," the woman's shrill tones cut Gregory's throat. "But—Do. I. Believe?"

"Honestly, Hortense," retorted Mr. Fine, sitting up straighter. "Aren't you in a better place? It weren't my fault you contracted the Spanish Flu. I did my utmost to save you."

"You did at that," Hortense answered, her voice less shrewish. Gregory shook his head, but it was Hortense controlling his movement. "I have been looking out for you from here—beyond the veil. I know you must move on, but I had hoped you would hold me forever in your heart." Gregory moved the hand holding Irene's indicating his chest.

"I -- I say," Fine relaxed and sat up straighter. "There is one thing you might do to help me. What can you tell us about the future of the stock market? Will things turn 'round as Hoover and the Fed say?"

"Do I look like a fortune teller?" Hortense retorted. "There is no hint of change here for good or bad. I may look out for your soul, but I have no resources where your money is concerned. If you've moved on, so must I."

Participants around the table murmured after hearing Hortense's answer. Miss Brannigan said softly, "No idea about the Market?"

Mr. Stanley, a rotund man of about fifty, shook his head. "Is Hoover doing too much? Not enough?" He tsked.

Gregory felt Hortense slip from him. He took several deep breaths, clearing his mind. "Is there another spirit wishing to speak?" he asked after a moment. The words barely left his lips when he felt another spirit take hold of him. "Hannah, dearest Hannah," came from his mouth in a thick German accent. "My *liebchen*, you are married?"

"Papa, Big Papa is that you?" Mrs. Lipshultz asked incredulously. In a softer voice she hissed, "Nikoli, I think its him." To her grandfather she said, "His name is Nikoli. He is a good man, an honest man."

"My darling granddaughter," Gregory seemed to swell in size with each word, "Good news to have such a husband."

"I've missed you, Pappa," Mrs. Lipshultz said. "But Pappa, I need you to tell me where the treasure is – the one from those story's you told me as a young girl."

"But, why?" the spirit asked, "some things are better left alone."

"You can feel no shame connected to it, especially now, Pappa," Mrs. Lipshultz insisted. "You were too upstanding a man to have stolen or killed for it. So, why can't you tell us?"

The ghost wailed straining Gregory's vocal cords. "I would not want to destroy my reputation or standing. Why is that money so important to you?"

Nikoli spoke up before his wife could, "We are broke. We have lost everything since the Market failed. If she doesn't find that money, we will be out on the street living in a cardboard box and selling apples."

The outburst caused the other participants to speak. "Oh no!" Irene gasped.

Others exclaimed, "How terrible," or "Horrible," or "No worse than we are."

Mrs. Lipshultz begged, "Please, Pappa, tell us."

"That blood money will bring you nothing but pain," the spirit moaned. *A bleakness came into the room, surrounding them all.* Gregory noticed most because he was Pappa and himself both at the same time. And, at the far end of the table, a round man of medium height – Mr. Banbury, Gregory recalled, blinked nervously behind his small, round glasses.

"But we must know," Nikoli pleaded.

"There is a small cask buried under the third oak behind your father's house – the home where you grew up, Hannah." The spirit moaned again communicating a great sadness. "If you truly need that money, you shall find it. May it be sufficient to resolve your difficulties because it is cursed. That is why I buried it in the first place. I'm sorry for your pain, *liebchen,* remember I love you." Gregory once again felt the spirit sliding from his body, returning his control and voice.

"*Schatzi,*" Nikoli said to his wife, 'we must go to your father's house at once. No one needs that money more than we do."

Mrs. Lipshultz nodded her agreement. They released the hands of their neighbors and made to stand.

Gregory thought a moment. Harrison or Teddy would have known who Hannah Lipshultz's grandfather was. Perhaps he had been a hatchet man from the past, tainting that money he had hidden with blood. "Yes, go as your conscience dictates," he told the Lipshultzs. "That will be all tonight. I am too tired to do more. Please speak with Mr. Klein. He will arrange for another night."

The guests around the table began speaking at once. The clamor made Gregory's head throb. Irene moved closer to him; her Jasmine and Heliotrope perfume surrounded him. She gently placed a hand on his shoulder, rubbing in tiny circles. Her touch soothed him until he suddenly stiffened. He tried to move, but couldn't and the people in the room, who had been gathering up their things to leave, stopped and stared at him. Gregory felt his throat tighten and get that tingly, tickle signaling a visitation.

"Damnation!" Deanie O'Banion yelled through Gregory's mouth.

Irene flinched and stepped back quickly. The small bell on her charm bracelet tinkled in the near silence of the room as she trembled.

"Why hasn't Moran taken down Capone?" Cousin Deanie's anger rushed into the parlor like a harsh wind, and a few of the women – Miss Brannigan in particular, shivered in fright. "I *know* he has the will. Is he waiting for the *Untouchables* to do the task for him?"

Irene, seeing the torment O'Banion caused his cousin, rounded on the spirit. "Hasn't there been enough violence in this city?"

"There is never enough when me own family harbors spirits like his" Deanie rasped, making Gregory point an accusing finger at the Lipshultzs who had not yet made it out the door. "Her Pappa's partner was Frankie McErlane – the most vicious hired killer in all Chicagoland. That money he hid? T'was blood money from using the Tommy gun for the first time to take down five men at once, ya follow?"

The Lipshultzs slowly turned around to face Gregory. Their faces were as white as the rest of the participants in the room. All except for Banbury, whose rosy face had grown decidedly more red. O'Banion's rage seemed to fill the room like a fog resting on the ground, bringing a moist, deep cold.

Banbury stiffened and stared murderously at Gregory whose unblinking eyes finally rested upon him. "You!" Banbury pointed, drawing a 38 mm. from his coat pocket. Everyone in the room gasped.

Clarice and Letty, who had slipped in to watch, drew their pearl handled pistols, aiming at Banbury. "Drop your weapon," they commanded.

"No!" Banbury shouted, shifting his aim towards Letty.

"You bastard, McErlane!" Deanie O'Banion snarled, recognizing the man for who he was and sending a breeze throughout the room. O'Banion, in Gregory's body, launched himself across the table almost reaching the chair where McErlane stood. Gregory's hands moved as if they had tightened around McErlane's throat. "Murderer!"

Gregory could sense Deanie's fingers closing, digging into the loose, double chins quivering above the man's black bow tie. "Why won't you die?!" Deanie rasped.

McErlane hissed and gurgled, reaching his free hand up towards his throat as if to wrench something free. His gun went off wildly, sending a bullet close to the small chandelier on the ceiling. Crystals rained down and Miss Brannigan screamed. "You," cough, gag, "I got you once. You can't stop me," McErlane gasped.

"Watch me, boyo!" Deanie said in slow, deliberate words. "I know we spirits haunt you—hunt you." Gregory's fingers moved as if squeezing tighter and tighter. "This is for me and all those others you've murdered!"

Gregory sensed his cousin's grip around his killer's throat, rage and terror building inside him. Deanie's anger was palpable, much stronger than the fear Gregory felt.

McErlane reddened further as he struggled against the supernatural force choking him. He made burbling sounds and only bubbles of saliva came from his lips. He finally dropped his gun, raising both hands to his neck and then to his heart. His eyes bulged as his large body sank down into the chair. Clarice and Letty ran forward to stand over him, guns still pointed at his head.

"He's had a stroke," Clarice said, touching the man's neck to feel for a pulse.

Around the room, men and women pressed handkerchiefs to their noses and mouths. McErlane's stench caused Gregory to gag.

"McErlane will die tonight because he fears *me*. I *will* get vengeance for my people!" Deanie yelled, pushing Gregory back to stand at his own place, and bang a fist on the table. The wood felt so smooth and solid beneath his skin, so real. "Ghosts of those he has killed haunt him; they haunt Capone too. They are bullies as well as murdering bastards. I take pleasure in riding the world of McErlane, but Capone is harder to reach. I am relying on Moran."

"Moran hasn't taken Capone out! But he has `offed'-- as they say-- so many South Siders." Irene clenched her fists at her side. *Was Irene thinking about the threat the mob wars created for the likes of Teddy and Carlo?* Gregory couldn't help believing she was.

"Not enough, for me, m'darlin'" O'Banion retorted. "I'll not be sending the likes of m'cousins after Capone—in person, mind ye, but there's some who could provide evidence for those government men."

Gregory strained, managing to squeak out in his own voice, "If O'Brien..."

"...talks to Ness about Geoff," Irene picked up because she recognized how difficult it was for Gregory to speak for himself when he was being used as a spirit vessel, "we can put evidence before them to arrest Capone. Will that appease?"

A moment of silence griped the room. No one moved.

"Tis a start, me boyo," Deanie replied almost calmly. "Tis a start. That man is more slippery than an eel. It will take more than evidence of poor Geoff's murder to bring him down."

Gregory dropped into his chair and crumpled forward onto the table, his cousin's ghost leaving him empty, drained of energy. He scarcely heard Klein and Irene usher the participants of the séance from the room. *Here was their chance to get justice for Geoff. O'Brien needed to meet with Ness, convince him that Capone was behind Geoff's murder. Would that give the Untouchables enough evidence to gain a conviction?*

23

Several hours after Deanie's appearance and the conclusion of the séance, Irene knocked on Gregory's bedroom door. "Baby, it's me. Let me in."

"Give me a minute," he called softly. Gregory shook himself awake, slowly getting to his feet. Switching on his bedside lamp, a yellow glow filled his bedroom. He noticed that Irene had slipped his suit jacket onto the back of the wooden chair near his chest of drawers. After putting on the jacket, shaking his shoulders to settle the fit, Gregory ran a comb through his hair. Checking the mirror, he decided he looked good enough and strode over to open the door for Irene.

She stood just outside, one hand gripping her other arm above her elbow. Her pale floral chiffon frock, clung to her slight figure and sported a wide belt around her hips. Irene's blonde curls had relaxed some since he had seen her earlier, but her kohl lined eyes remained stunning. *Wowzer,* he thought. "Come here, baby," Gregory said, pulling her into his arms.

Irene settled tightly against him, filling his head with Heliotrope and Jasmine. He would never smell those flowers again and not think of her. With one hand he lightly rubbed her back, with the other he cupped her chin, tilting her bowed lips to his.

"Are you all right?" he asked, moving slightly away, but allowing his arms to remain around her.

She nodded, leaning her forehead against his sternum. "Are you? I cannot believe the nerve of your cousin!"

"Down kitten," he laughed, "watch those claws."

She smiled up into his eyes. "Father needs to go to the Prohibition department."

"No, baby. He needs to see the Untouchables. His evidence won't nail Capone into a coffin, but as Deanie suggests, it will be a start." Gregory turned her, keeping one arm looped around her waist and guided her toward the steps. "Let's go talk with Harrison and come up with a plan."

They hurried down the flights of stairs, heading for Harrison's office at the back of the *Hair of the Dog*. Surrounded by clusters of well-turned-out patrons, Clarice and Letty were performing a duet near the piano on stage when they entered the club. Gregory noted it was a nice rendition of "Nobody Knows You When You Are Down and Out," with Clarice singing alto and Letty taking soprano and the back-up players "wawww, wawwing" on the trumpets, harmonizing on sax and clarinet. The patrons joined in when the gals reached the line, "If I ever get a dollar again," the entire club joined in, singing slightly off key, "I'm going to hold on to it until those eagles grin." Clarice nodded at Gregory and Irene as they moved past towards Harrison's office.

Gregory nodded back, smiling. "Come on," he whispered to Irene, "while everyone is busy."

The singing receded slightly once they reached the short, narrow hallway between the club and the office. From down the plaster walled hallway, they could hear the crackling on Harrison's small radio set. President Hoover was talking. "Any lack of confidence in the economic future or the basic strength of business in the United States is foolish," he said, right before Harrison plunked his feet off his desk top and onto the floor, snapping off the radio. Harrison tilted his fedora and grinned at Gregory and Irene.

"What's hopping?" Harrison asked, grabbing a cigar out of the box on his desk.

Gregory glanced at Irene. "You tell him," she said, and Gregory did.

"So, you're telling me Deanie caused McErlane to have a stroke?" Harrison looked more relieved than surprised. That's when Gregory remembered that Harrison had witnessed Deanie's murder, and McErlane's part in it.

"Yes," Irene was saying in response to Harrison's question. "Clarice and Letty took care of him afterwards. They are a remarkable pair. If they hadn't suspected *Mr. Banbury,* McErlane's disguise might have worked."

"But not on Deanie!" Harrison slapped his knee. "Well, good riddance to McErlane!! He was a real piece of work. Good for Cousin Deanie!"

With McErlane gone, Harrison would be safer. Gregory thought.

His mood rather mercurial tonight, Harrison shifted from delighted to incredulous as he asked, "Deanie yelled at you?"

"Well not at me, per se," Gregory rubbed the back of his neck. "But he definitely wanted Moran to have taken Capone out by now." He shook his hand. "But that's not the real point."

"No," Irene chimed in. "He wants Father to –"

"--talk to Eliot Ness and the Untouchables about Geoff," finished Gregory.

"Well, O'Brien has us in his good books, ya savvy?" Harrison toyed with the tip of his cheroot. "He would most likely do anything *you* asked him to right now." Biting down on the cigar, Harrison took up a lighter and set the end aflame.

Gregory and Irene looked across the desk cluttered with piles of ledgers. Harrison leaned toward them, gripping the cheroot between two fingers and blew out smoke before he said, "Ok. Ok. I know my onions. You—" he pointed the cigar first at Gregory and then at Irene, "want me to go with you." He laughed then good humoredly. "How about tomorrow morning?"

Gregory and Irene exchanged a glance. "Sounds lovely," Irene responded. Gregory placed a soft kiss on the top of her head.

"Fine, fine," Harrison made a shooing motion with his hands. "I'll see you both in the front hall at 10am. Go on now. You kids have some fun."

Gregory guided Irene before him towards the door. He glanced over one shoulder. "And, Harrison? Don't believe what you hear from President Hoover."

Harrison looked back up from his open ledger. "Not on the radio or anywhere else," he told them. "Not anymore."

They nodded, then closed the door to keep the volume of the club down inside the office.

The next morning dawned warmer than usual as the rest of the fall had been, which should have put Gregory, Irene, and Harrison is a jovial mood, but they each carried their own concerns as to why O'Brien might not agree to see the authorities.

When Saunders announced them, O'Brien rushed out into the hallway to greet them. "You are always welcome," he told them, waving them into his office. "Sit, sit please."

Irene brushed a kiss on her father's cheek before taking a chair. Gregory settled on the arm, placing his hand protectively on her shoulder. "Good morning, Father."

"Sir," Harrison rushed in, before O'Brien could say anything. "We had a visitation last night from Cousin Deanie."

O'Brien sat up taller in his chair behind his desk. "O'Banion? At the séance?"

Irene nodded while Gregory and Harrison said, "Yes, sir."

Stroking his chin, O'Brien thought a moment. "And?"

"He wants you to see Eliot Ness," Irene blurted. "Take him everything connected to Geoff and his murder."

O'Brien began shaking his head. He raised his hands, palms outward.

"We know the danger," Gregory said quietly. "Deanie seems to think he can protect us, even from beyond the grave."

Harrison sat forward, leaning toward O'Brien. "He caused McErlane to have a stroke. Offed that hatchet man. Revenge for his own murder!" Harrison's eyes gleamed.

O'Brien's ruddy features whitened. "He did?"

"No baloney!" Harrison replied.

"He really wants you to turn everything over to Ness." Gregory coughed. "Deanie believes with enough evidence they will be able to convict Capone."

"You must go, Father," Irene said. "Capone already controls too much of this city. With everyone's money troubles, things will just get so much worse." She wrung her hands, helplessly.

O'Brien tugged on his pursed lips. "Let me think about it." When Gregory and Harrison began to protest, O'Brien raised his hands again. "At least let me have time to compose what I will say to the man."

Gregory and Harrison nodded. Irene spoke up softly, "Don't wait too long Father. Each day Chicago suffers more and more. As a politician, you have responsibilities, as you've always told me."

O'Brien nodded. "As I said, give me a little time. I'll report back after I've seen him."

After the meeting with Ness later that week, O'Brien visited them all at the farm house. Klein ushered the larger man into the front foyer, where O'Brien took the loveseat as his own. Gregory, Irene, and Harrison joined him, while Klein brought in a small tray of refreshments.

"Ness seems a capable egg," O'Brien told them over a mouthful of cigar. "The task force is having trouble making a case stick. Even with the ring, the finger bone, and the other materials I gave them, he was unable to predict whether or not the Justice Department could get a conviction for murder."

"How could they not?" Harrison asked from his club chair.

"Capone has been very clever covering his tracks and Geoff's case is over five years old," O'Brien explained, repeating what he had heard. "The task force is now pursuing another tactic in addition to the racketeering and liquor charges. If anything gains a conviction, our Geoff will get justice."

"What tactic?" Gregory asked from his place perched on the arm of the chair where Irene sat, next to his brother.

O'Brien leaned forward towards the other three. "Tax evasion," he whispered. "You boys are paying your taxes, aren't you?" O'Brien looked suddenly worried.

"As a matter of fact, we have been," Harrison admitted. "Running this place? We don't want coppers putting their nose in where it don't belong. We run a legit operation here; government gets its share." Harrison beamed.

"As Teddy would say—you slay me," Gregory chuckled. *Justice for Geoff would settle things for Irene and her father.*

O'Brien went on to discuss politics and business with Harrison while Gregory and Irene excused themselves. Irene planned to move into the farm house, taking the second-floor rooms Teddy and Carlo had used. Her roommates were finding more and more trouble keeping employment as the economic conditions worsened. Irene agreed she would stay on their lease until the end of November, but after that the gals were on their own. Gregory cranked up the Ford and handed Irene up into the passenger seat.

"Marshall Field's has new windows up," Irene told him, her eyes flashing with excitement. She clasped his hand closest to her.

"Let's go see them," Gregory smiled across the narrow seat. He causally patted the pocket of his jacket where he had concealed the small, purple velvet box with the hand furthest from Irene. His heart skipped a beat when he thought about what he wanted to do. *She was the cat's pajamas – there was no one else he ever felt this way about.* That thought gave Gregory courage as he drove through the outskirts and then central Chicago toward State Street and the huge Marshall Field's department store. The tall, white stone, building dominated the block, its sign high overhead. Gregory parked the Ford on the street, handing Irene down so they might walk and enjoy what the window dressers had designed.

The sidewalk around them was crowded with people, but fewer than in the tent village close to Irene's former flat. Many people raced past them, but a few remained clustered near the tall, broad windows under brown fabric awnings which shielded pedestrians from sun and rain. Gregory's long tweed coat swirled around his legs in the wind. He looped his left arm around Irene's waist and held her left hand in his right, pulling her close, not just to keep her warm, but also because he enjoyed having her close.

"Look!" gasped Irene. "That window has a small marry-go-round and a miniature Ferris wheel." Gregory looked where Irene was now pointing, her excitement building. In front of several art deco lights, the window dresser had positioned dolls as if they were at a fair. Like Irene, Gregory was charmed by the sight.

"Isn't it the leopards spots?"

"Oh, yes," Gregory said, but he was no longer looking at the window.

Irene took only a heartbeat to realize the man beside her was no longer interested in the display. "Gregory?" she asked, an eyebrow raised.

Not caring about the people around him, Gregory dropped to one knee, retaining Irene's hands in his clasp. "Baby nothing compares to you" he said, looking at her intently. Pedestrians flowed around them. He dropped her hands with his right hand in order to grope in his suit pocket for the purple velvet box. Once he had the box, Gregory held it out to her, popping the clasp open with his thumb. A large 1.5 carat, square cut diamond surrounded on each side by two diamond chips all in a platinum setting winked in the sunlight as it rested on purple velvet.

Irene gave a small gasp, but she didn't move.

"Irene O'Brien, you are the cat's pajamas," Gregory cleared his throat. "I adore you, please say you will make me the happiest of men – that you will marry me?"

"Yes," she exhaled.

Gregory slid the ring from the box and onto Irene's left hand. "Good thing your father gave his permission," he said, smiling.

Once the ring was securely on her finger, Irene tugged at his hands, pulling Gregory to his feet. "You are the cat's pajamas, Gregory. I'm over the moon for you."

"You love me?" he asked just to be clear, pressing his lips on her folded knuckles.

"I do," she said into his mouth as they kissed, fiercely, passionately for a few seconds that felt at once like forever, and not nearly long enough.

Gregory murmured. "Together we are going to make the future a better place."

"Wowzer!" Irene moaned, before surrendering again.

Someone cat whistled behind them, while other pedestrians laughed. A small boy pointed at them. His mother shushed him, dragging him to the other side of the street. Cars honked. Gregory savored the feel of Irene against him, their hearts racing in the same rhythm.

They broke apart, looping their arms around one-another's waists. They had time to savor their budding relationship. *No need to rush.* For now, they enjoyed the creativity of the window dressers and dreamed of their life together. The streets of Chicago were far from being paved with gold, but so long as they had each other, Gregory and Irene could create their own riches.

Author's Note

Chicago during the 1920s definitely had an underbelly of violence and ugliness hidden beneath the veneer of culture and social progressiveness. While all the personages in this story are fiction, or fictionalized versions, the beer wars between the Southside and Northside gangs were very real. Dean O'Banion, the leader of the Northside gang, was actually murdered in his flower shop. While Frank McErlane did not have a heart attack during a séance (something that fit well into my story), according to witnesses, he did suffer a heart attack and die in an alley, shouting that the ghosts of his past murder victims were killing him.

Also by Jean Luntz

The Bequest (A Regency Romance)

Coming soon:

If There Be Witches, Spirits Will Walk

Also coming soon in audio:

The Bequest (A Regency Romance)

Hair of the Dog

About the Author

My name is Jean Luntz, and I always wanted to be an author. I started in fifth grade with a novel entitled *The Nose Knows* – a mystery; wrote several short plays, short stories, poetry, and several magazine articles. After attending Northwestern University, and the University of Texas at Austin, I rounded out my education with a Master in Library and Information Science, conferring the highest level of professionalism, as if I had not been devouring history and other books all my life.

As an adult, I began writing romances – historical and modern, because I am a sucker for a happy ending, but have expanded into mystery and fantasy genres to develop more complicated storylines. Furthermore, my novels contain ghosts, mysticism, suspense, and fantasy elements. In addition to writing, I train dogs for competitive dog sports such as agility, scent-work, and obedience. The thrill of working with my canine partners never wears thin.

Made in the USA
Monee, IL
19 November 2023

46802992R00184